PHYSICAL EDUCATION UNIT PLANS FOR GRADES 1-2

Bette J. Logsdon, PhD / Luann M. Alleman, MEd
Sue Ann Straits, PhD / David E. Belka, PhD
Dawn Clark, EdD

Human Kinetics

Library of Congress Cataloging-in-Publication Data

Physical education unit plans for grades 1-2 / Bette J. Logsdon . . .
[et al.].--2nd ed.
    p.   cm.
   Rev. ed. of: Physical education teaching units for program
development, grades K-3, c1994.
   Includes bibliographical references.
   ISBN 0-87322-782-4
   1. Physical education for children--Curricula.   2. Physical
education and training--Study and teaching (Primary)--Curricula.
3. Curriculum planning.   I. Logsdon, Bette J.   II. Physical
education teaching units for program development, grades K-3.
GV443.P472 1997
372.86--dc20

                                             96-38313
                                              CIP

ISBN: 0-87322-782-4
ISBN: 0-88011-697-8 (set)

Copyright © 1986 by Lea & Febiger
Copyright © 1994, 1997 by Bette J. Logsdon

This book is a revised edition of *Physical Education Teaching Units for Program Development: Grades K-3*, published in 1986 by Lea & Febiger.

Acquisitions Editors: Rick Frey and Scott Wikgren; **Developmental Editors:** Christine Drews and Julia Anderson; **Assistant Editors:** John Wentworth and Alesha G. Thompson; **Editorial Assistant:** Jennifer Hemphill; **Copyeditor:** Bonnie Pettifor; **Proofreader:** Erin Cler; **Graphic Designer:** Judy Henderson; **Graphic Artist:** Angela K. Snyder; **Cover Designer:** Jack Davis; **Photographer (cover):** Wil Zehr; **Photographers (interior):** Jim Kirby and Terry Fell; **Illustrators:** Craig Ronto (Mac Art) and Paul To (Line Drawings); **Printer:** United Graphics

Printed in the United States of America   10 9 8 7 6 5 4 3 2

Human Kinetics
Web site: http://www.humankinetics.com/

United States: Human Kinetics, P.O. Box 5076, Champaign, IL 61825-5076
1-800-747-4457
e-mail: humank@hkusa.com

Canada: Human Kinetics, 475 Devonshire Road, Unit 100, Windsor, ON N8Y 2L5
1-800-465-7301 (in Canada only)
e-mail: humank@hkcanada.com

Europe: Human Kinetics, P.O. Box IW14, Leeds LS16 6TR, United Kingdom
+44 (0)113-278 1708
e-mail: humank@hkeurope.com

Australia: Human Kinetics, 57A Price Avenue, Lower Mitcham, South Australia 5062
(08) 82771555
e-mail: humank@hkaustralia.com

New Zealand: Human Kinetics, P.O. Box 105-231, Auckland Central
09-523-3462
e-mail: humank@hknewz.com

Contents

Second Grade Gymnastics

Second Grade Dance

Preface

Over the years, we have met a host of caring, capable, and knowledgeable teachers who believed they needed to do more to fully challenge their students' movement potential. Many teachers were quick to point out that they felt their program lacked not only breadth and depth but also progression. Some of them were frustrated by the time required to plan, develop, and evaluate quality programs for children of many different grades and levels of development. Others were overwhelmed by the awesome task of planning for scope and sequence throughout the early childhood and elementary school curriculum.

We have shown many teachers our materials for teaching physical education, and invariably they have expressed appreciation and encouraged us to make the materials widely available. In 1986, we developed a two-book set with lesson plans for grades K through 6. These books have been used by teachers in both public and private schools in urban, suburban, and rural areas in the United States and abroad. Freed from the burden of long-range planning and some of the daily preparation, teachers who use the books have been able to focus more on enhancing their instruction methods to meet their students' individual movement needs. Spending less time on the question, *What am I going to do today, and how will it lead to what I want to do tomorrow?* allows them to spend more time answering the question, *How can I help each of my students benefit most from the time they spend in my class?*

The units in the two-book set served us well for ten years, but it's always the case that the more familiar you become with materials, the more ways you find to improve them. The most obvious changes are that this edition includes units for preschool children and that the set has grown from two books to four, each containing plans for two grade levels: Preschool & Kindergarten, 1 & 2, 3 & 4, and 5 & 6. We have redeveloped, re-edited, and revised the instructional units in three program areas—games, gymnastics, and dance. To help us establish models for quality teaching and program planning, we have developed and tested the units in real-life movement and physical education settings. Each of the four books features an introductory perspective on different aspects of physical education, addressing "Movement as Content" (Preschool & Kindergarten); "Developing the Program Overview" (Grades 1 & 2); "Developing Unit Plans and Lesson Plans" (Grades 3 & 4); and "Accommodating Individual Needs" (Grades 5 & 6).

Our objectives for each unit are consistent with the National Standards for Physical Education (NASPE Standards and Assessment Task Force 1995) and the National Standards for Arts Education (Consortium of National Arts Education Associations 1994). To help you determine whether or not children have met these objectives, we have added assessment tools that correspond to the national standards. These tools will help you collect evidence of student achievement and make judgments about student learning and teaching effectiveness—a process that is essential in order to develop *performance* standards that indicate the level of achievement required to meet *content* standards (NASPE Standards and Assessment Task Force 1995). Assessment can also help you identify content progression, for example, which parts of a unit have been well learned, which skills and concepts require more practice or need revisiting in a different way, or which children show control and variety in their movements and which do not (McGee 1984).

Of course the goal of this edition remains the same as it was for the first edition: To promote active and healthy lifestyles while helping each child to fulfill his or her personal movement potential. To achieve this goal, we have integrated into many of the units important physical fitness concepts and skills that children really have fun doing.

We welcome this opportunity to help you teach. We hope our efforts help you provide your students with the kind of meaningful movement experiences that stimulate development.

ACKNOWLEDGMENTS

We would like to acknowledge the help so willingly given by the following teachers in sensitively critiquing the units in this book and the other three in this series and who also permitted us to interrupt their classes to photograph their students at work: Ann Black, Glendale-Feilbach; Sara Davison, Walbridge; Amy Kajca, Beverly; Karen Keener, McKinley; Jane Lyon, Harvard; Kay Siegel, Franklin; Becky Summersett, Reynolds from the Toledo, Ohio Public Schools and Janet Frederick, Liberty Center, Ohio. We would also like to acknowledge the cooperation of the principals, teachers, parents, and students in the above schools as well as Terry Fell, Director of Media at the University of Toledo for the photographs of children in games and gymnastics.

Our gratitude is extended to Kathleen Landfear, Director of Reston Montessori School, and to teachers and parents affiliated with this private school in Reston, Virginia, for allowing us to photograph the children during dance experiences. Our grateful thanks are given to Brian Ziegler, Theatre and Dance Specialist, Arts Focus Project–Lake Anne Elementary School in Reston, Virginia (and to the administrators, teachers, and parents of this Fairfax County School) for their enthusiasm and support during the dance photo shoots. A special thank you is given to Jim Kirby, photographer, who brought life to our dance units by providing us with a photographic record of learning experiences. Thanks are also due to Ann Erickson, Curriculum Leader, Art Program of Studies–Fairfax County Public Schools, and to Patty Koreski, Visual Arts Teacher, for their assistance in providing children's artwork from Armstrong Elementary School and Lake Anne Elementary School, Reston, Virginia.

We would also like to thank Human Kinetics and their publishing staff, especially Chris Drews, John Wentworth, Angela Snyder, Judy Rademaker, and Alesha Thompson, for their infinite patience and professional attitude and expertise during the completion of this instructional series.

Finally, we are deeply grateful to family and friends for their moral support during the final stages of this project.

Introduction: Developing the Program Overview— Phase 1 in Planning

CREATING TEACHING MATERIALS

Organizing physical education programs based on progressively challenging concepts appropriate for children is never an easy task. Selecting and organizing content, especially by those who are just developing a commitment to progression in program planning in physical education, may be an overwhelming undertaking to launch with no assistance. This introduction has been designed to *suggest* guidelines and to provide *samples* to facilitate the early stages of program planning in an attempt to make this initial task less awesome.

The following approach to planning has been developed in response to college students and practice teachers who have asked for help in formulating teaching materials, saying they need specific guidelines to trigger their thought processes. Please understand we perceive that planning for teaching that progressively challenges children can be as individual as the person doing the planning as long as learning principles applied developmentally to motor activities are not violated. The approach outlined in this series of four books is founded on a philosophic position basic to an educational approach to teaching physical education. Content progression basic to program planning is presented through movement themes that reflect maturing stages in growth and development. Planning as described here may seem to be lock-stepped, with no alternatives. *Not true.* Teachers and university students alike, using this series of four books, should feel free to design their own formats for planning. The ideas developed in this introduction are provided to assure similar processes are stimulated in planning, even though formats may vary widely. Also, the format used in planning by any one teacher is predicted to change as the user matures and becomes more practiced in implementing plans when teaching.

PLANNING: THREE QUESTIONS TO GET YOU STARTED

If your planning is to be meaningful to you, the teacher, and challenging for the students you teach, at least three questions must be answered to initiate the beginning process of planning prior to selecting, organizing, and developing content. These questions are: *Who am I teaching, why am I selecting the content,* and *how will I teach?*

WHO AM I TEACHING?

Before beginning to plan at any level, it is important to establish an awareness of the students for whom the plan is to be written. There will be times when you will not know the children for whom you are writing a unit or a lesson. Outlining the following information about the children is crucial to effective planning:

- Chronological age
- Grade level
- Developmental needs
- Special characteristics
- Previous experiences

If you do not know the children and real data is unavailable, you need to develop hypothetical data before you go any farther, so as you plan you can identify with specific needs and characteristics.

WHY AM I SELECTING THE CONTENT?

Arriving at the answer to this question when you begin to plan for teaching physical education can be found in reviewing the goals of physical education. The goals of physical education are to:

1. Move skillfully, demonstrating versatile, effective, and efficient movement in planned and unplanned settings.
2. Become aware of the meaning, significance, feeling, and joy of movement, both as a performer and as an observer.
3. Gain and apply the knowledge that governs human movement.

The decisions relevant to the "why" you select specific content for teaching physical education at every grade level should always be reflective of these goals. A conscious, concerted effort must be made to plan for the development of skillful, versatile movers in instructional, educational settings that nurture the joy and understanding of movement. In addition, care must be taken to see that the *content you select is appropriate* for the motor abilities, age, and social and mental development of the children and relevant to the *objectives* or *purposes* you are trying to achieve.

HOW WILL I TEACH?

Each teacher has a philosophy, whether written or unwritten, that lies at the heart of their answer to the question "How will I teach?" The following philosophy was written to help chart and maintain an approach to teaching physical education reflecting a philosophy that promotes a full commitment to the education of the student as well as to the goals of education. It has been used effectively by university students in teacher preparation settings as well as by experienced teachers in public and private schools in rural and urban settings. Working to implement this philosophy requires understanding the meaning each statement has for teaching and a concerted effort as you teach to keep each decision and every moment with students reflecting this philosophy.

Statement of Philosophy

As instructors, we believe that

1. Students are individuals and their individuality varies from day to day, task to task, and moment to moment.

2. Teachers must respect the integrity of the student and accept responsibility for the education of this whole being.
3. Teachers need a sincere dedication to each child in order to help all children achieve their full potential by permitting them to become increasingly independent learners.
4. Students are capable of making decisions, and education is responsible for helping students develop the ability to make reasoned and wise choices so that they can adjust their role appropriately as their social and physical surroundings change.
5. Understanding skills essential to progression can be developed by students at different times through different experiences.
6. Physical education, to share meaningfully in education, must provide experiences that improve the ability to move, that engage thought processes, and that contribute positively to the development of a value system and the esteem in which students regard themselves and others.

PHASES IN PLANNING

There are three phases in planning—three time frames for which planning ultimately must be thoughtfully conceived when developing and implementing a physical education program. These are:

- Developing the Program Overview
- Developing Unit Plans
- Developing Lesson Plans

The second and third phases are discussed in the introduction to the third book in this instructional series.

PHASE ONE IN PLANNING—DEVELOPING THE PROGRAM OVERVIEW

The Program Overview is the largest time frame for which plans are outlined. It identifies the content to be taught and projects the progression for teaching the content from grade to grade. The Program Overview spans the entire time period for which the physical education program is to be taught. For example, in a school that enrolls children from preschool through sixth grade, an 8-year Program Overview is needed. In planning the Program Overview, the teacher must have an awareness of the scope and sequence of the content to be taught and an appreciation for the learner and the teaching-learning process essential to understanding the problems and the needs inherent in planning and teaching for progression.

The chart on page xi was designed to provide a broad outline of content progression to aid in the selection of content needed in planning appropriate progression when developing a Program Overview. The dotted lines on the chart identify at which grade level, preschool through 6 grade and beyond, content from each theme is first appropriate. The heavy lines indicate the grade level where content from the theme is emphasized and should be the main focus of the units. Thin arrows illustrate that the volume of content related to each theme is so great that it continues to be appropriate beyond grade six. Content from these themes can remain a challenge on a continuing basis throughout the life of an adult. We recommend that you use this chart to guide your selection of themes when planning an appropriate Program Overview for each grade.

THEMES—A SCHEME FOR ORGANIZING CONTENT

The ability to accomplish long-range planning may be facilitated greatly by personal experience acquired through broad, alert participation in sports, gymnastics, and dance and by studying and understanding movement and the progression essential to achieving success in these program areas. The content for the teaching of games, gymnastics, and dance in this series is organized into themes to assist you in understanding the sequence for the development of skillful, versatile movement when selecting and outlining program progression. Knowing which movement themes are appropriate for various grade levels—as illustrated in the chart on pages xiv-xv—and an understanding of the Movement Framework (pages xii-xiii) will help you select appropriate content for each grade. The basic content taken from the Movement Framework and the list of themes recommended for grades 1 and 2 are included here to provide other essential information needed in preparing a Program Overview.

You will need to study carefully the content in the sample games, gymnastics, and dance units in this book and select the units that best suit your individual teaching situation. This list of themes in games, gymnastics, and dance most appropriate for Preschool through Grade 6 is provided so you can see the scope of content and identify where the content for Grades 1 and 2 fits into this outline of progression.

THEMES APPROPRIATE FOR PRESCHOOL THROUGH GRADE 6

Games Themes
Theme 1   Introduction to Basic Body and Manipulative Control
Theme 2   Introduction to Space
Theme 3   Introduction to Movement Quality (Effort)
Theme 4   Movement Flow
Theme 5   Introduction to Basic Relationships
Theme 6   Advanced Body and Manipulative Control
Theme 7   Introduction to Complex Relationships

Gymnastics Themes
Theme 1   Introduction to the Body
Theme 2   Introduction to Space
Theme 3   Introduction to Time
Theme 4   Relationships of Body Parts
Theme 5   Introduction to Weight
Theme 6   Flow and Continuity of Movement
Theme 7   Relationships to Others
Theme 8   Introduction to Rhythm

Dance Themes
Theme 1   Introduction to the Body
Theme 2   Introduction to Weight and Time
Theme 3   Introduction to Space
Theme 4   The Flow of Movement
Theme 5   Introduction to Relationships
Theme 6   Instrumental Use of the Body
Theme 7   The Basic Effort Actions
Theme 8   Occupational Rhythms
Theme 9   The Awareness of Shape in Movement
Theme 10 Transitions Between the Basic Effort Actions

Movement Themes: A Guide for Planning Teaching Progression

	PK	K	1	2	3	4	5	6
Theme 1								
Games	Introduced	Emphasized	Emphasized	Emphasized	Emphasized	Emphasized	Continues	Continues →
Gymnastics	Introduced	Emphasized	Emphasized	Emphasized	Emphasized	Emphasized	Continues	Continues →
Dance	Introduced	Emphasized	Emphasized	Emphasized	Emphasized	Continues	Continues	Continues →
Theme 2								
Games	Introduced	Introduced	Emphasized	Emphasized	Emphasized	Emphasized	Emphasized	Continues →
Gymnastics	Introduced	Emphasized	Emphasized	Emphasized	Emphasized	Emphasized	Continues	Continues →
Dance	Introduced	Emphasized	Emphasized	Emphasized	Emphasized	Emphasized	Continues	Continues →
Theme 3								
Games			Introduced	Emphasized	Emphasized	Emphasized	Emphasized	Emphasized
Gymnastics			Introduced	Emphasized	Emphasized	Emphasized	Emphasized	Continues →
Dance		Introduced	Emphasized	Emphasized	Emphasized	Emphasized	Emphasized	Continues →
Theme 4								
Games				Introduced	Introduced	Emphasized	Emphasized	Emphasized
Gymnastics				Introduced	Emphasized	Emphasized	Emphasized	Continues →
Dance		Introduced	Introduced	Introduced	Emphasized	Emphasized	Emphasized	Continues →
Theme 5								
Games					Introduced	Emphasized	Emphasized	Continues →
Gymnastics				Introduced	Emphasized	Emphasized	Emphasized	Emphasized
Dance				Introduced	Emphasized	Emphasized	Emphasized	Emphasized
Theme 6								
Games					Introduced	Emphasized	Emphasized	Emphasized
Gymnastics					Introduced	Emphasized	Emphasized	Emphasized
Dance					Introduced	Emphasized	Emphasized	Emphasized
Theme 7								
Games					Introduced	Emphasized	Emphasized	Emphasized
Gymnastics					Introduced	Emphasized	Emphasized	Emphasized
Dance					Introduced	Emphasized	Emphasized	Emphasized
Theme 8								
Gymnastics						Introduced	Emphasized	Emphasized
Dance						Introduced	Emphasized	Emphasized
Theme 9								
Dance					Introduced	Introduced	Emphasized	Emphasized
Theme 10								
Dance							Introduced	Emphasized

Key for content selection: -------------- Introduced
■■■■■■ Emphasized
————→ Continues

The Movement Framework

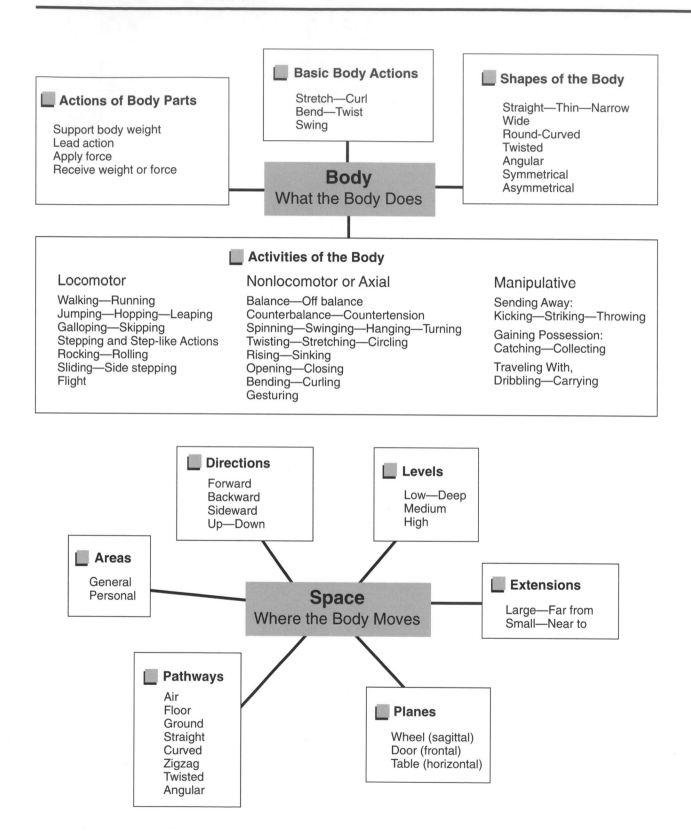

Actions of Body Parts

Support body weight
Lead action
Apply force
Receive weight or force

Basic Body Actions

Stretch—Curl
Bend—Twist
Swing

Shapes of the Body

Straight—Thin—Narrow
Wide
Round-Curved
Twisted
Angular
Symmetrical
Asymmetrical

Body
What the Body Does

Activities of the Body

Locomotor

Walking—Running
Jumping—Hopping—Leaping
Galloping—Skipping
Stepping and Step-like Actions
Rocking—Rolling
Sliding—Side stepping
Flight

Nonlocomotor or Axial

Balance—Off balance
Counterbalance—Countertension
Spinning—Swinging—Hanging—Turning
Twisting—Stretching—Circling
Rising—Sinking
Opening—Closing
Bending—Curling
Gesturing

Manipulative

Sending Away:
Kicking—Striking—Throwing

Gaining Possession:
Catching—Collecting

Traveling With,
Dribbling—Carrying

Directions

Forward
Backward
Sideward
Up—Down

Levels

Low—Deep
Medium
High

Areas

General
Personal

Extensions

Large—Far from
Small—Near to

Space
Where the Body Moves

Pathways

Air
Floor
Ground
Straight
Curved
Zigzag
Twisted
Angular

Planes

Wheel (sagittal)
Door (frontal)
Table (horizontal)

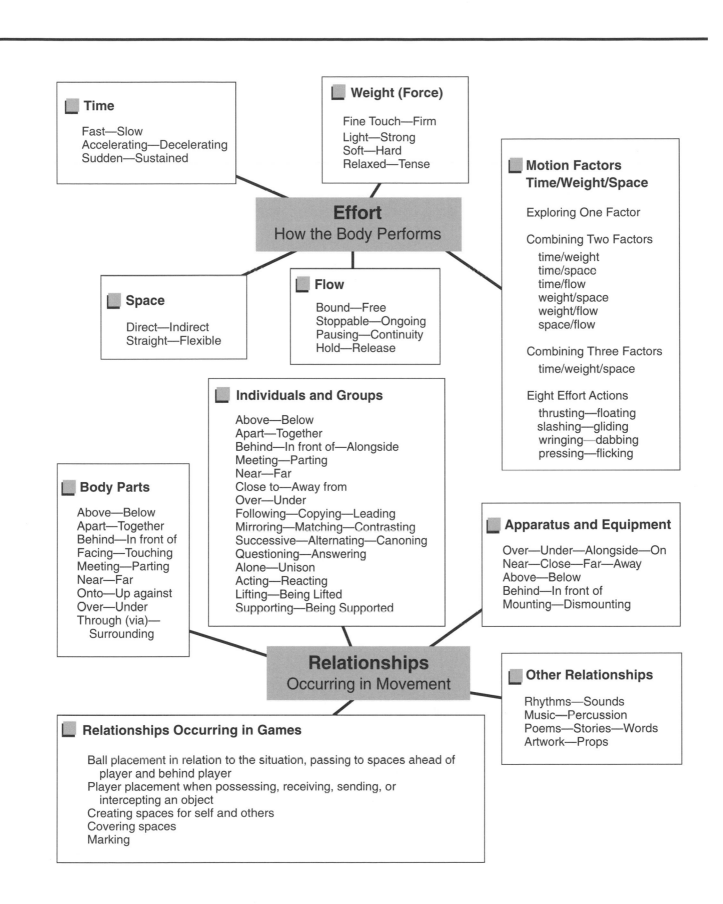

Time

Fast—Slow
Accelerating—Decelerating
Sudden—Sustained

Weight (Force)

Fine Touch—Firm
Light—Strong
Soft—Hard
Relaxed—Tense

Effort
How the Body Performs

**Motion Factors
Time/Weight/Space**

Exploring One Factor

Combining Two Factors
time/weight
time/space
time/flow
weight/space
weight/flow
space/flow

Combining Three Factors
time/weight/space

Eight Effort Actions
thrusting—floating
slashing—gliding
wringing—dabbing
pressing—flicking

Space

Direct—Indirect
Straight—Flexible

Flow

Bound—Free
Stoppable—Ongoing
Pausing—Continuity
Hold—Release

Individuals and Groups

Above—Below
Apart—Together
Behind—In front of—Alongside
Meeting—Parting
Near—Far
Close to—Away from
Over—Under
Following—Copying—Leading
Mirroring—Matching—Contrasting
Successive—Alternating—Canoning
Questioning—Answering
Alone—Unison
Acting—Reacting
Lifting—Being Lifted
Supporting—Being Supported

Body Parts

Above—Below
Apart—Together
Behind—In front of
Facing—Touching
Meeting—Parting
Near—Far
Onto—Up against
Over—Under
Through (via)—
    Surrounding

Apparatus and Equipment

Over—Under—Alongside—On
Near—Close—Far—Away
Above—Below
Behind—In front of
Mounting—Dismounting

Relationships
Occurring in Movement

Other Relationships

Rhythms—Sounds
Music—Percussion
Poems—Stories—Words
Artwork—Props

Relationships Occurring in Games

Ball placement in relation to the situation, passing to spaces ahead of
    player and behind player
Player placement when possessing, receiving, sending, or
    intercepting an object
Creating spaces for self and others
Covering spaces
Marking

Movement Themes and Basic Content
for First and Second Grades

Educational Games *

Theme 1   **Introduction to Basic Body and Manipulative Control**
Fundamental motor skills basic to becoming a games player are gradually introduced at maturing developmental levels.
Basic Content:
Manipulative activities—striking, throwing, catching, collecting, carrying, dribbling (hand and foot)
Locomotor activities—traveling and stopping, running, jumping, sidestepping
Body parts—hands, feet, shins, knees, hips, shoulders, chest

Theme 2   **Introduction to Space**
Introduction to the games environment is highlighted by exploring different ways to use the available space. (This theme is always taught in conjunction with content from Theme 1.)
Basic Content:
Areas—general, personal
Levels—high, medium, low
Extensions—near to, far from
Directions—forward, backward, sideward, upward, downward
Pathways—ground, air, curved, straight

Theme 3   **Introduction to Movement Quality (Effort)**
The focus is on the quality of movement—how the movement is being performed; how "efficient" is the movement. (This theme is always taught in conjunction with content from Theme 1.)
Basic Content:
Force—strong, light
Speed—fast, slow
Space—small, large

Educational Gymnastics

Theme 1   **Introduction to the Body**
This theme centers on creating environments in which children are encouraged to try, discover, invent, see, practice, refine, learn, and develop a movement vocabulary appropriate for gymnastics.
Basic Content:
Locomotor activities—rocking, rolling, sliding, jumping, swinging, flight, step-like actions

Theme 2   **Introduction to Space**
Content focuses on learning to be responsible for and understanding where their bodies are in space. (This theme is always taught in conjunction with content from Theme 1.)
Basic Content:
Areas—general, personal
Levels—high, medium, low
Directions—forward, backward, sideward, up, down
Pathways—straight, curved, zigzag

Theme 3   **Introduction to Time**
The main purpose of this theme is to improve the efficiency or effectiveness of movement by creating experiences that involve the purposeful production and regulation of speed. (This theme is always taught in conjunction with content from Theme 1.)
Basic Content:
Time—fast, slow; accelerating, decelerating; sudden, sustained

Theme 4   **Introduction to Relationships of Body Parts**
This theme places full attention on the relationships of body parts as a child performs in gymnastics. (This theme is always taught in conjunction with content from Theme 1.)
Basic Content:
Relationships of body parts to each other—above, below; apart, together; behind, in front of, alongside; near, far; over, under
Relationships of body parts to apparatus—over, under; near, far; above, below, behind, in front of, alongside, arriving on, dismounting from
Roles played by body parts—support body, lead action, apply force, receive force (weight);
Body shapes—angular, straight; wide, round, twisted; symmetrical, asymmetrical

Educational Dance

Theme 1   **Introduction to the Body**
This theme focuses on becoming increasingly aware of their bodies and at the same time gaining a feeling for producing motion and stillness.
Basic Content:
Locomotor activities—walking, running, skipping, galloping, leaping, stepping, jumping
Nonlocomotor activities—rising, sinking; opening, closing; turning, spinning
Body parts—leading body actions, supporting weight, receiving weight

Theme 2   **Introduction to Weight and Time**
This theme involves learning the dynamics of movement.
Basic Content:
Time—sudden, sustained
Weight—firm, fine touch

Theme 3   **Introduction to Space**
This theme teaches how to use space in a dance environment and how to "feel" space to create a particular mood or feeling. (Space is not taught alone. Like content for each of the remaining themes, space is always taught in conjunction with basic content emphasizing the body.)
Basic Content:
Areas—general, personal
Directions—forward, backward, sideward, up, down

Theme 4   **The Flow of Movement**
The emphasis is on the quality of movement while introducing the motion factors of flow and space. (Children are becoming more aware of a movement phrase.)
Basic Content:
Flow—bound, free
Space—direct, indirect

* Adapted from Barrett 1984, pp. 200-215, 154-173; Logsdon 1984, pp. 246-272.

STRUCTURING THE PROGRAM OVERVIEW

Determining the number of instructional periods of physical education to be taught annually to a class is the first essential in initiating preparation of a Program Overview. This number is determined by multiplying the number of weeks in the program by the number of lessons you need for each class per week. For example, if there are approximately 36 weeks in the school year, the following calculations show the number of lessons needed annually for each grade for programs that have 1, 2, 3, 4, or weekly lessons.

Number of Lessons Needed Annually

36 weeks x 1 lesson per week = 36 lessons annually
36 weeks x 2 lessons per week = 72 lessons annually

36 weeks x 3 lessons per week = 108 lessons annually
36 weeks x 4 lessons per week = 144 lessons annually
36 weeks x 5 lessons per week = 180 lessons annually

After the required number of annual lessons is determined, a series of units are selected for the year from those in this book, from the curriculum guide provided by the school, or from those written by you, the teacher. The games, dance and gymnastics units are noted, with a specified number of lessons approximated for each unit. Then the order in which the units is to be taught for each grade level is determined by considering such variables as geographic location of the school, availability of equipment and facilities, as well as individual school calendars affecting scheduling. You can see it is difficult to develop one yearly schedule that is appropriate for every school even within one school system. Of course, planning will always have to be adjusted to fit the needs of the children, the school schedule, and the availability of facilities and equipment.

SAMPLE PROGRAM OVERVIEW

An illustration for charting program overviews is included on page xvii to demonstrate one possible format that may be used. It outlines the program for Grades 1 and 2 as developed in this book. It is formatted in three columns so the reader can see at a glance the progression for the teaching of games, gymnastics, and dance as well as any interrelationships occurring in content across the three program areas. Often it is beneficial to know if the concepts you are teaching in one program area (games, gymnastics, or dance) have been previously introduced or will be taught later in another program area. Listing the unit foci side by side for games, gymnastics, and dance helps the reader to see when a concept is introduced and where it is being applied in another area. See if you can find content being introduced for the first time and places where it is being revisited in the same program area or in a different area. Ultimately your personal preference will determine the format you use in charting the overview of your program.

HOW TO USE THE UNITS

All the units in this series of four books are organized around Laban's (1948) movement themes and movement framework. We have described this framework in the introduction to each of the books.

How the Units Are Organized

We have divided the teaching units for each grade level into three program areas: games, gymnastics, and dance. Within those three areas, we have arranged units to progressively develop skills.

Each unit has a series of major learning experiences, numbered 1.0, 2.0, 3.0, and so forth, that usually move from simple to complex, developing the unit content. Following each major learning experience are subtasks, numbered 1.1, 1.2, and so forth, generally proceeding from simple to complex as well. They provide a variety of situations and the practice time needed to extend the children's abilities to perform or understand the skill or concept the major learning experience introduced.

Grade 1 Teaching Units

Game Units

1. Dribbling, passing, and stopping a ball with the feet
2. Developing a forceful overhand throw with a small ball
3. Traveling and stretching to catch a ball
4. Tapping a bouncing ball with the hand(s)
5. Dribbling with either hand, changing directions, and stopping
6. Sharing self-selected throwing, striking, and kicking activities with others
7. Passing and trapping a soccer ball

Gymnastics Units

1. Refining the forward roll
2. Traveling on different body parts, emphasizing changing speeds and directions
3. Combining rolling with taking weight on hands
4. Jumping, landing, and rolling, emphasizing controlled body in the air
5. Traveling into and out of a variety of balances on different body parts and surfaces

Dance Units

1. Exploring body shapes while traveling and while staying in place
2. Combining traveling and turning with stillness while creating body shapes
3. Skipping and pausing changing directions, levels, and shapes to musical beats
4. Changing body shapes and the size of movement through extensions in space
5. Traveling and pausing, changing speed, and responding to musical phrases

Grade 2 Teaching Units

Game Units

1. Dribbling and passing the ball in different directions with the feet
2. Reaching to catch while keeping one foot stationary
3. Dribbling a large ball with either hand while traveling in different directions
4. Tapping a bouncing ball with the dominant hand
5. Throwing and catching fly balls and grounders
6. Bouncing a ball forcefully and traveling under or over it at different levels
7. Punting and kicking a ball high and far
8. Batting a ball off a tee and fielding grounders

Gymnastics Units

1. Traveling in a variety of ways
2. Developing the backward roll
3. Combining balancing, rolling, and stepping
4. Creating different body shapes while balancing on and traveling off or over apparatus
5. Stepping with feet and hands

Dance Units

1. Exploring different directions by marching and traveling with step-like actions
2. Rising and sinking to musical phrases while changing directions, pathways, and expressing characters
3. Combining action words into short dance phrases, contrasting locomotor and nonlocomotor movements
4. Changing the relationship of body parts while traveling and while staying in place

How to Organize the Teaching of Units

Whether integrating this series with an existing program or adopting it as a total program, we urge you to review the introduction and the material written for the grade level you are preparing to teach before selecting your first unit.

If your current program lacks progression, you may need to choose units dealing with similar content from an earlier grade to develop introductory skills, understanding, and attitudes. Consider revisiting units introduced earlier to provide additional practice and refinement of skills needed to enjoy success in later grades. Classes showing advanced levels of motor development may benefit from instruction based on units one grade level higher. Base these decisions on careful observations of the children's movement skills and assessment of their developmental needs.

Though the units in each of the three program areas appear in a logical progression, no one order will satisfy all situations. We have found that rotating the units from games to dance to gymnastics satisfies most students, as this way no one area is the focus of study for an extended time. There are times when studying a concept in one area will carry over to the same concept in another area, such as symmetrical and asymmetrical shapes in dance and gymnastics. In this case, you may want to teach these units back to back to reinforce the concept. The order and length of units will also depend largely on you and your teaching situation—you might need to adjust the order of the units in each area to accommodate differences in climatic conditions, facilities available, and class capabilities.

Unit Components

The following presents the eight components, each with a brief description, that we have used to develop each unit in this series.

- Length of unit: Shown beneath the unit title, we approximate the number of lessons we think it will take to develop the content of the unit. Remember, situations vary. Some students will take fewer lessons and others may need more lessons to accomplish the objectives. Practice over time has a positive influence on skill development.
- Unit focus: Here we identify the main content of a unit to help you plan for progression and skill integration, not only from unit to unit, but also on a yearly basis.
- Themes: We list the relevant themes to help you determine if the unit will meet the developmental needs of *your* students. Refer to the theme and content chart on pages xiv-xv, keeping this information in mind when planning lessons.
- Motor content: You can easily see the specific movement content to be studied in each unit. Sometimes the content is new. Other times, the units focus on concepts you have previously covered. This gives you and your students the opportunities to expand, polish, and apply skills acquired in other units.
- Objectives: Based directly upon the National Standards for Physical Education (NASPE Standards and Assessment Task Force 1995) and, specifically for dance, on the National Standards for Arts Education (Consortium of National Arts Education Associations 1994), we include the unit objectives to help you identify the affective, cognitive, and motor objectives relevant to the content and appropriate for your particular group of students.
- Equipment and materials: You can tell at a glance what you need to gather for each unit, helping you prepare for the daily demands of teaching one class after another.

- Learning experiences: These are prepared in detail to provide a model for developing effective teaching to help you purposefully and safely nurture the cognitive, affective, and motor aspects of your students' development. Use and adapt these in ways that fit your style of teaching and meet the needs of your students.
- Fitness: Keeping in mind that fitness is a lifetime pursuit—not merely a unit in physical education class—we intersperse fitness concepts and activities that children can practice at home.

To personalize the units, freely add your own ideas for subtasks and new learning experiences. We encourage you to develop additional units, selecting content appropriate for your students and locale. Follow the seven-step format when developing your own units to ensure you include each of these vital components.

First Grade Games

Unit 1 — Dribbling, Passing, and Trapping

3 to 5 lessons

FOCUS Dribbling, passing, and stopping a ball with the feet

MOTOR CONTENT

Selected from Theme 1—Introduction to Basic Body and Manipulative Control

Body

Manipulative activities—dribbling, passing, and stopping a ball with either foot

OBJECTIVES

In this unit, children will (or should be willing to try to) meet these objectives:

- Dribble, looking for empty spaces by taking short running steps and pushing the ball lightly with the feet to keep the ball close in front of them.
- Place a supporting foot at the side of the ball with toes pointed toward the direction of the pass and swing the kicking leg toward the target.
- Learn how to stop the ball by placing the bottom of the nonsupporting foot lightly at the back of the ball.
- Avoid others while dribbling by looking for and traveling into empty spaces.

EQUIPMENT AND MATERIALS

One 8.5-inch vinyl, foam, or partially deflated playground ball; traffic cones, beanbags, rubber discs, or plastic bottles for each child; receptacles for the balls.

LEARNING EXPERIENCES

[If class is taught outdoors, be sure to mark off the working area with cones or other markers.]

1.0 Let's see if you can keep up with a ball as you dribble the ball by pushing it sometimes with one foot and then with the other. Stop the ball with one foot when you hear two claps. Carefully get a ball and begin to dribble with your feet, being very careful to avoid others. [Start and stop them many times, changing the length of time the children dribble before giving the stop signal.]

1.1 Try dribbling and stopping again. This time, take short running steps when dribbling. Push the ball very lightly with the inside and outside of your feet while looking for and traveling into empty spaces.

1.2 Stop the ball by placing the sole of your foot very gently on the back of the ball. [Demonstrate by placing the stopping foot behind the ball with your heel close to the ground and the sole wedging the ball between your foot and the ground. To prevent falling, place little or no weight on your stopping foot.]

Proper foot placement for stopping the ball.

1.3 Let's travel again and see if you can stop the ball quickly. Each time I clap, have your ball with you. [Check spacing often to develop and maintain a safe working environment.]

1.4 See if you can dribble into empty spaces for 30 seconds without letting your ball touch another ball or person. [Repeat several times.]

1.5 Now change your pathway each time I clap.

1.6 Everyone remember to stay on the balls of your feet and take quick, short running steps, pushing the ball lightly ahead of you. [Look for children who are staying on the balls of their feet and have them show the class how easily they can maneuver the ball.]

1.7 I just noticed [Christopher] lifting his arms out to his sides to help him keep good balance as he dribbles. Give it a try and see how your arms can help you be a better dribbler.

1.8 Running lightly on the balls of your feet and letting your arms help you balance, let's see if you can dribble into empty spaces for one minute without you or your ball touching anyone or another ball. [Repeat several times to sustain practice.]

2.0 [Place cones all about the space.] Dribble your ball about all the cones in the room without letting it touch anyone else, a cone, or another ball. Look for empty spaces as you dribble.

Can you dribble your ball about the room without letting it touch anything?

2.1 Each time you come to a cone, dribble around it. If necessary, stop the ball to keep it from touching the cone. Keep looking for an empty space and then dribble to a new cone.

2.2 Control your ball by staying close to your ball and pushing it with quick, short taps with different parts of your feet. You are the boss of your ball. Take the ball where *you* want to go rather than letting the ball take you where *it* wants to go.

2.3 You each have five points to start our game. Whenever your ball touches a cone or another ball, you lose one point. If you stop your ball with your foot or shin [touch shin] when I clap my hands, you add one point to your score.

2.4 This time, see if you can dribble your ball to one cone and, just as your ball is about to touch the cone, quickly change the direction of the ball. Sometimes change directions with your left foot and sometimes, with your right foot.

2.5 This half of the class take a seat near the wall and observe the dribblers as they look for empty spaces. Observers, see if you can find dribblers who are looking for empty spaces and not bumping into other balls or classmates. [Be sure to give the observers something specific to observe.] Observers, who dribbled without bumping anyone? [Answer: Children who dribbled with their heads up and eyes looking for open spaces. Change roles several times.]

3.0 You are all controlling the ball and getting to be pretty good dribblers. Are you ready for another challenge? This time, try to pass the ball to the wall [or your partner] with the inside of your foot and stop it with any part of your foot. [If working with a partner, put one ball away and begin.]

3.1 Turn your passing foot sideways to contact the ball with the inside of your foot. Always stop the ball before you pass it back. [Have a child demonstrate.]

3.2 Swing the inside of your foot straight toward the wall [partner] after you contact the ball to help your pass go right where you aimed.

3.3 If one foot is getting good at passing, give your other foot practice so you can pass accurately with either foot.

3.4 Practice stopping the ball with different parts of your feet. Can you try using the inside, the outside, the bottom [sole], and the top [instep] of your feet?

3.5 Try pointing your supporting [nonkicking] foot in different directions as you pass the ball. Sometimes point it to the left and sometimes to the right. See how often your ball goes where the supporting foot points?

3.6 Count and see how many times you can send your ball to the wall [partner] and stop it when it comes back without chasing it or touching it with your hands.

4.0 If you have been practicing passing the ball to the wall, join with a partner now and put one ball away. Let's all find a good working space and pass the ball back and forth. Remember to stop the ball only with your feet.

4.1 Some of you are passing accurately. You are sending the ball right to the stopping foot of your partner. Let's see if everyone can pass the ball 10 times without touching it with their hands.

4.2 Receivers, move to a different place in your work space and see if your partner can send the ball straight to you each time.

4.3 If you want a greater challenge, ask your partner to pass the ball a little faster and see if you can still stop it with your foot.

4.4 Remember how you moved your feet quickly to get in front of the ball to catch it with your hands? Let's see if you can move quickly to get in front of the ball to stop it with your foot. Passers, send the ball to the side to make your receiver travel two or three steps to stop the ball.

4.5 Receivers, move quickly to get your body in front of the ball. Reach your foot out in front and wedge the ball between the sole of your foot and the floor to stop the ball. After you stop it, pass it straight back to the front of your receiver, making your kicking leg swing toward the spot where you are aiming.

4.6 Count the passes you and your partner complete while making each other travel a bit to receive each pass. Remember to control your passes to keep the ball in your own working space.

ASSESSING DRIBBLING AND STOPPING BALLS				
Class list	Dribbles, pushing ball with either foot while running. [scale, date]	Uses different parts of foot to stop ball. [scale, date]	Points nonkicking foot in direction of intended pass. [scale, date]	Aligns body to path of ball when receiving a pass. [scale, date]
Ables, Chris	2 9/10	2 9/10	1 9/24	3 9/24
	4 9/24			
Brenning, Pat	5 9/10	4 9/10	3 9/24	5 9/24

Scale: 5 = *Consistently*   4 = *2/3 or more of the time*   3 = *Half of the time*   2 = *1/3 of the time*   1 = *Rarely or not at all*

Unit 2

Overhand Throw

3 to 5 lessons

FOCUS Developing a forceful overhand throw with a small ball

MOTOR CONTENT

Selected from Theme 1—Introduction to Basic Body and Manipulative Control and Theme 3—Introduction to Movement Quality (Effort)

Body

Manipulative activities—overhand throw with a small ball

Effort

Force—strong

OBJECTIVES

In this unit, children will (or should be willing to try to) meet these objectives:

- Improve the overhand throw through increasing power by transferring weight to the foot opposite the throwing arm and by increasing hip and torso action.
- Learn that twisting the upper body and transferring body weight to the opposite foot creates more throwing power because more body parts are working.
- Help create and maintain a safe, friendly working environment by handing stray balls back to their owners and waiting until no one is in front of them before throwing.

EQUIPMENT AND MATERIALS

One 4- to 5-inch yarn, Nerf, or sock ball for each child in the class; four to six receptacles for the balls. [Use jump ropes or beanbags to define class space if outside.]

LEARNING EXPERIENCES

1.0 Today, we are going to work on throwing a small ball overhand as far as we can. Who can tell me two things you remember from last year that helped you throw the ball far? Yes. You must make your throwing hand go high over your shoulder and step forward on the foot that is opposite your throwing hand. Now that you are older and stronger, let's see how far back you can stand from the wall and still hit the wall with the ball. Remember, do not throw your ball when anyone is in front of you retrieving a ball. Start out by facing one of the end walls. Take about 10 to 12 steps back away from the wall before you throw.

FLEXIBILITY AND WARMING UP

Hold your arms out to your side as high as your shoulders. Make small, slow circles with your arms. Now circle your arms in the other direction. Go forward again, making the circles larger and a little faster. Let's make 10 circles backward. Ten forward, larger and faster. Ten backward, larger and faster. This helps your shoulders warm up for throwing. Can you remember to do these at home each day this week?

[If outside, designate a line to throw over.] Get a ball and practice your best throws.

1.1 Always be caring about others when you throw your ball. Look before you throw. Throw only when no one is in front of you.

1.2 If you are hitting the wall, take a few steps farther back, and see if you can still hit the wall. Move a couple of steps closer if your ball doesn't quite get to the wall.

1.3 Let's see if everyone's ball can hit the wall by making your throwing hand and arm come high over your shoulder as you release the ball. [Record the names of those who are having trouble getting their throwing hand high over their shoulders.]

1.4 Get far enough away from the wall to make you really work to hit the wall.

1.5 You will get more power in your throw if you make your whole body help you throw the ball fast. Most of you are making your throwing hand go high over your shoulder as you throw. Now, work hard to get your throwing hand to go faster over your shoulder by stepping forward toward the target on your foot that is opposite your throwing hand. [See photo, page 8.]

1.6 If you are still having trouble making your ball hit the wall, look at a spot higher on the wall and try to hit it.

1.7 You really have shown you care about the others in the class by waiting for them to get their ball before throwing. Continue to think about safety and showing politeness to your classmates as you make high, overhand throws.

2.0 [Observe for children who are showing opposition as they throw and let them show the class.] You need to get both sides of your body working if you want to throw the ball fast and far. Look at [Jimmy] and see how he makes both sides of his body work by throwing with the hand on one side of his body and stepping forward on the foot on the side that is opposite his throwing hand. Look at your throwing hand holding the ball. Step forward with the foot opposite your throwing hand as you throw the ball.

2.1 Talk to your opposite foot. Say, 'Step forward as I throw.' This will help you put more power into your throw.

2.2 As you step forward on your opposite foot, don't forget to make your throwing hand go very fast as you throw.

2.3 Take turns being teacher and student with the person next to you. One of you be the teacher, the other, the student. Teachers, check to see if your student steps forward on the foot opposite of the throwing hand. [Change roles.] Doesn't it make you feel good when you help someone else?

2.4 Teachers, see if you can help your student hit the wall five times in a row without missing by reminding them to step forward on the opposite foot and to make the throwing hand go very fast over the shoulder. [Change roles.]

2.5 See how many steps you can be away from the wall and still hit the wall. Remember, we are all trying to make both sides of our bodies work as we throw. That means you throw with your favorite hand and step forward with the foot on the opposite side of your body. Make both sides of your body work.

2.6 This half of the class sit and watch the throwing hand and the stepping foot of the throwers. See if they make both sides of their bodies work. [Reverse roles.] Okay, can you make both sides of your bodies work, too?

3.0 Let's try to make our ball go farther. Each time we throw and hit the wall, take a step back and try again. If the ball misses the wall, move closer to the wall. [Observe for those not using opposition.]

3.1 To get more speed as you throw, make your arm whip forward over your shoulder very fast.

3.2 Try two throws. First, make your hand go very slowly as you throw. Then make your throwing hand go very fast as you throw and see what happens. Which throw made the ball come closer to the wall? Right—throwing fast made your ball go farther.

3.3 Take your elbow on your throwing arm way back when you throw and see if you can get more speed. Don't forget to have your eyes look at the spot where you want the ball to hit.

4.0 You must remember that your whole upper body has to move and work to put power into the overhand throw. Try twisting, turning your shoulder and hips back along with your throwing arm and hand as you prepare to throw. Then twist forward as you step forward and throw. [Help a child demonstrate. Keep a record of those having trouble with the twist and give individual feedback.]

4.1 Twist back as you drop your throwing shoulder back to make your nonthrowing shoulder point toward the wall. Practice this twist to help you get in position to throw the ball hard.

4.2 Keep your eyes looking at a spot on the wall that you want your ball to hit. Don't take your eyes off the spot when you take the ball back to throw. Twist, keep looking at your spot, and . . . throw!

4.3 Now as you twist to take the ball back, let your body and shoulder lean back, shifting [putting] most of your weight onto your back foot. Then, make that ball *fly* as you step forward onto your opposite foot.

4.4 You are really beginning to look like baseball pitchers. Pitchers twist, lean back, and let the ball fly. See how far away from the wall you can be and still hit it.

4.5 Can anyone tell me the important things to remember to help you throw the ball far? Yes! Twist, taking your hand, throwing shoulder, and hip back; keep your eyes focused on the target. Great! Now step forward on the opposite foot; make your throwing hand go high and fast over your shoulder, and release the ball when your hand is high in the air.

4.6 Some of you may like to see if you can catch the high throw of your partner. [You may give this challenge of throwing and catching with a partner to individuals who appear to you to be ready or you may choose to open the choice to the entire class. Teach those throwing and catching with a partner to position themselves safely. If you hold class indoors, have the class form two lines with partners facing each other, with their backs toward the side walls.]

Stretch your throwing arm way back. Tell your opposite foot to *step forward as I throw.*

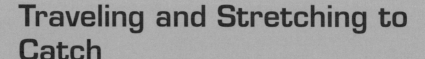

Unit 3 — Traveling and Stretching to Catch

3 to 5 lessons

FOCUS — Traveling and stretching to catch a ball

MOTOR CONTENT

Selected from Theme 1—Introduction to Basic Body and Manipulative Control

Body

Manipulative activities—throwing overhand, traveling to catch
Locomotor activities—traveling to catch

OBJECTIVES

In this unit, children will (or should be willing to try to) meet these objectives:

- Reach to catch a ball, bringing it toward the body as they catch it.
- Throw a small ball or beanbag overhand and travel to catch it.
- Learn that errors made in throwing and catching are usually not made intentionally so they should be patient with their partners and themselves.
- Remain in their own spaces while working and retrieve balls or beanbags by going around, not through, the working space of others.

EQUIPMENT AND MATERIALS

One small "soft" ball or beanbag for every one or two children.

LEARNING EXPERIENCES

1.0 [It is best to teach this unit outside where children have more space to run and catch safely.] In your own working space, try hard to do your best throwing and catching. Choose a partner, one ball [or beanbag], find your own working space, and see how many times you can throw and catch the ball [beanbag].

1.1 Try to throw overhand by making your hand go over your shoulder. Really try to send the ball [beanbag] right to your partner.

1.2 As you throw, remember to step forward with the foot that is opposite your throwing hand. Help each other to remember to take this step.

1.3 Catchers, try to make your partner look like a good thrower by trying to catch every ball they throw. Reach with your hands and fingers to catch. Travel to get to the ball if it doesn't come to you. Partners, move farther apart if you are both catching successfully. Move closer to your partner if you are having trouble catching. [If using a ball, tell them to allow the ball to bounce if they are having trouble catching.]

1.4 Catchers, think about what you do with your fingers as you try to catch the ball. Remember to point your fingers up, thumbs close together, if the ball is high [above your waist] and point fingers down, little fingers close together, when you catch low [below your waist].

1.5 If you have been throwing a ball, trade with someone who has a beanbag and see if you can still be a good catcher.

1.6 If the ball has been going to the side of your partner, see if you can make it go straight to your partner by making your hand point to your partner as you release the ball.

1.7 Good throwers always keep their eyes on their targets. Keep your eyes focused on your partner all the time while you are throwing the ball.

1.8 Stay on the balls of your feet ready to travel in any direction to catch the ball. See if you can look like a baseball player in the field ready to catch a fly ball!

1.9 Catchers, be ready to move your feet if the ball does not come to you.

2.0 Throw the ball to the side of your partners to make them travel a little to catch it.

2.1 Throwers, if you want the catcher to move to catch, you will have to think about making your throwing hand reach out and point to an empty space to the side of your partner as you release the ball. Remember to stay in your own work space. Go around other people's spaces to get the ball if it gets away from you.

2.2 Catchers, see if you can tell where your partner is going to throw the ball and get ready to run to the spot where it will come down.

2.3 You people are doing a super job of caring for others in the class by being very careful not to send your ball into the work space of others and walking around work space to retrieve your ball. Keep up this good work!

Point fingers up, thumbs close together to catch a high ball.

If the ball doesn't come to you, step and reach to catch it.

2.4 Catchers, give with your hands by bringing them toward your body as the ball touches your hands. This helps take the speed off the ball and keeps the ball from bouncing out of your hands.

2.5 Be sure you are throwing to an empty space and not to the catcher. This will give the catchers good practice in running to catch.

2.6 See if you can throw the ball so it will make the catcher run forward to catch it.

2.7 Throwers, give your catcher more time to catch the ball by throwing the ball high in the air.

2.8 Catchers, bring the ball into your body, catching as quietly as you can.

3.0 Check your space. You may need to spread away from other partners a bit. Be careful you don't run into the space of others as you practice to see how far you can make each other run to catch.

3.1 If your partners are not catching the ball, did you throw it too far away from them? Make your partners feet run to catch, but don't throw the ball too far away from them. Work hard to make sure they can catch every ball.

3.2 Try to catch every ball thrown to you. Take pride in being a good catcher. See how many catches you can make in a row.

3.3 Change partners and see if you can make your new partner a good catcher.

3.4 Catchers, if you can, try to throw the ball back carefully as soon as you catch it but remember to throw it so your partner can run to catch.

4.0 How high in the air can you throw the ball? You will have to lean far back at your waist and make your throwing shoulder drop down in back of you as you prepare to make a very high throw.

4.1 When throwing high overhand, let go of the ball when your throwing hand is high. [If a child has trouble throwing the ball high overhand, have him try to make the ball hit above a line 15 to 25 feet high on the wall or stand 10 to 15 feet in front of him with your hand raised and ask him to try to throw the ball far and high over your hand.]

4.2 Make your hand go fast over your shoulder to make the ball go faster, sending it high in the air. Sending the ball or beanbag high helps your partners catch more balls because it gives them more time to catch.

4.3 Catchers, if your partner sometimes throws the ball over your head, stand farther back from them. You can run forward to catch much easier than backing up to catch.

4.4 Throwers, see if you can make the catcher travel to one side and then to the other side to catch. Catchers, remember to get your hands ready to catch the ball by pointing your fingers up with your thumbs touching for a fly ball.

4.5 Mix up your throws so the catcher is traveling into different spaces to catch each time.

4.6 Count and see how many good running catches you and your partner can make without either of you missing. Set a new catching record!

4.7 Let's see if you and your partner can improve your record.

ASSESSING CATCHING PROCESS				
Class list	Fingers up, thumbs close for high catches. (scale, date)	Fingers down, thumbs apart, for low catches. (scale, date)	Consistently reaches to meet the ball with two hands. (scale, date)	"Gives" to bring ball, partly or wholly, to chest. (scale, date)
Jones, James	4 9/15/97	4 9/15/97	3 9/17/97	3 9/17/97
Locke, Sue	3 9/15/97	3 9/15/97	2 9/17/97	2 9/17/97

Scale:　5 = Always　4 = Frequently　3 = Sometimes　2 = Rarely　1 = Never

Unit 4 — Tapping a Ball With the Hand
3 to 5 lessons

FOCUS Tapping a bouncing ball with the hand(s)

MOTOR CONTENT

Selected from Theme l—Introduction to Basic Body and Manipulative Control

Body

Locomotor activities—traveling to return the ball
Manipulative activities—tapping a bouncing ball underhand

OBJECTIVES

In this unit, children will (or should be willing to try to) meet these objectives:

- Tap a bouncing ball underhand with the palm of the hand(s), sending it so it bounces in front of a receiver to be tapped back.
- Direct each ball to a spot in front of the receiver and adjust body position to return each ball tapped to them, trying to keep the ball in play as long as possible.
- Learn that they can control the direction of the ball by reaching out the tapping hand toward the spot where they want the ball to land.
- Listen and work willingly with others to help create and maintain an effective learning environment.

EQUIPMENT AND MATERIALS

One 8- to 10-inch vinyl plastic ball for each pair of children, one short rope for each two children.

LEARNING EXPERIENCES

1.0 Let's see if you can gently toss a ball underhand so that it bounces in front of your partner. Try to toss it so it bounces up to about your receiver's waist. Today, you will need a working space away from others, a partner to work with, and one ball for the two of you.

1.1 Some of you are one or two steps too far apart. Move closer and see if all of you can toss the ball so that it lands and bounces about one step in front of your partner. This way, everyone can catch the ball without moving their feet.

1.2 [Observe the children carefully. Often a few children may need a new challenge before the whole class is ready for it. Children who are able to catch the ball at waist height are ready for this task.] Now, one of you be a tapper. When your partner tosses the ball and makes it bounce one step in front of you, see if you can tap it with two very flat hands so it bounces up to your tosser's waist. Tossers, catch the ball and toss it again. [Change roles quickly several times so both partners can practice tapping and tossing.]

1.3 Tossers, look at a spot on the floor about one step in front of your partner. Try to make the ball land right on that spot. Remember, the job of the tosser is to help the tapper practice tapping by being a careful tosser.

1.4 Tappers, you can make the ball go right to the spot on the floor in front of your partner, too, if you make your tapping hand reach out for that spot as you tap.

1.5 Some of you might also have to watch your power as you tap. If your catcher catches the ball before it bounces or if it goes past him in the air, you need to tap it more gently. [Have the children change partners often to see if they retain their skills as they work with others and to give them practice in adjusting to the skill levels of others.]

1.6 Tappers, try to swing your tapping arm close along the side of your body and hit up underneath the ball—not down on top of the ball. [Go for an underhand hit, not overhand. Occasionally, a child with more mature striking skills may be ready to control the sidearm hit with the hand and arm swinging more parallel to the floor.]

2.0 You have all been such caring partners. Now let's see if you can both be tappers and keep the ball bouncing back and forth between you, letting it bounce on the floor before you tap it back.

2.1 Tap the ball, making it bounce right up to your partner's waist, just as you did when you tossed it and made it bounce in front of your partner.

2.2 Remember when you are tapping, you must be the boss of the ball. Make the ball bounce right to your partner by carefully reaching out toward the spot in front of your partner as you tap the ball.

2.3 Let's stop a moment. It is difficult to always tap a ball perfectly so that it lands in front of your partner. Sometimes the receiver has to help a little and move quickly to get in front of the ball to return it. Let's remember no one is perfect yet. Be up on the balls of both feet ready to move to the ball if it isn't going to bounce in front of you.

2.4 Let's see how many times you can tap the ball back and forth without either of you catching or chasing the ball.

2.5 Change partners and see if you can help your new partners set a new record number of taps.

2.6 Receivers, be alert [pay attention]. Keep your eyes on the ball and your feet ready to travel to the ball. Both of you try very hard to return every ball.

2.7 See if the two of you can tap the ball back and forth without making your partner have to travel to tap it back to you. You might want to start close and, when you are successful close-up, move back a little. Be the master of the ball and make it go right where you want it to go.

3.0 You and your partner may want to place a rope down on the floor in between the two of you and see if you can tap the ball back and forth over the rope. Try very hard to tap with only one hand.

3.1 See how many times you can tap the ball back and forth over the rope. Remember, let the ball bounce before you tap it.

3.2 Let's see if you can help your partner set a new record. Make every tap bounce right in front of your partner. Carefully watch your power.

Make your tapping hand reach out for the spot on the floor right in front of your partner.

4.0 [You may wish to reserve the following tasks to challenge more advanced children. These tasks often require children to adjust body position to give the tapper access to the bouncing ball.] Some of you might like to work by yourself. If you do, get a ball, find space near a wall, and tap the ball against the wall. Catch it after it bounces once or tap it back to the wall again.

4.1 Notice where the ball bounces on the floor and move to get your body, hitting arm, and hand behind the ball to be ready to tap it back against the wall instead of catching it.

4.2 Count how many times you can tap the ball against the wall without catching it, letting it bounce after each tap.

4.3 If you would like, join with someone and put one ball away. It can be fun to play this game with another person. Take turns hitting the ball against the wall.

Unit 5

Dribbling, Changing Directions, and Stopping

4 to 5 lessons

FOCUS Dribbling with either hand, changing directions, and stopping

MOTOR CONTENT

Selected from Theme 1—Introduction to Basic Body and Manipulative Control and Theme 2—Introduction to Space

Body

Manipulative activities—dribbling a ball with either hand

Space

Areas—general, personal
Directions—changing directions, forward, backward, sideways

OBJECTIVES

In this unit, children will (or should be willing to try to) meet these objectives:

- Change directions while dribbling a ball with either hand, keeping their eyes focused on the space in front of them—not on the ball.
- Learn that they should push with the hand, wrist, and elbow rather than slap with the hand to dribble the ball.
- Keep the ball below the waist, making changing directions easier.
- Show an awareness for the safety of others by keeping their ball close and moving into empty spaces as they dribble.

EQUIPMENT AND MATERIALS

One 8.5-inch playground ball for each child, 10 to 15 traffic cones or beanbags.

LEARNING EXPERIENCES

1.0 Remember some of us last year bounced a ball while making our feet do different things as we traveled about the room? This year, we are going to try to make our dribbling even more exciting. Everyone on this side of the room may politely walk over and get a ball, find a working space, and begin to dribble the ball with your hand. Now let's see if the other half of the class can be as polite and caring as you get your ball, find a space, and begin.

1.1 Try to dribble by pushing your ball toward the floor with a cupped hand. Don't slap the ball—push it.

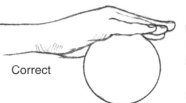

Correct

Incorrect

1.2 As you dribble, try to feel the ball with your whole hand as you push the ball toward the floor. Stop when I clap my hands twice. [Clap twice. Check to see if the children are spaced away from others. Comment about spacing and get them started dribbling again quickly.]

1.3 [Look for those who are slapping and not pushing the ball. If necessary, have them listen to see if they can hear their hands hit their ball or feel the hard slaps of their hands on their ball.] Try not to slap the ball. Push the ball as you dribble. Make your hand ride the ball down toward the floor and up again. Bend your elbow to ride the ball up and straighten your elbow as you push the ball down toward the floor.

1.4 Dribble again, traveling slowly. Each time you hear the signal to stop, try to be in a big space all by yourself. [Stop the children often. Comment on spacing and restart quickly.]

1.5 Look for an empty space and dribble to it. When you get to an empty space, stop traveling but keep dribbling your ball as you look for another empty space. See how many empty spaces you can find. Stop, look, then start traveling to each new empty space.

1.6 To be safe, you must look where you are going as you dribble so you don't bump into others. As you dribble, focus your eyes out in front of you. Make your eyes look for empty spaces. Stop when you hear my hands clap twice.

1.7 Try not to let the ball bounce up higher than your waist as you push the ball toward the floor. Keep your eyes looking straight ahead.

2.0 I believe some of you can dribble with either hand. See if you can sometimes push the ball with one hand and then push it with the other hand. [You may need to say 'change.'] When I say 'change,' give one hand a rest and use your other hand.

2.1 Some of us have a favorite hand. Let's see how long you can dribble with your opposite [other] hand, sometimes traveling and sometimes standing still.

2.2 Now, try to dribble to an empty space with your favorite dribbling hand and stop. Change hands and dribble to a new space with your opposite hand and stop. Keep looking for new spaces as you dribble.

2.3 Remember to push your ball with your whole hand. See how long you can dribble your ball into many new empty spaces, changing hands every time you get to your new space. I'll time you for one minute. Ready? Begin.

2.4 Listen to your hand. See how quietly you can push the ball with your hand. Is it making a slapping noise or is it pushing the ball very quietly toward the floor?

3.0 You are getting to be good dribblers, and some of you are even changing hands as you dribble. Try traveling a little faster this time. To travel faster, you will have to push the ball farther out in front of you—not straight down, to make you run as you dribble.

3.1 Let's check to see if you are still looking for empty spaces as you dribble. When I clap my hands twice, stop and check your spacing.

3.2 [Scatter cones or beanbags about the space.] As you dribble, see if you can look out for the cones [beanbags] and your classmates at the same time. I'm going to watch your eyes to see if they are watching the ball or looking for open spaces and other classmates.

3.3 Try to dribble to a cone, change hands, and go to another cone and change hands. Change hands without stopping each time you get near a different cone.

3.4 Dribble to a cone. Circle around the cone while you are still dribbling, then travel to another cone. Keep going until you have gone to every cone in the room.

3.5 Let's play follow the leader as we dribble. You will need a partner. One person will be the leader and dribble with either hand about the room. The follower must watch the dribbling hand of the leader and use the same hand. This is going to be hard for the followers. They have to carefully watch the

Looking for lonely cones.

leader change hands and keep from bumping into anyone else. Get a partner, decide who will be the leader, and begin. [Change leaders several times.]

4.0 What kind of step do you take that lets you go to the side? Yes, a sliding step or a sideways gallop. Let's all try to dribble sideways by sliding.

4.1 Try to stay on the balls of your feet so you can move lightly and quickly. Remember to dribble the ball by pushing—not slapping—as you travel sideways.

4.2 Some of you may want to really challenge your skill in dribbling by changing hands each time you come to a different cone.

4.3 Let's see if you can safely dribble a little faster and still change hands. Don't forget to push the ball toward the floor, then let your hand ride the ball back up to your waist. Make your elbow bend and straighten as you dribble.

5.0 Let's play follow the leader again but, this time, see if you can dribble sometimes forward, backward, and sideways. Work with the person closest to you. Take turns being the leader. [Change leaders frequently.]

5.1 Remember to try to change your dribbling hand and your direction each time your leader changes.

5.2 I like the way you are being careful of others. Leaders, watch for changes in direction by other groups and be ready to dribble to an open spot.

5.3 Leaders, change your direction often. See if you can lead forward, backward, and sideways.

Unit 6   Throwing, Striking, and Kicking

4 to 5 lessons

FOCUS   Sharing self-selected throwing, striking, and kicking activities with others

MOTOR CONTENT

Selected from Theme 1—Introduction to Basic Body and Manipulative Control

Body

Manipulative activities—striking, kicking, dribbling, tossing, rolling

OBJECTIVES

In this unit, children will (or should be willing to try to) meet these objectives:

- Explore a wide selection of manipulative activities, including striking and kicking stationary or moving objects with a hand, foot, or an implement, and tossing and rolling balls while staying in teacher-designed areas.
- Show they can share by selecting an alternate choice when all equipment in an area is in use, looking especially for experiences that they have not had yet on a particular day.
- Leave the equipment where they found it and move quickly to a new choice when the teacher asks them to do so.
- Work well with anyone who comes to share in the same activity area so that everyone may have mutually rewarding learning experiences.

EQUIPMENT AND MATERIALS

The following is a sample of equipment and activities for a class of 30 children.

Learning Area	Equipment	Number of Children and Description of Activity
A	one large balloon, a rope or string and two standards	four to eight children tapping a large balloon with their hands over a string or rope tied onto two standards 3' or 4' high
B	one plastic bat, one traffic cone, one yarn ball	one child batting a ball off the traffic cone, one child retrieving the ball
C	two bowling pins, two hockey sticks, one yarn ball	two children with hockey sticks sending a yarn ball back and forth between the bowling pins
D	six short paddles, six small, round balloons	six children tapping small, round balloons with the paddles
E	six 8" playground balls, six traffic cones	six children dribbling a ball with hands or feet around and about the traffic cones
F	four softballs, eight bowling pins	two children rolling balls at bowling pins
G	nine beanbags, three small boxes	three children tossing beanbags into small boxes

This type of unit requires you to select sensitively and arrange equipment carefully to create diverse learning areas. Each area needs its own equipment and sufficient working space. Arrange the equipment so that the children can perceive quickly the activity you want them to do with it. Either you or the children may change the equipment periodically during the teaching of the unit or leave it the same throughout the unit. Safety, however, must be your first consideration.

LEARNING EXPERIENCES

[This unit is different from most others because it allows children to explore a wide range of activities, using many different types of equipment, manipulative skills, and social skills. The children will need little instruction in how to perform the activities. Instead, focus on the social interaction of the children, managing the situation carefully. Transitions from area to area are the toughest to manage. You must ensure safety, teach children to share, and help some children make new choices. Otherwise, let the equipment and the environment teach the manipulative skills. You can use tasks such as the following, with modifications, for each lesson.]

1.0 [On the first day, arrange the equipment. Introduce each piece of equipment and identify the activity for each work area.] Today, let's sit down and look around at the many things we can do. See the big balloon [at station A]? [Tap it up.] Several of you can enjoy tapping the balloon back and forth over the rope. Now look at the ball on top of the traffic cone [at station B]. One person bats the ball off the tee into the corner. Another person picks up the ball and puts it on the tee and becomes the next batter. See these hockey sticks [at station C]? Two people pass the ball [puck] back and forth between the goals [pins]. Can you see how to use these paddles [at station D]? [Pick up a paddle and tap a balloon up in the air.] Here [at station E] you can practice dribbling the ball around and about the traffic cones. Now watch here [at station F]. You get to practice rolling the ball to knock over the pins. [Pick up a softball and roll it at two pins.] Look over here at the beanbags [at station G]. Three of you get to see how good you are at tossing the beanbags into the boxes. [Pick up a beanbag and try to toss it into a box.] Oh! There are so many exciting things to do. Let's listen to four rules for today. Rule one: If you get to an area and others already have the equipment, you will need to look for lonely equipment and pick it up and use it. You may not stand and wait to work. Rule two: We must use and return the equipment right back to the same place where we find it. Rule three: Always look and be sure no one is around you to get hit with any of the equipment you use. Rule four: Work quietly and walk.

1.1 This half of the class may walk and choose their equipment and begin. Look for the equipment not being used. Now this half choose your equipment. [Some things you need to do each time children select equipment are (1) comment on how courteous children were in selecting equipment, (2) monitor the batting areas carefully to be sure balls are batted into the corners and the retrievers are not in the way of a swinging bat, (3) check to see if students are waiting at favorite areas and remind them when the equipment is in use to find unused equipment, (4) remind children that several of them can be on either side of the rope tapping the large balloon, (5) help children having difficulty getting started,

Children working at two stations.

(6) notice the favorite and least favorite areas, and (7) complement children working together effectively. Use these suggestions each day that you teach the unit.]

1.2 [Highlight different activities each time you stop the children before having them move to a different activity. This encourages the children to change equipment and try different things with less hesitation. If you notice a less popular area, calling attention to the activity in this way may increase its popularity. Clap hands twice for all children to stop.] Thanks for stopping so quickly. Have a seat. Let's watch this group [name equipment and activity]. See how they are making [name the activity] a really fun game. Everyone return your equipment to right where you found it. Remember to share—don't work with the same equipment twice. When I say go, let's have the boys and girls working on this side of the gym walk and find new equipment and begin. Go! Now this side may find a place and begin. [Monitor and intervene immediately where needed for switching and sharing activities, noise, batting areas for safety (i.e., remind children to hit into the corner), and children having difficulty restarting.]

1.3 [When you observe a group working and sharing beautifully, clap hands twice for the children to stop.] Many of you are sharing and working so well together. Boys and girls with the [big balloon] stand up and show how you share the [balloon] and make it fun for each person. Now everyone carefully place your equipment where you found it, find a new place to work, and begin. [Observe and improve behavior where needed (i.e., putting equipment down where they found it before moving to a new area, children who may quarrel over equipment, and batting areas). Constantly monitor the whole area to maintain a safe environment. You may need to repeat 1.1, 1.2, and 1.3 several times during a lesson, depending on the length of the class period.]

1.4 [You may need to have and to explain an explicit plan for putting the equipment away at the end of the class.] This time, show me how you can carefully place your equipment exactly where you found it and quietly prepare to leave.

2.0 Revisit this unit by introducing child-designed activity areas. You and the children could invent new equipment arrangements or variations on activities that challenge skills in throwing, striking, and kicking and promote safe play.

AFFECTIVE ASSESSMENT				
Class list	Joins quickly with those selecting same activity.	Stays within designated area sharing equipment by limiting turns.	Arranges equipment without guidance before leaving area.	Selects alternative area when equipment is in use.
Colt, R.	3	3	3	1
Baker, M.	5	5	5	3

Scale: 5 = *Does consistently* 3 = *Does inconsistently* 1 = *Does rarely*

Unit 7

Passing and Trapping

4 to 5 lessons

FOCUS Passing and trapping a soccer ball

MOTOR CONTENT

Selected from Theme 1—Introduction to Basic Body and Manipulative Control

Body

Locomotor activities—traveling to stop a ball, stopping the ball with the sole and front of either foot

Manipulative activities—passing a large ball with the inside and outside of either foot

OBJECTIVES

In this unit, children will (or should be willing to try to) meet these objectives:

- Pass a large ball, making it roll by contacting it with a flat surface of the inside or outside of either foot.
- Travel to trap a rolling ball.
- Travel to stop a rolling ball.
- Learn that to start traveling quickly, they must be on the balls of their feet with their weight balanced.
- Show consideration for the work of others by going behind classmates to retrieve balls that stray.

EQUIPMENT AND MATERIALS

One 8 inch soccer ball, foam or playground ball and one cone for every child.

LEARNING EXPERIENCES

1.0 [Try having the children kick from tape marks on the floor about 15 feet from the wall to encourage them to develop a forceful kick.] Today, let's see if you can make your ball roll straight to the wall and back to you by kicking the ball with the inside or outside of your foot. Stop the ball with a foot before you send it back to the wall.

1.1 Try to stand with your toes and shoulder on your nonkicking side pointing to a spot on the wall straight out in front of you each time you kick the ball.

1.2 Pass the ball by kicking it with the inside of your foot. The flat, inside of your foot will make the ball roll and hit the wall down low—not up high.

1.3 Place your nonkicking foot near the side of the ball as you step forward to kick. Then pass the ball with the inside of your foot. Try to contact the ball just above its center.

1.4 Have some of you played or seen someone play soccer? What body parts usually are not supposed to touch the ball in soccer? Right, your hands! Maybe we had better practice stopping the ball using only a foot by quickly positioning your body and foot directly in front of the ball.

1.5 Count how many times you can pass the ball to the wall with the inside of your foot and stop it with just your foot when it comes back to you.

1.6 The ball got away from some of you because your kick sent the ball too high. See if you can make the ball roll by contacting it with the flat, inside of your foot instead of kicking up under it with your toes.

1.7 If you have been successful in passing the ball low with the inside of your foot, you may want to try passing the ball with the outside of your foot.

1.8 Great! Most of you have your ball rolling to the wall. Now, see how many times you can pass and stop the ball without chasing it or touching it with any body part except your feet. Feet only!

Use the inside of your foot to kick the ball.

2.0 You can teach both feet to be good, low kickers and stoppers if you change feet each time you stop or kick. Begin to pass and stop the ball first with one foot and then with the other.

2.1 Make your kicking foot and ankle nice and firm as you swing your foot back and through the ball.

2.2 Whether you pass the ball with the inside or outside of either foot, aim your kick by pointing the toes on your supporting foot toward the spot on the wall where you want the ball to go and by swinging your kicking foot toward that same spot.

2.3 Most of you have been stopping the ball with the sole of your foot. Try stopping it with the top of your foot [the instep] by moving to line up your foot with the ball, pointing your toes down near the ground in front of the ball, and giving as the ball touches your foot.

2.4 You have to stay on the balls of your feet with your weight leaning forward to be ready to get the toes of one of your feet pointed down behind the ball to kick.

2.5 Count and see how many passes you can make without having to chase the ball or touch it with your hands.

3.0 Let's work on passing the ball straight to a partner. When I count to five, choose someone close to you, put away one ball, find a space, and begin.

3.1 Try to make each pass roll exactly to your partner. Straight passes won't make your partner travel to stop them.

3.2 Don't forget to give both feet practice in passing and stopping the ball.

3.3 Get your weight forward on the balls of your feet ready to travel quickly to line up with the ball. See how much faster you can stop the ball and pass it when you are ready?

3.4 Some of you might like to set a record: See how many times the two of you can stop the ball without either one missing. Remember, put your weight forward on the balls of your feet and travel quickly to get the front of your body and your stopping foot in line with the ball.

4.0 This time, the receivers are going to point to where they want the ball to come. Passers, be alert and watch for the signal. Try to send the ball to the target by pointing the toes of your supporting foot straight toward the target.

4.1 Receivers, practice your best ready position so you can give both feet practice in stopping the ball. Lean forward on the balls of your feet.

4.2 Passers, choose your passing foot carefully. Sometimes pass the ball with the inside of your foot and sometimes the outside.

4.3 If you are passing the ball three or four times without missing, take a step or two back and see if you can still make accurate passes to the spot where your partner is pointing.

4.4 People with the ball stand very still. Those without a ball move to a new partner close to you who has a ball. Work hard to see how many passes you and your new partner can make without missing.

4.5 Passers, if your receiver is having to chase the ball, try aiming your pass more carefully by pointing the toes of your supporting foot toward the center of your partner's body and swinging the inside of your kicking foot straight out toward your partner.

4.6 Stay alert when you are trying to stop the ball. Be ready to travel quickly to line up your body and stopping foot with the front of the ball. Point the toes of your stopping foot down near the ground and pull your whole foot back just as the ball touches it. Bringing your foot back helps the ball stay right in front of you so you do not have to chase it. Remember to teach both feet to stop and pass the ball.

4.7 Some partners may want to place two cones in the middle of your space about three steps apart and try to pass the ball between the cones. When you get good at aiming your passes between the cones, you may want to move back a little farther or move your cones a bit closer to each other to make you aim your passes even more carefully. Remember to send the ball by contacting it above its center.

5.0 [Before giving this task to the entire class, you may choose to group and challenge children with the task who are passing and stopping the ball with either foot and completing several passes in a row.] Boys and girls, I've noticed your passes getting straighter, and I have seen many of you giving both of your feet great practice in stopping and passing the ball. Some of you may wish to join with another set of partners so that you have a group of four. If you do, put away one ball and find a working space and begin.

5.1 Share the ball with everyone and see how long the four of you can keep the ball in your own area, passing and stopping the ball with just your feet. In your group, count your completed passes. Try to set a new record each time you start over.

5.2 Help make stopping a little easier for your receiver by contacting the ball with a flat inside or outside surface [area] of your foot to make the ball roll when you pass it.

5.3 Don't get too excited when you are working in a larger group. Remember to point your supporting foot toward the receiver and make your kicking foot swing right out to your receiver. Try to give both feet equal practice in stopping and passing the ball.

5.4 See how quickly you can pass the ball to someone else. Try not to send it back to the person who passed it to you. Why do you think I am suggesting you send it to a different person? Right! Everyone needs lots of practice to get better.

5.5 This time, all four of you are to sit down immediately when anyone has to chase the ball or touches it with a hand. Let's see which group can pass and stop the ball the longest. [Restart the class whenever everyone is sitting. Repeat several times. Ask those sitting how they could improve their skills.]

5.6 This time, each of you tell the others in your group what you can do better to help your group make more completed passes. After each of you have shared, get up and count again to see if your ideas help you beat your record.

5.7 [You may want to select different groups to share the things they are going to do to help complete more passes. Then pick out one or two of the specific hints they give and suggest that other (or all) groups might like to try working on these improvements.]

ASSESSING TRAPPING AND STOPPING BALLS				
Name	Can use either sole to stop balls. (rating, date)	Gives with front of foot to trap. (rating, date)	Moves quickly to the side to stop balls. (rating, date)	Consistently stops or controls balls close to self. (rating, date)
Town, Emma	4 9/25 5 10/9	3 9/25 4 10/9	4 10/9	4 10/9

Scale: 5 = *Always*   4 = *Frequently*   3 = *Sometimes*   2 = *Rarely*   1 = *Never*

First Grade Gymnastics

Forward Roll

3 to 4 lessons

MOTOR CONTENT

Selected from Theme 1—Introduction to the Body

Body

Locomotor activities—forward roll

Space

Directions—forward

OBJECTIVES

In this unit, children will (or should be willing to try to) meet these objectives:

- Improve their forward rolls by remaining tucked, reaching forward with their hands, and jumping up to finish.
- Roll in a straight line by pushing equally with their feet and hands.
- Accept responsibility for developing a positive work attitude by staying focused on the task.
- Share space on a mat, not interfering with others.

EQUIPMENT AND MATERIALS

One large (4- by 6-foot to 5- by 10-foot) mat for each four children or a small mat for each child. (Because the children use only the floor space covered by the mats and a small space surrounding each, it is often easier to manage the class if you keep the mats as close together as safety allows.)

LEARNING EXPERIENCES

1.0 Come in and sit on the floor near a mat. [Designate number to be at each mat, depending on its size.] Who remembers some of the safety rules we learned last year? Right! Spread out. Start your roll from the same side of the mat and roll straight across to the other side. Stand on the side of your mat where your back is to the wall and show your best roll across the mat.

1.1 Look at the space right in front of you. See if you can make your roll go straight across your own space on the mat so [three] of you can practice safely at one time.

1.2 To help you make your forward roll go straight, after you squat down, press your hands flat on the mat, with fingers and thumbs pointed straight forward and close to the space in front of your feet. Tighten your arm muscles to make your arms strong. Push with both hands, keeping your arms strong, roll, and stand up. Try to keep from relaxing an arm because an arm that relaxes will make you roll crooked. [Repeat verbal cues as children practice.] *Tuck*, stay in a ball, *roll*, and *reach* for the wall.

1.3 Remember, place your hands flat on the mat and keep your arms strong. Now, lift your seat, tuck your head, and roll. Check—did you roll in a straight line?

2.0 Some of you are coming out of your curled position. You are showing your tummy to the ceiling after you roll onto your back. Uncurling as you roll makes you finish your roll sitting or lying on the mat with your legs stretched out in front of you. Keep your knees tucked close to your chest. Try to hide your tummy as you roll from your shoulders onto your back.

2.1 To hide your tummy, you need to stay round like a ball as you roll. Make your leg muscles press your knees to your chest and keep your head close to your knees to help keep you round like a ball.

2.2 To start your roll, push off with your toes, keeping your hands hard and flat on the mat with your fingers pointing straight out in front of you.

Tuck, roll, and reach for the wall.

3.0 You are staying so round as you roll that I can't see anyone's tummy now until you stand up! Let's begin to see if you can stand up quickly right after you roll.

3.1 Remember, don't let your knees straighten while you are rolling. Keep your knees bent and your head tucked close to your knees until your feet are flat on the floor.

3.2 Only let your hands touch the mat once just as you start your roll. Then, as you are rolling, reach both your hands and arms forcefully toward the other side of your mat to help you come to your feet.

3.3 Really poke those hands and arms toward the other side of the mat. Make that reach so strong that it pulls you off your seat right onto your feet.

3.4 Hear your hands touch the mat just one time. Touch! Roll! Reach! And stand up! Coach yourself. Say to yourself, 'Touch, roll, *reach*, stand up!'

3.5 Try to touch, roll, reach, and stand up all in one smooth movement without stopping until you stand up.

4.0 Let's really show you are excited when you have finished a splendid roll. Instead of just standing up, can you jump up and land softly on your feet after you touch, roll, and reach?

4.1 [Two or three] at each mat, see if you can perform with me as I give you the magic words. Ready? Touch, roll, reach, and pop up! [Repeat, giving cues several times.]

4.2 As you pop up, stretch those arms and hands way up over your head.

4.3 Let's show another kind of finish to your roll. Roll, stand up, and glue your feet to the mat. Don't end with a pop-up so you can feel the difference between just standing up after your roll and popping up.

4.4 Now, exaggerate your pop-up, making it even higher. Swing your arms forcefully up over your head just like the cheerleaders and ball players do when their team wins. Really show you have done something you think is great.

4.5 Can you roll, pop up, land, and freeze? Try it.

4.6 Let's have this half of the class share how they can roll, pop up, land, and freeze. Observers, watch carefully to see if the performers are freezing after they pop up. [Change rolls and have the observers watch for straight roles and high pop-ups.]

ASSESSING THE FORWARD ROLL					
Class list	Pushes with hands; tucks head. (scale, date)	Transfers weight onto shoulders and rounded back. (scale, date)	Holds tuck to complete roll. (scale, date)	Rolls in a straight line. (scale, date)	Hands reach forward to end roll on feet. (scale, date)
Harris, T.	3　12/17	2　12/17	2　12/17	3　12/18	2　12/18
Marks, S.	4　12/17	3　12/17	3　12/17	2　12/18	4　12/19

Scale: 5 = *Always or almost always* 4 = *Frequently needs additional practice* 3 = *Sometimes needs reminding and additional practice* 2 = *Rarely needs instruction and additional practice* 1 = *Never; needs special instruction or a different task*

Unit 2

Traveling on Different Body Parts

4 to 6 lessons

FOCUS Traveling on different body parts, emphasizing changing speeds and directions

MOTOR CONTENT

Selected from Theme 1—Introduction to the Body, Theme 2—Introduction to Space, and Theme 3—Introduction to Time

Body

Locomotor activities—rolling and step-like actions

Effort

Speed—traveling at different speeds

Space

Directions—forward, backward, sideways, up, down, changing directions

OBJECTIVES

In this unit, children will (or should be willing to try to) meet these objectives:

- Control the change of speed and direction while performing selected gymnastic movements.
- Know that they need to use muscle tension to develop, control, and change speed and direction.
- Recognize when they or others alter speed or direction.
- Accept the responsibility for changing speed and direction and gain satisfaction by improving their ability to do so by showing a willingness to experiment.
- Work quietly to maintain a safe environment.
- Move back from the starting area, making sure the space in front of them is clear before starting for safety.

EQUIPMENT AND MATERIALS

One mat and one bench for each four to six children, one hoop or jump rope for each child. (Rather than having more children working at a mat, provide better learning experiences by having half of the class continue to work at individual hoops or ropes while the other half works at the mats, rotating the groups two or three times during a lesson.)

LEARNING EXPERIENCES

1.0 Raise your hand and help me remember the name of one direction. Forward! Right! Another? Backward. Sideways. Up. Down. Let's see how each of you can travel in different directions going in, out, over, and around your hoop. Show each other how you can place your hoop on the floor in a spot away from other hoops and the wall. Walk, get a hoop, place it in a big space just for you, and begin.

1.1 Each time we stop, be sure you sit outside of your hoop with your hands in your lap so you don't get the hoop in trouble. I have been seeing mostly forward movement. See if you can move in every direction but forward and try to stay a little closer to your own hoop. [Observe the direction used most frequently and encourage traveling in another direction.]

1.2 Stop and have a seat. It's great to see so many of you remember to sit outside your hoop and not touch it. See if you can change your traveling direction each time I say 'change.' Try to make your muscles firm and strong. Begin. Change. [Pause.] Change. [Repeat often.]

1.3 Can you name the traveling directions of others? One person sit away from the hoop and watch the other travel. Each time your partner changes directions, name the direction. Watch if your partner collapses or is strong. [Change roles.]

1.4 I think you will have fun naming the direction you want your partner to travel and seeing your partner change direction. One of you tell your partner a direction to travel and the other be the performer. Mix up the directions to make your performer change directions frequently. [Change roles several times.]

1.5 [Ask all children to travel in a specific direction. Naming the direction is a good technique to use when assessing the responses.]

2.0 [Check to see if the placement of hoops ensure safety and allow each child freedom of movement.] See how you can do one of your favorite gymnastic movements going over or in and out of your hoop. Try to do the same movement several times.

2.1 As you repeat your gymnastic movement, pay close attention to the speed of your movement. I am going to ask some of you whether you think your speed is fast, slow, or medium. [Go from child to child, asking each to verbalize his speed.]

2.2 [Recall which children had been moving fast, slow, or medium.] Let's sit down away from your hoop and watch [Jonica] [a child who was doing a fast movement] and see if you can name the speed she is showing in her movement. [Continue by asking a child who was doing a slow movement and one who was performing at a medium speed to demonstrate, asking the observers to name the speed.] That was good that you could name the speed of the movements by [Christopher, Emily, and Joel] because it is important to be able to see the different speeds. Remember that each of you can do the same movement at different speeds. Isn't it fun to see how different the movement looks when the speed changes?

2.3 Start by repeating your favorite movement. Everytime I say 'change your speed,' see how you can show a definite change in your speed. [Give cues several times.]

2.4 Select another gymnastic movement and do it three times. First, do it very slowly, then, very fast, and then, medium. Try to make the changes in speed of your three movements look very different. [It is helpful if you name a specific speed, but it is also important to give the option for changing the speed back to the children.]

2.5 [To change 2.0 to 2.4, name different gymnastic movements (e.g., cartwheel, rolling, and so on) for the class to perform. Have different children demonstrate each movement before the class performs. Repeat variations of 2.0 to 2.4 several times.]

2.6 You are really going to need to think very hard this time. See if you can do the same movement three times at different speeds without stopping.

2.7 Try to show a definite difference between the fast and slow movements by making your slow movement *very* slow.

2.8 Sit down away from your hoop and think a moment about what you had to do to make your muscles help you show fast, slow, and medium movements. [Pause.] Did you feel your muscles tighten and get strong as you changed your speed? Go back and try to show more clearly that your mind is talking to your muscles, making them work harder to slow down or speed up your movements.

3.0 Let's see if you can show fast, slow, and medium speeds each time you take your turn on the mat. Start your turn at the end of the mat. Give the workers safe working space in front of the mat. Try to stand about three steps away from the mat when you are standing waiting your turn. No more than [four] to a mat. Go to a mat, count your number, and begin.

3.1 Some of you may have to change your direction as you travel on the mat to be able to show three speeds. People waiting, watch carefully. Start your turn after the performer in front of you walks away from the mat.

3.2 Each time you take your turn, select a different gymnastic movement and experiment with making your muscles work to change the speed of that movement three times.

3.3 Watch the person in front of you. Make your gymnastic movement different from that person. Everyone still try hard to perform each new movement fast, slow, and medium.

3.4 Those of you who are waiting, sit down two or three steps away from the end of the mat and see if you can name the speed of the performer at your mat. Performers, listen to the observers name your speed and try hard to help them see fast, slow, and medium movement in your performance.

3.5 Some of you may be able to include both a change in speed *and* a change in direction.

3.6 If you have started out by traveling forward, try starting by going sideways or backward. Then show a change in both your direction *and* your speed.

4.0 Let's add a bench to the mat and see if you can show a definite change in your speed as you travel back and forth over the bench and across the mat.

4.1 Think about and select your starting speed carefully before you begin. Plan and show a definite change in your speed when you are halfway down the bench.

4.2 People waiting in line, say 'change' when you see the speed of the performer change.

4.3 This time, let's play 'listen and move.' I will call out the speed. Performers, see if you can change your speed and move at the speed I name. People waiting, you watch closely and see if the performers match the speed when you hear the speed named. Performers ready? Start very slow. *Change* to medium! [Draw out the word "change" to give them time to change.]

4.4 You are changing speed and direction nicely. Now begin to experiment with different kinds of traveling. Try to include both rolling and weight on hands as you change speed while on the bench and mat.

5.0 Begin to travel back and forth over the bench by placing only your hands on the bench. Remember to still work on changing speed as you travel over the bench.

Change your speed as you travel over the bench.

5.1 When you are traveling slowly, see how high up in the air you can take your feet safely before they land on the floor. See if taking your feet low and close to the bench helps you speed up your movement as you travel back and forth over the bench. Make your arm muscles strong to help you move safely.

5.2 Concentrate on making your arms and hands stronger. Grip the sides of the bench with your hands as you try to take your feet slow and high or fast and low while going back and forth over the bench.

5.3 Keep moving your hands down on the bench to regrip the bench. Moving your hands to regrip can help you travel down the bench.

5.4 Keep your feet close to the bench and push with your feet against the floor to help you spring up onto your hands as you go back and forth over the bench. Landing close to the bench and pushing with your feet will also help you develop speed or height for your next movement.

5.5 Take care to include fast and slow movements on the bench. When you get to the mat, show at least two changes in direction as you travel.

5.6 Stop and sit down two or three steps behind your bench. Let's have a gymnastic show for your own group. One at a time, each of you show your very best changes in speed and direction. Make your demonstration the very best work you can possibly do to encourage everyone else to be a good performer.

ASSESSING TRAVELING AND USE OF DIRECTIONS AND SPEEDS						
Date: 4/19 Class list	Shows variety traveling in 3 major directions.	Differentiates speeds.	Changes speeds to achieve variety.	Controls speed.	Can perform same movement at different speeds.	Allows child in front space to work safely.
R. Sinbad	4	3	3	3	2	5
S. Mishan	5	4	4	3	3	5
T. Petty	3	2	2	2	2	5

Scale: 5 = *Always* 4 = *Frequently* 3 = *Sometimes* 2 = *Rarely* 1 = *Never*

Unit 3 — Rolling and Weight on Hands

4 to 5 lessons

FOCUS Combining rolling with taking weight on hands

MOTOR CONTENT

Selected from Theme 1—Introduction to the Body

Body

Locomotor activities—combining rolling with weight on hands
Actions of body parts—careful placement of the feet on the floor

OBJECTIVES

In this unit, children will (or should be willing to try to) meet these objectives:

- Pull the knees and abdomen closer together, improving their ability to make a ball shape when rolling.
- Transfer their weight onto their hands following a roll, remembering to spread their fingers and keep their eyes focused on their fingertips.
- Tighten their abdominal muscles to bring their feet slowly back to the floor near their hands.
- Understand that they are trying to control the placement and speed of their feet as they return them to the floor after taking weight on their hands.
- Stay on task and share work space with others, taking pride in improving their skills and in helping others to learn.

EQUIPMENT AND MATERIALS

One large (4- by 6-foot to 5- by 10-foot) mat for each four children or smaller, individual mats for each child. (Place mats on floor to give you the best observation point while still providing for the safety of children in rolling and taking weight on hands.)

LEARNING EXPERIENCES

[The number of children working at one time at a mat will vary, depending on the size of the mat, the ability of the children to control their bodies, and the task. Some children may be able to do some of the tasks safely on the floor.]

1.0 Working on your part of the mat, spread your fingers and place your hands flat on the mat. Make your arms straight and strong. See how you can take your feet up in the air and bring them down softly. Remember your fingers, hands, and arms have to be strong if they are to hold you up. Always keep your eyes focused on your fingertips when your feet are up in the air.

1.1 Everyone sit a moment and face me. Make your fingers on both hands point toward the ceiling and press them very firmly against each other. [Demonstrate.] Really push! Now ease off and just barely push. Keep changing from pushing forcefully [hard] with your palms and fingers to pushing gently. Feel the difference in pressure you can make against your hands?

1.2 Try to place your hands about shoulder-width apart with your fingers spread apart, pointing forward and pressing firmly against the mat. Tighten your arm muscles. Make them very hard and strong. Push off the floor with both of your feet and try, when you bring your feet down, to land on your feet—not on your shins or your hips.

1.3 If you stay tucked by keeping your knees bent when trying to take weight on hands, you may be able to feel your hips go right over your hands when you push off the floor with your feet.

1.4 Now think about bringing your feet down after you take weight on your hands. Try to control the speed of your feet and where they land. Tighten your tummy muscles to help your feet come down slower.

1.5 Some of you are letting your feet fall after you get them in the air. Try to take charge of your feet and return them softly onto the mat [or floor]. It will be easier to bring your feet down softly if you try to place them close to your hands.

1.6 Let's listen to [Nathan's] feet. His tummy muscles and arms were so strong he was able to control his feet so we couldn't hear them touch the floor. Everyone see if your feet can be as quiet as [Nathan's].

Feel your hips go right over your hands.

STRENGTH

See if you can remember to practice this activity at home this week. Get your hips over your hands by placing your hands flat on the floor about as wide as your shoulders with your fingers spread and pointing forward. With your hips over your hands, take your feet off the ground and slowly bring your feet down. Practice taking your feet in the air and taking them down slowly 10 times each day at home, either outside or inside in a big, safe space.

2.0 Remember your best tucked roll. See if you can roll once and come quickly to your feet.

2.1 Try to feel your tummy and leg muscles squeezing close together to make your whole body curl tightly as you roll.

2.2 As you finish your roll, stay curled and tucked to see if you can end up on your feet in a squat position with your hands reaching out in front of you.

2.3 Most of you have been doing forward [backward] rolls. Everyone work on your best forward roll and try ending your roll by forcefully stretching your hands out in front of you to help you finish up on your feet.

3.0 Remember when you pushed against your hands and felt the difference between pushing gently and pushing really strong? We did this to help you learn to take your weight on your hands. Take a moment and think about pulling your feet down after taking all your weight on your hands. Don't let your feet fall. Tighten your stomach muscles to pull your feet down. This will help you control where you place your feet on the mat [floor]. When you don't tighten those stomach muscles, your legs come crashing down. Right where you are, pull your stomach muscles in. Feel them tighten and then relax? Now, after you finish your forward roll, see if you can make your hands push against the mat to take your weight up onto your hands with your feet in the air. Then, tighten your stomach muscles to help you place both feet back down slowly and softly on the mat [floor].

3.1 Each time, after you take your weight on your hands, pull those stomach muscles in tight and see how slowly these muscles help you bring your feet down.

3.2 After you take your feet up in the air, carefully make your feet come down gently, one at a time.

3.3 Remember, you must be in charge of your feet. Take your feet up only as high as you can control them when they land. Some of you are taking your feet too high, and you are not showing me that you are able to control their landing. [This often results in getting their weight going past their hands, which is the base of support, causing them to collapse or fall flat on their backs. It is called an "overthrow"; teach them to avoid overthrows.]

3.4 See if you can choose a spot near one hand and bring your feet down softly on that spot by twisting your hips. Don't end up falling onto the mat.

3.5 To help you really control your feet and take weight on your hands safely, try to make those stomach muscles pull both feet down close to the side of one hand. Next time, see if you can control your feet when placing them close to your other hand.

4.0 Boys and girls, let's watch [Samantha] take three blocks and show how she would stack them one on top of another to keep them from falling. [Samantha], think of the bottom block as your hands, the middle block as your hips, and the top block as your feet. Good! [Samantha] has stacked the hip block—the middle block, right over the first block, which is the hands block. Then she stacked the third block, which is the feet block, right over the hip and hands blocks. Too many of you have been trying to get your feet up in the air without thinking first about getting your hips over your hands.

4.1 Remember, the hip block had to be right over the hands block to keep the tower balanced. This time, concentrate on feeling your hips stacked up over your hands. Try staying tightly curled when practicing taking your hips over your hands—it might help you balance. [Children will need to practice this often and can benefit by your feedback as they work.] [Kay] got all three blocks—hands, hips, and feet—stacked straight up. Oops, [Shirley], you didn't send your hips high enough to get up over your hands.

4.2 [Twisting can prevent an overthrow.] Now, some of you might like to try adding a twist when your hips are over your hands. [Have a child demonstrate a twist of the hips and point out the twist and placement of the feet near one hand. Then have others who are ready add the twisting of the hips.] Remember, when you feel your hips high over your hands, twist your hips to one side and place your feet down near your hand on that same side.

4.3 Don't forget, you have to take charge of your feet. Place them on the mat [floor]; don't let them fall after you twist. Control your feet by tightening your tummy muscles to pull both feet down close to one hand.

5.0 Finish your roll in a squat position on your feet with your hands reaching forward. Then see if you can place both hands on the mat in front of you and go right into weight on hands. Make your arms and hands strong and push off the mat with both feet taking your hips into the air. [You may need to encourage some to stay tucked when moving their hips over their hands.]

5.1 Push your hands flat on the mat after you roll to take weight onto your hands. Stay curled, feeling your hips coming up over your hands and your arms being strong. Don't be in a hurry to take your feet high.

5.2 Don't relax and collapse. Remember to be tight and strong in your arms and legs as you roll. Keep your eyes on your fingertips when you take weight on your hands.

5.3 Remember to make your hands flat on the mat and try to push off with both feet at the same time as you roll. Look for a spot in front of you to place your hands.

5.4 After you roll and reach both hands out in front of you, see if you can go right into weight on hands without stopping after you roll.

5.5 After taking your hips up into the air, try to bring your feet down slowly and softly. Only you can be in charge of your feet.

5.6 [This is an additional challenge.] After you finish your roll and take your weight on your hands, some of you might like to stand and travel sideways on your hands [like a cartwheel] by bringing your hands then your feet down one at a time. [Some children find it easier to travel to the right by touching their right hand to the floor first, others prefer the left. If you observe children having difficulty, you might suggest they try the cartwheel in another direction to discover which direction is easier for them.]

5.7 Let's take time to enjoy how much we have learned. Those on this side of the room, safely show your best tight roll and go right into weight on hands. The rest of you watch for the tight roll. Look carefully to see the hips going right over the hands and how well they control the placement of the feet when they land. Now let's have the watchers share their best work, too. [You may want to change the focus of the sharing time each time you use this task, suggesting new things to watch for.]

Unit 4

Jumping, Landing, and Rolling

3 to 5 lessons

FOCUS — Jumping, landing, and rolling, emphasizing controlled body shapes in the air

MOTOR CONTENT

Selected from Theme 1—Introduction to the Body

Body

Locomotor activities—jumping, landing, rolling, making shapes with body

OBJECTIVES

In this unit, children will (or should be willing to try to) meet these objectives:

- Willfully control their body shapes in the air, landing on their feet, either holding their positions or going into a roll immediately following their landings, all the while maintaining control of their bodies.
- Learn that their feet should be spread only about a shoulder-width apart to prevent the force of their landings from putting too much stress on their knees.
- Allow the person in front of them to leave the mat before mounting the apparatus to maintain a safe environment.
- Keep their arms strong and tuck their heads when performing a forward roll, taking responsibility for their own safety.

EQUIPMENT AND MATERIALS

One landing mat and one piece of apparatus to mount and dismount for every four to six children.

LEARNING EXPERIENCES

1.0 Everyone, see if you can practice your very best roll by rolling straight across the mat from one side to the other. Boys, please find a place by the side of the mat and have no more than two boys [depending on the number of boys in the class] at any one mat. Girls, join the boys at the mats and see if you can have no more than [four] workers at a mat.

1.1 Don't forget to place the palms of your hands flat on the mat, fingers pointing forward, and make your arms nice and strong to start your roll.

1.2 Take care of your head as you roll. I am going to be watching to see who remembers to tuck their head and let their shoulders touch the mat without touching the top of their head on the mat.

Land with your feet shoulder-width apart.

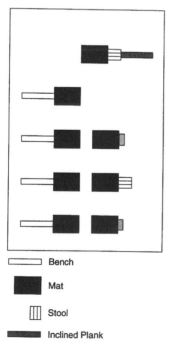

☐☐☐ Bench

■ Mat

▥ Stool

▬ Inclined Plank

▨ Vaulting Box

1.3 Make your body nice and round as you roll seeing if you can hug your knees close to your body.

1.4 Who can add a beautiful, springy, pop-up by jumping nice and straight right up into the air after you roll?

2.0 See how high you can jump as you pop up after you roll.

2.1 How many of you can change the shape of your body during your pop-up after you roll?

2.2 Let's see if you can reach your arms way above your head as you pop up and make a long, straight shape with your arms, body, and legs, pointing your toes straight toward the mat. [Have a child demonstrate.]

2.3 Some of you might like to try tucking your knees while you're still in the air to make your body round like a ball before you land on your feet.

2.4 Keep thinking of a different, new shape to make in the air each time after you pop up.

2.5 Watch your landing after you make the shape in the air. Land with your feet about as far apart as your shoulders. If your feet are too close together, it is hard to hold your balance when you land. If they are wider than your shoulders, your feet won't be under your shoulders and the force of your landing can hurt your poor knees.

2.6 Really exaggerate that shape you are making. If you are making a wide shape, take those legs and arms very far apart in the air but remember to land with your feet shoulder width apart.

2.7 Let's watch some of these body shapes in the air following our nice rolls. [Call on several children, one at a time, to share their roll, pop-up, and body shape in the air. After each demonstration, give the observers a chance to try making the shape they just observed. Then call on another child for a demonstration of a different shape in the air.]

3.0 [Add a piece of apparatus to each mat. Children can help arrange most apparatus, but you must give them explicit directions to make this a safe experience. Tell them the number needed to carry the apparatus, to lift with arms and back straight and carry the apparatus traveling forward, and where each apparatus should stand. This will take time at first, but eventually it saves time because the children will know how to manage the apparatus safely. Monitor their behavior closely and reinforce your directions as each group takes its turn to set up their apparatus.] Let's see how you have remembered to stand back away from the performer and the apparatus to give the performer lots of room. Take turns and practice mounting the apparatus and landing softly on your feet on the mat.

3.1 Remember to land with your feet about shoulder-width apart to be nice to your knees.

3.2 To help you remain on your feet after you land, try to keep your back straight up and down like a wall, keeping your head over your feet. Don't let your head tip forward.

3.3 I am going to watch your knees when you land and see if you bend them a little as your toes touch the mat to help give you a nice, soft landing.

3.4 Leaning forward makes you fall when you land. Try very hard to keep your back straight up and down like the wall and your head right over your feet when you land. This will help you hold your balance on your feet as you land.

STRENGTH

Rock back and forth on your back, staying as tightly tucked as possible. After three or four rocks, try to pop up and land on your feet. When you pop up, see if you can change your shape in the air, always landing quietly on your feet by bending your knees as you land. See if you can do 20 pop-ups each evening this week.

3.5 Now after you land with your back straight up and down, see if you can spring right up into a high pop-up and land right on your same landing spot.

3.6 Some of you are rushing and crowding the performer. Try to stand at least four steps away from the apparatus to give the person in front of you running room to practice a nice, clean mount so they don't have to crawl up on the apparatus.

3.7 Can you jump high in the air off the apparatus and land safely on your feet with them spread about shoulder-width apart?

3.8 To help you get more height in your jump, try to land closer to your apparatus and not so far out on the mat.

3.9 When you dismount, try to bend your knees and swing your arms up high above your head as you push hard with your feet on top of the apparatus. This will help you jump higher.

4.0 Think of all the different shapes you have been making. [Name a few.] As you dismount and come off the apparatus, see if you can make one of these shapes in the air with your body before you land.

4.1 Remember to land with your feet about shoulder-width apart. [Instruct children landing from a twisted shape to make their base a little wider to maintain stability in their landing.] If you make a twisted shape in the air, try landing with your feet a little farther apart to help you keep your balance.

4.2 Begin to exaggerate the shape you are making. Take your body parts farther away from each other or bring them closer together.

Make a different shape in the air each time you have a turn.

4.3 Try to make a different shape each time you have a turn. [Be sure to monitor each child carefully for a variety of shapes. Teachers often mistake variety within a group or class for that of the individual child's variety. To ensure broader practice of a variety of shapes, you may choose to (a) name a shape (wide, straight, round, twisted) and have all of the children try to make the shape; or (b) have different children demonstrate a shape and ask the class if they can copy the shape.]

4.4 Remember, when landing to keep your back straight up and down like a wall, keeping your head over your feet. Don't let your shoulders and your head tip forward.

4.5 Spread your arms out to your sides about as high as your shoulders when you land to make your arms help you keep your balance.

4.6 Try to feel your muscles really tighten into a full-stretch or a tucked-ball shape. Don't feel loose and saggy when you make your shapes in the air.

5.0 If you are making lovely shapes in the air and finishing with a nice cushioned [soft] landing by remembering to bend your knees, try adding a roll after you land quietly on your feet.

5.1 Watch carefully and tighten up those leg muscles when you feel your knees give [bend] a bit as you land so you can go into your roll without banging your chin on your knees.

5.2 Prepare your hands to receive your weight on the mat in your roll by spreading your fingers out and placing both hands flat on the mat, fingers pointed in the direction you are rolling.

5.3 After you roll, see how quickly you can come to your feet.

5.4 Take turns being the leader in your groups. Leaders, try very hard to mount your apparatus quickly, do a fine shape in the air, land, and then perform a beautiful, tight roll with a pop-up at the end.

5.5 Followers, watch the way your leader mounts the apparatus and be sure you copy it. Leaders, do your best work. Make your shapes, landings, and rolls worth copying. When you do your best work, it helps everyone in class get better because everyone will be copying only gymnastic work that is very special.

ASSESSING LANDING QUALITY				
Class list	Lands with feet shoulder-width apart. (rating, date)	Keeps head and back nearly vertical over feet during landing. (rating, date)	Hips, knees, and ankles extend to hold balance after landing softly. (rating, date)	Ankles, knees, and hips extend forcefully to create springy pop-up. (rating, date)
J. Johnston		4 11/15 5 12/10	3 11/15 3 12/10	4 11/15 4 12/15
R. Isaac		3 11/15 3 12/10	3 11/15 4 12/10	3 11/15 3 12/15

Scale: 5 = *Always* 4 = *Frequently* 3 = *Sometimes* 2 = *Rarely* 1 = *Never*

Unit 5

Traveling Into and Out of Balances

4 to 6 lessons

FOCUS Traveling into and out of a variety of balances on different body parts and surfaces

MOTOR CONTENT

Selected from Theme 1—Introduction to the Body

Body

Locomotor activities—rolling, stepping
Nonlocomotor activities—stretching, curling, lowering, balancing

OBJECTIVES

In this unit, children will (or should be willing to try to) meet these objectives:

- Know that they must hold the body very still when balancing.
- Name the parts of the body that make up a base of support.
- Stretch free body parts upward, away from the base of support, showing clarity and control while balancing.
- Lower body parts slowly to the floor when coming out of a balanced position.
- Look for open spaces as they travel, sharing space safely.

EQUIPMENT AND MATERIALS

Charts with these headings: Balance, Base of Support, Free Body Parts, Stretch, Curl, and others appropriate for class and content. Mats and pictures illustrating different body parts and surfaces serve as bases of support. (Children may cut out pictures or draw them to enhance understanding of the "base of support" concept.)

LEARNING EXPERIENCES

1.0 Move freely about the room, traveling carefully on your hands and feet. Stop when you hear me say 'and stop.' Hold your position very still. [Start and stop the children often commenting on spacing, stillness of stopped position, and noise level.]

1.1 See how you can travel sometimes making your feet go high into the air and sometimes making them go close to the ground.

1.2 It's great the way you are listening, stopping quickly, and holding very still. This time, look for and move into empty spaces so you always keep a big, safe space around you as you travel.

BALANCE

This is a good activity to do at home. Move and then stop *all* body parts to hold a balance as still as you can while you count to 10. Try this five or six times. If you like, try to hold the balance perfectly still as you count to a higher number.

1.3 You are stopping your hands and feet. See if you can also stop your head, your arms, and your whole body when you freeze. Stay strong and try not to let any body part move. Ready? Travel! [Pause.] Freeze! [Repeat several times, commending their performance.]

2.0 [Discuss "base of support" with the children, having them name body parts serving as the base in some of the pictures.] Staying just on your feet, travel about the room and be prepared to stop. Ready? Travel! [Pause.] Stop! Now lower one arm or hand carefully and place it on the floor. Let the arm or hand you select help your feet become a part of your base of support along with your feet. [Repeat cues several times, asking for different body parts to become part of their base.]

2.1 Again, use one hand or arm and two feet as your base of support. Every time you hear the signal to stop after you travel, place your arm or hand on the floor in a new place so you make a different shape as you balance.

2.2 Each time you stop, try to lower a different body part to the floor to make a new base of support along with your two feet. Be sure you know how many body parts make up your base if I should ask. [Ask children to have two, three, four, or more body parts as a base.]

2.3 As you place your body part on the floor, move some of your weight onto that body part so you can feel your body pushing down on the floor with your new body part and both of your feet. Your new base of support should feel like it is gripping the floor while the rest of your body is stretching up and away from this base.

2.4 This time, when you stop, make one hand a part of your base, pushing your hand flat on the floor with fingers spread. Try to stretch all free body parts far away from your base as you hold very still. Now carefully relax and see what happens to your stretched shape. [Observe and ask, "What happened?"]

2.5 What other balanced shapes can we make when we have only one hand and two feet on the ground? See if you can look very wide or narrow—maybe straight, twisted, or curled.

2.6 Everyone have a seat and let's watch [Timmy] share his work. When he is finished, see if you can tell us what you liked about [Timmy's] balance.

Simple bases of support. Children should challenge themselves to make different bases as they progress through tasks 2.0 - 2.7.

2.7 You have done a super job noticing good stretches and gripping with the body parts on the floor. After you travel, see if you can press or grip the floor nice and firmly and stretch the free body parts far away from the base as you balance. All of you travel, stop, and hold a balance. Ready? And go! Travel . . . , balance . . . , stretch and hold—one, two, three, four, five. [Repeat.]

3.0 [Children could use individual mats; however, the children tend to grip better on the floor, taking more care not to collapse when coming out of their balances.] Everyone, try to find different balances with three body parts on the floor as your base of support. Remember to stay in your own working space.

3.1 Make sure you count the number of body parts touching the floor.

3.2 See how high in the air you can reach with all of your body parts not touching the floor. *Stretch*! Keep your muscles very strong, always coming out of your balance slowly as you return to a standing position.

3.3 [Name and describe balances you see.] I see balances that look like bridges with the tummy and the chest high in the air and others with tummy down and hips high in the air. See if you can try different balances by changing where you stretch your free body parts.

3.4 Now keep choosing different body parts for your base. Remember each part that is on the floor should feel the pressure of your weight. It should be gripping and pushing against the floor to keep you still.

4.0 See how you can travel, then balance on four body parts. Now, carefully try to take one part off the floor, still holding your balance by shifting your weight to the other parts of your base.

4.1 Slowly lift that free body part high in the air and let the other three parts work to support you.

4.2 Keep traveling and taking balances on four body parts. Then take away one part very slowly, very carefully, shifting your weight to the three remaining parts. Try to be very strong so you have no sagging parts. Try to always take the free body part you are lifting straight up over your base.

4.3 Let's all watch [Johnny]. [Susie], name the four parts that make up [Johnny's] base of support. Everyone think of a body part [Johnny] could lift and still hold his balance. [Zach], what body part do you think [Johnny] could lift off the floor and still be balanced? [Johnny], take your balance again and see if you can lift the body part [Zach] suggested and try to hold your balance steady.

4.4 Find a partner. One of you take a balance while the other names the body part to lift. [Have children change roles.]

4.5 When we make our base smaller by having fewer body parts on the floor, it makes our balance harder to hold. Everyone, on your own, see how you can make different balances, working hard on trying to balance on three, two, or one body part. Remember to press the body parts supporting you against the floor to make your base very strong so it can hold you very still.

4.6 Let's look at some of your balances on one, two, or three body parts. [Have different children share.] Some of you might like to try some of the balances you have watched.

5.0 [Scatter individual mats, if available, about the room.] Think about your favorite balance. When I say, 'travel carefully,' travel, then take your balance, stretch, and hold. Travel carefully. Take your balance. Stretch. And hold. Now slowly curl your body into a ball, lower it carefully to the floor, roll over, and pop up to your feet. [Talk the children through this several times. Don't hesitate long

Each time you stop, make a new base of support.

after saying "take your balance" because some may be using difficult bases of support and others may not be able to hold any balance very long.]

5.1 On your own, practice taking your balance. Stretch when you are in your balance, hold it, then curl to the floor, roll, and spring up to your feet.

5.2 Some of you are forgetting to hold your balance very still. Show me a very still picture before you roll. Count to three before you find a way to curl and roll out.

5.3 Let's share our balance, curl, and roll sequences. Observers, watch for a still balance before the curl and roll.

ASSESSING BODY SUPPORTS				
Class list	Names supporting body parts. (scale, date)	Holds balance with active stillness. (scale, date)	Stretches free body parts upward away from base. (scale, date)	Changes supporting parts slowly and smoothly. (scale, date)
Ables, Chris	5　3/15	4　3/15	4　3/15	4　3/15
Monnet, K.	4　3/15	3　3/15	3　3/17	2　3/17

Scale:　5 = Consistently　4 = 2/3 or more of the time　3 = Half of the time　2 = 1/3 of the time　1 = Rarely or not at all

First Grade Dance

Unit 1 — Making Shapes With the Body

2 or 3 lessons

FOCUS

Exploring body shapes while traveling and while staying in place

MOTOR CONTENT

Selected from Theme 1—Introduction to the Body and Theme 3—Introduction to Space

Body

Basic body actions—bend, stretch
Shapes of the body—wide, straight, thin, narrow, rounded or curved, twisted, angular

Space

Levels—high, medium, low
Extensions—small (near the body), large (far from the body)
Directions—up, down

OBJECTIVES

In this unit, children will (or should be willing to try to) meet these objectives:

- Create and feel muscular tension needed to hold still body positions.
- Design a simple movement sequence with a beginning, middle, and end, combining favorite body shapes with a variety of traveling actions (reflects National Standards in Dance 2a, 2c, and 4a).
- Recognize that wide shapes result from body parts opening away from the midline of the body and narrow shapes are formed by bringing body parts close to the midline.
- Recognize that rounded shapes have curved lines with soft edges and angular shapes have straight lines with sharp corners.
- Create a variety of body shapes at low, middle, and high levels (reflects National Standard in Dance 1c).

EQUIPMENT AND MATERIALS

Drum or wood block (or other percussive instrument), gong or triangle (or other instrument capable of producing sustained sounds). *Optional:* Selection of visual aids to enhance children's comprehension of shape and form, such as (a) objects: narrow (bone, stick); wide (starfish, shell); rounded (pebble, bubble, shell); and angular (crystal, fossil); (b) art exhibiting strong lines and shapes; (c) geometric forms illustrated in picture books, such as the legend *Arrow to the Sun: A Pueblo Indian Tale* by Gerald McDermott or *The Amazing Book of Shapes* by Lydia Sharman; or (d) geometric objects hidden inside a mystery bag or box.

LEARNING EXPERIENCES

1.0 [Begin by showing objects having different shapes (see equipment and materials list). Identify and describe characteristics of these shapes, making sure the children understand the movement vocabulary you will use in this unit.] Find your own space and stretch as long, narrow, and thin as you can. Pull your arms in close and your legs together tightly. Now open your body and reach out far to make a *wide* shape.

1.1 See if you can make a skyscraper-tall shape! Touch the sky with the top of your head. Make your straight shape even taller by reaching your arms up and stretching your fingers.

1.2 Jump up quickly! Shoot your arms straight up to the sky like a long, thin arrow [Elicit children's responses.] . . . like a rocket in space. 10, 9, 8, 7, 6, 5, 4, 3, 2, 1—blast off! Pierce the space above you!

1.3 Think of a shape that is very long and narrow, but low to the ground instead of up and down. Show me a *long* stretched-out shape. Another narrow

Move from closed, narrow positions to open, wide shapes.

shape near to the floor. A different long shape. [Repeat. Observe for variety of narrow shapes at a low level.]

1.4 Make low, deep, *wide* shapes this time. Stretch body parts far apart, staying low to the ground. Keep changing the body parts supporting your weight.

1.5 Tighten your muscles to hold clear, strong shapes. Create many different *wide* shapes at a low level.

1.6 Surprise us with sudden jumps! Can you show *wide*, stretched shapes in the air? Jump out as straight and wide as you can! Keep jumping high. Reach out to make your shape extra *wide*! Watch out for your neighbors.

2.0 Let's mix up our body shapes. Make narrow and wide positions at different levels. Begin with your favorite *wide* shape . . . now show a narrow shape at a different level. Keep changing from wide to narrow and back to wide. [Move with the children, talking them through.]

2.1 Be sure your body shapes are at different levels. Make some shapes low and others high. How can you use space in the middle to create wide and narrow shapes?

2.2 Draw an imaginary line down the midline [middle] of your body [Demonstrate]. Show clear differences in your wide and narrow shapes. Wide, wider, widest! Stretch arms and legs far apart and away from your body. Now make skinny, thin, narrow shapes. Pull or squeeze body parts together, close to your imaginary line. [Repeat many times, talking children through tasks. Demonstrate to reinforce the concept.]

2.3 Support your weight on different body parts as you make closed, narrow shapes and open, wide shapes. Move onto your front [back, side] to make a shape. On your seat. Now your knees! Make long, *narrow* shapes, balancing on your feet and arms. Now *wide* shapes, balancing on your shoulders, chest, or back.

2.4 Try many wide and narrow shapes on different bases of support at different levels. Thick spread-out shapes. Thin, pulled-in shapes.

2.5 Think of two different-looking narrow shapes and perform one, then the other. Keep practicing until you can move quickly from one shape into the next without stopping. This is your 'narrow shape dance.' [Share ideas.]

2.6 Think of two different wide shapes and perform one, then the other. See if you can move *slowly* and smoothly from one shape to another. Now everyone has a 'wide shape dance.'

2.7 Listen as I play these sounds. [Alternate two quick taps on drum with two sustained sounds on gong. Support or suspend drum and gong for ease in playing two instruments.] When you hear two drumbeats, quickly show me your two narrow shapes. Fast as the drum! When you hear the triangle, *slowly* and smoothly move into your two *wide* shapes.

2.8 Let's watch our narrow and wide shape dances. This half of the class have a seat. Each of you watch just one of the performers. Does your performer make two or more very different shapes? I'll tap the drum and gong to tell the performers when to make narrow and wide shapes. [Play two soft drumbeats and two light taps on gong, or simply give verbal cues. After two or more repetitions, change roles.]

3.0 In your own space, make your arms curve into a *rounded* shape. Imagine wrapping your arms around something very big [use imagery of a giant soap bubble, beach ball, rainbow, and the like]. Hold that space! What other body parts can wrap up the space around you?

3.1 With each tap of the gong [long, sustained sounds], curve your body parts to make different rounded shapes. Can you smooth out all those sharp edges? '[Tap:] Show me a curved shape with one arm . . . [tap] use the other arm, rounding out your elbow . . . [tap] a curved shoulder . . . [tap] a rounded hip . . . [tap] a round shape with your legs . . . .'

3.2 Give me a round-eyed look—eyes wide open with alert bodies! See if you can round your back into a curved shape. Bend forward carefully. What other body parts can you curve? Discover and invent ways with your chest [sides of the body, neck, arms with hands].

3.3 Each time you hear a long, sustained sound [tap gong], change the body parts holding you up as you make new, rounded shapes. Here we go: '[Tap:] Change your base of support . . . [tap] change again . . . [tap] keep changing the body part[s] holding you up . . . [tap] change.'

3.4 How can you *curve* your whole body? Show some shapes where both the inside and outside of the shape are curved. Think of a bagel, doughnut, tire, or wheel. [Allow children to explore task on their own time with no accompaniment.] Circle your body round. Capture some space. Now, release that space and make new curved shapes.

3.5 [Divide class in half and take turns performing and watching.] Demonstrate your two favorite curved shapes. See if you can change from one shape to another without stopping. Show your roundest body shapes!

4.0 *Angular* shapes have very sharp corners where two straight lines come together. Show me angular shapes with your arms or legs. Watch those corners—make them pointed and sharp!

4.1 Create many angular shapes using different body parts to make sharp corners—head-to-toe angular shapes. Tilt or tip your head. Bend at your elbows, wrists, waist, knees, ankles.

4.2 [Tap sharp, sudden sounds on drum or wood block.] With each tap, show me a totally different angular shape. Move your *whole* body. Make all your corners sharp and pointed!

Practice changing your base of support.

Show angular shapes with your arms or legs as you create an "angle dance."

4.3 Change your body parts touching the floor. Make up a lot of different angular shapes. [Tap drum and say, "Change," encouraging children to change their bases of support often.]

4.4 Create an 'angle dance' by joining two of your favorite sharp-cornered shapes. Go from one shape to another without stopping. Practice until you can do it quickly.

4.5 Add an angular jump to finish your dance. Curl and twist your body into a knot, then jump and explode into the air! Show sharp lines and corners in the air. Great ending! [Repeat entire dance.]

ASSESSMENT: NARRATIVES

Write three sentences to explicitly describe how the children (as a class) performed in dance based upon progress toward dance objectives. Refer to these when planning subsequent dance experiences to build on strengths and improve weak areas. Decide whether to include the following learning experience based on children's progress.

5.0 As I tap the drum, carefully travel through empty spaces. Then, when you hear the quiet triangle, stop and slowly make a still shape. [Play even and uneven drum rhythms for traveling parts; tap triangle or gong softly for body shapes.]

5.1 Listen carefully. The triangle will tell you to make several shapes. Change your shape with each sound.

5.2 [Immediately after last tap on triangle.] Let's try traveling in the shape you just made. Feel your muscles working to hold onto your wide, narrow, curved, or angular shape even as you travel. I see many different ways of traveling—rolling, jumping, sliding. Keep traveling. The triangle will tell you when to change your shape.

5.3 Let's make up a shape dance that travels. Choose three of your favorite shapes. Begin, 'Shape number one and travel to an open space . . . . Next, shape number two and travel . . . . Now, shape number three and hold your still position!' From the beginning, 'Number one . . . number two . . . number three.'

5.4 Your shape dance has a beginning, a middle, and an end. You start with, '[Tap triangle:] Shape number one and [drumbeats] travel . . . [tap triangle]. This is shape number two and [drumbeats] travel again . . . [tap triangle]. Finish in a strong pose [position] with shape number three!' Ready to repeat your shape dance exactly the same way? Curtain going up!

5.5 Try to move in different ways during the traveling parts—dancing up and down, hopping or skipping forward, jumping backward or sideways, turning round and round. Make your feet do something different each time you travel!

5.6 As we practice our dances, try to remember how your muscles tighten to hold still positions and how different each shape feels.

5.7 This half of the class, come sit down by me. As this half performs, the audience will look for three things: Does each shape look different? Can I name the four shapes—wide, narrow, rounded, or angular? Are those magic muscles working to hold still shapes?

6.0 Let's try to make two different types of shapes at the same time with different parts of your body. Think of the possibilities: wide, curved arms and bent, angular knees; or narrow, pulled-together legs and angular arms. Right where you are, show one type of shape with your upper body and a different shape with your lower body.

6.1 Make one shape with the bottom half of your body and hold it. With each tap of my drum, change the shape of just the upper part of your body. Now, let's try the opposite: Hold those magic upper body muscles very still in one shape, but keep changing the shape of your lower body with each tap.

6.2 Sometimes we can change magically from one shape to another in slow-motion. Each of you make a shape. With each quiet tap [on triangle], *slowly* change into a different shape. Keep moving and forming different shapes. [Compare to "transformer" toys.]

6.3 Listen to the faster drumbeats. Try to quickly change your upper and lower body shapes. Here we go: '[Tap:] Change! . . . [Tap.] Change! . . . [Tap.] Change!' [Repeat many times.] Now find a partner and take turns performing for each other. Say, 'Change' to tell your partner when to change shapes. See if you can get new ideas for making your own shapes.

ASSESSING DANCE

Videotape short segments from one or more classes for each major unit. These can be used to (1) assess the classes' performances on selected tasks, (2) provide a baseline for subsequent assessing, (3) enable the children to begin to evaluate their own performances, and (4) explain dance instruction and goals to parents or other groups.

Unit 2

Traveling, Turning, and Body Shapes

3 to 5 lessons

FOCUS Combining traveling and turning with stillness while creating body shapes

MOTOR CONTENT

Selected from Theme 1—Introduction to the Body and Theme 3—Introduction to Space

Body

Locomotor activities—running, skipping, galloping, turning
Shapes of the body—freezing in various shapes

Space

Levels—high, low

OBJECTIVES

In this unit, children will (or should be willing to try to) meet these objectives:

- Push off from the balls of their feet as they run, skip, gallop, and turn to create light, buoyant locomotor movements (reflects National Standard in Dance 1b).
- Create still, firm shapes at high and low levels (reflects National Standard in Dance 1c).
- Move to a musical beat, demonstrating quick changes in traveling and stillness (reflects National Standard in Dance 1f).
- Travel to open spaces, showing concern for the safety of themselves and others.

EQUIPMENT AND MATERIALS

Drum, tambourine, or other percussion instrument, such as claves, rhythm sticks, sandpaper or wood block, clappers, or hollow coconut shells. *Optional music:* Select one (or more): Selection A—Bartok: *For Children,* "Vol. 1, Nos. 1, 4, or 10" or an instrumental folk dance piece with a fast, lively tempo and even rhythm for running steps; Selection B—"Square Dance," "Red River Valley," or "Oh! Susanna!" (sel. and arr. for piano by Palmer, Manus, and Lethco) or any square dance music in 2/4 or 4/4 time with a moderately fast tempo; Selection C—"The Snail," a French song-play (see Resources for recorded music or piano arrangement on page 56); Selection D—Schumann: "The Wild Horseman" from *Album for the Young* (arr. for piano by Levy); Selection E—Kabalevsky: *The Comedians, Op. 26,* "Comedian's Galop." *Optional story: Pecos Bill* by Steven Kellogg (see Resources).

The Snail

LEARNING EXPERIENCES

1.0 [Familiarize yourself with music Selections A, B, or C for inventing sequences of traveling and freezing.] Let's see how quietly you can run to the soft beat of the drum. Find all the empty spaces in the room. Don't let your feet make a sound as they touch the floor. Stop when you hear two loud beats. [Alternate a series of soft, even beats with two loud, quick beats.]

1.1 Don't touch anyone else. Show you care about others as you run quietly to the soft drumbeats. [Repeat this many times. Comment on spacing, running softly, and stopping quickly.]

1.2 Make your running soft and light by staying forward on the balls of your feet. Relax your ankles as you run. Stop the moment you hear the drum stop.

1.3 Really push off the floor with your feet as you run! Feel your whole leg bend and stretch farther with each push (takeoff).

1.4 Make your arms look powerful as you run. Show us you are a very strong runner, but remember to run quietly. [Practice.] Swing those arms forward—a big, easy swing.

1.5 What else can you do to look strong and powerful when you run? [Big running steps, strong leg muscles, front knee lifts, a spring run.] [Michael] said that taking big running steps makes you a strong runner. Try big running steps and see if your run feels stronger, faster. [Use three or four children's ideas, then let everyone choose the idea that makes them feel strongest running.]

1.6 Take four big running steps, then freeze for four counts in a strong shape. Ready? *And*, 'Run, two, three, four; freeze, two, three, four.' [Play even drumbeats, repeating verbal cues several times.]

1.7 Let's work on our frozen shapes. Can any part of your body move if it is frozen? [No!] Sometimes, I can see fingers, eyes, arms, or heads moving as I look at frozen shapes. Surprise me this time. Don't let me see even one body part move a tiny bit. Hold as still and strong as you can. Ready? *And*, 'Run, two, three, four; freeze, two, three, four.' [Repeat cues, coaching them to "Get ready to freeze when you hear count 4." Select children to demonstrate still, firm shapes.]

1.8 Run for four counts, then freeze for four counts in a medium shape with your arms way out from your body. Ready? *And*, 'Run, two, three, four; freeze, two, three, four.' [Repeat cues several times.]

1.9 This time, freeze in a high curved or angled shape. [Cue and tap drumbeats.]

1.10 Freeze in a strong, low shape or a strong, high shape. Ready? *And*, 'Run, two, three, four; strong shape, two, three, four.' [Repeat many times, encouraging children to create a variety of shapes at different levels.]

1.11 Let's try running and freezing with the music. [Play an excerpt from music Selection B or C.] I'll help you the first few times, then we'll see if you can remember the dance by yourself. Four counts to go. Ready? Count with me, 'One, two, three, four; run, two, three, four; freeze, two, three, four; run, two, three, four; freeze, two, three, four.' [Repeat; say cues and counts several times with the children, then have children respond on their own.]

2.0 Take a low shape near the floor that really looks strong. Turn and move out of your low shape into a high, strong shape. Keep trying it on your own. Turn around on one spot and rise until you are standing very tall.

Try little steps as you turn, then big steps. Which size steps do you like?

2.1 Remember to hold your low, medium, and high shapes strong and still.

2.2 Hold your arms up and out and up as you take your turning steps. This helps you keep your balance.

2.3 As you turn around, make your turning steps take you to another spot in the room. Now you are traveling as you turn. [Keep the traveling time brief so children manage turning safely. Slowly repeat:] 'Turn, 2, 3, 4, hold, 2, 3, 4.'

2.4 When you get to your new spot, travel with slow turning steps back to your own [home] spot. Step out with one foot in the direction you are going and turn your whole body around in a circle. Keep looking at the spot where you are going. [Tap drum and cue as in 2.3.]

2.5 Choose big turning steps, or little turning steps, or some of each as you travel to a new spot and back. Can you turn for four counts, hold or freeze for four counts, travel back to your old spot for four, and freeze for four? [Repeat several times.]

2.6 Take a high or low frozen shape. Be ready to travel with your turning steps. Ready? *And*, 'Turn, two, three, four; freeze, two, three, four.' [Play music Selection B or C. Repeat phrase three times with cues to help children turn and freeze with the music.]

2.7 We are ready to add 'run and freeze' to our 'turn and freeze' phrase. Show me a strong, still body shape to start! [Play music Selection B or C.] Ready? *Begin*, 'Run, two, three, four; freeze, two, three, four; run, two, three, four; freeze, two, three, four.' [Repeat several times.]

3.0 [Play an uneven "*gal*-lop-ing" rhythm using a drum, wood block, or two hollowed-out coconut shells, accenting the first (*gal*) beat.] Listen to this rhythm. Show me how it makes your feet want to move.

3.1 Enjoy all the wide, open spaces—'*gal*-lop-ing, *gal*-lop-ing!' [Remind children to keep one foot out in front when galloping.] When I say, 'Change,' change your leading foot. [Change every eight or four steps.]

3.2 [Read one of the following poems to enhance children's enjoyment of high-stepping, grand galloping. Play music Selection D.] Gallop to the music, changing your lead foot *every* three or four steps. '*Gal*-lop-ing, *gal*-lop-ing, *gal*-lop-ing, change [and so on].'

Galloping Horses

Gallop and gallop and gallop around,
Horses take off like a merry-go-round!

The horses all gallop and race in the plains,
They jump over fences and shake their proud manes.

They chase and they play with small nips and small bites,
They kick and they buck in their playful mock fights.

Then thunder and lightning make all of them bolt,
Each stallion and mare and filly and colt.

Gallop and gallop and gallop they go—
There goes the herd like a wild rodeo!

—*Yolanda Danyi Szuch*

3.3 Let's try galloping to the words 'gal-lop, gal-lop.' Listen to the drum [beat an uneven long-short, long-short]. Off you go! 'Gal-lop, gal-lop, [and so on].' [Accompany with music Selections D or E, if desired. Another day, gallop to the words, "Gallop, and gallop, and gallop.]

3.4 [Replay music Selection B or C.] Some people like to skip to this music, others like to gallop. Wait for the music to start. See if you can fill all the empty spaces while skipping or galloping. Stop quickly when the music stops.

3.5 Let's all try skipping! Make your knees important. Lift one knee up high and then the other. Off you go!

3.6 Really push off the floor with the balls of your feet. Don't let your heels touch the ground as you skip.

3.7 Let your arms and hands swing high to help lift you up. Watch one arm swing up in front, then the other. Up, up, up, up! Look to see if your arm and opposite knee are high at the same time. [Check for opposition.]

3.8 Make your skipping light: Bend your ankle as you land and stretch the whole leg as you push off. Feel this lightness. Push off and up you go! A bubbly, sprightly skip! [Note developmental changes in leg and arm action since Kindergarten Dance Unit 5. Provide additional help for children at level one or in transition to level two.]

ASSESSMENT: DEVELOPMENTAL SCALE FOR SKIPPING

Child's Name: _____   Rater's Name: _____

Date	Grade	Unit	Tasks	Leg Action Step 1: One foot completes a step and hop (skip); other foot simply steps.	Leg Action Step 2: A step and hop on one foot, followed by a step and hop on other foot, landing from hop on total foot.	Leg Action Step 3: Two foot skip, landing from the hop on ball of the foot.	Arm Action Step 1: Both arms pump up and down together.	Arm Action Step 2: Arms sometimes swing in opposition to legs; other times, both arms are in front of body at same time.	Arm Action Step 3: Arms swing in opposition to legs; at no time are both arms in front of body at the same time.
9/97	K	#5	3.0-3.3 or 4.4	✔			✔		
12/97	K	#5	Revisit 4.4		✔		✔		
9/98	1	#2	3.8		✔			✔	
10/98	1	#3	1.5-1.7			✔		✔	
10/99	2	#4	1.0-1.4			✔			✔

Adapted from "Developing Children—Their Changing Movement" by M.A. Roberton and L.E. Halverson (In B.J. Logsdon, et al., *Physical education for children*, 1984, p. 58.) Developmental steps are based on sequences hypothesized by Halverson with Step 3 representing a more advanced skipping pattern. Adapted with permission of M.A. Roberton.

AEROBIC ACTIVITY

Jumping rope is another good activity to practice pushing off from the balls of your feet. You can jump alone with your own rope or three people can take turns turning the rope overhead or swinging the rope back and forth to jump over. Each day, try to jump more times without stopping.

3.9 Can you count and take four skipping steps and freeze? Think of all the different shapes you have created. Try to make an unusual shape at a low level. Ready? *And,* 'Skip, two, three, four; freeze, two, three, four.' [Repeat several times.]

3.10 Think of all the different shapes you can make at a high level. [Have children create high shapes during still moments. Encourage varied shapes, sometimes asking children to demonstrate. Observing gives children ideas for creating new shapes or samples to copy.] Let's watch [Jose]. He is using his arms and head to make a still, high shape. You might like to try [Jose's] or another one of your own ideas.

3.11 Everyone can make up their own skipping dance. You choose when to freeze in high shapes and when to freeze in low shapes. Ready? *And,* 'Skip, two, three, four; freeze, two, three, four.' [Repeat many times, seeing if individuals change levels.]

3.12 If your shape is low, stretch your hands and arms to reach for something on the ground. If your shape is high, pretend you are reaching for something way up high! Let me guess what you are reaching for. [Continue playing music or percussion.]

4.0 Let's put together a longer dance with running and freezing, turning and freezing, and skipping [or galloping] and freezing. I'll give you cues for each part of the dance. Ready? Four counts to go: 'Wait, two, three, four.' *Now,* 'Run, two, three, four; freeze, two, three, four; turn, two three, four; freeze, two, three, four; skip [or gallop], two, three, four; freeze, two, three, four.' [Repeat sequence several times.]

4.1 Make this your very own dance. Put your traveling and turning steps in any order you wish. Don't forget to hold very still on the freezes. I will call, 'Travel,' instead of 'Run, turn, skip, or gallop' so you can choose your own steps. Four counts to go: 'Wait, two, three, four.' *And,* 'Travel, two, three, four; freeze, two, three, four.' [Repeat several times to music Selection D or an uneven percussion rhythm.]

4.2 Let's create a dance with a partner. Join hands and see how many different ways you can travel together. Copy each others' movements exactly. Try hard not to get ahead of one another—travel side by side [next to each other]. [Play music Selection B or C.]

4.3 Let's dance with our partner again. Try to keep your steps the same size so you both can freeze at the same time right next to each other. [Continue music.]

4.4 How else can you travel with a partner? [One person leads, the other follows.] Try different ways—alongside, following, leading. Which way do you and your partner like best? Show us. [Music Selection B or C.]

4.5 Think of the stillness in your dance. Quickly decide who will freeze high and who will freeze low. Will your starting position [or ending] look the same or different? Can you think of other ways to make your body shapes more interesting? [Play music Selection B or C several times to give children a lot of practice working together.]

5.0 [Children enjoy dancing to poems about riding wild horses. Use percussion, reciting the poem as the children translate the words into movement.] Push off from the balls of your feet as you gallop and *ride!*

A Galloping Rhyme

I had a white charger,
Most splendid and bold:
His hoofs were like silver,
His mane was of gold,
He stamped his bright hoofs,
And he tossed up his mane
And he galloped away to the castles of Spain.

—*Anonymous*

Galloping Just So

Gallop, and gallop, and gallop, just so,
Hands held high, pull back and shout, Whoa!
Turning, and turning, and turning around,
Ropes twirl high and then to the ground,
Gallop, and gallop, and gallop, just so,
Hands held high, pull back and shout, Whoa!

—*Luann Alleman*

Gallop to the music!

5.1 [Have a chorus of children recite one of the poems with you while others dance, then change roles.]

5.2 [All children can dance at the same time or one partner could travel on the first stanza, the other on the second, and both on the third. Alternate starting roles to give everyone a chance to dance both galloping and turning steps. Children enjoy bringing riding hats, boots, handkerchiefs or bandannas, or making accessories to wear at the final performance. Ask the librarian or classroom teacher to read *Pecos Bill* by Steven Kellog or other legends and stories about wild horses and the Wild West. Emphasize that the American cowboys and ranchers were men and women who came from a mixture of cultural and ethnic backgrounds (i.e., Native American Indians, North Americans of primarily English, Spanish, and Irish descent, Mexican Americans, and African Americans).]

Skipping, Pausing, and Changing Body Shapes and Levels

3 or 4 lessons

FOCUS Skipping and pausing, changing directions, levels, and shapes to musical beats

MOTOR CONTENT

Selected from Theme 1—Introduction to the Body and Theme 3—Introduction to Space

Body

Locomotor activities—skipping, jumping
Nonlocomotor—balances
Body shapes—straight, thin, narrow, wide, round, curved, twisted, angular

Space

Levels—high, medium, low (deep)
Directions—forward, backward, sideways

OBJECTIVES

In this unit, children will (or should be willing to try to) meet these objectives:

- Look for and travel to open spaces about the room, demonstrating quick changes of direction and safe, controlled stops (reflects National Standard in Dance 1d).
- Show increasingly mature skipping patterns, keeping weight forward on the balls of the feet (or landing lightly on the total foot) and moving arms and legs in opposition or semi-opposition (reflects National Standard in Dance 1a).
- Willfully stop on the long (sustained) notes and create a variety of strong shapes at different levels (reflects National Standard in Dance 1c).

EQUIPMENT AND MATERIALS

Drum; recording of "Seven Jumps," a Danish folkdance. (See page 63 for the sheet music of "Seven Jumps.")

LEARNING EXPERIENCES

1.0 Today we are going to learn parts of a Danish folkdance, 'Seven Jumps,' once danced by men only. It is filled with stunts of strength and surprise. Find a space of your own. Stretch your arms way out to your sides; make sure you

Seven Jumps

Fine

Continue 5 times more *D.C.*
adding a measure each time

cannot touch anyone. Listen to the drum talk to your feet. It will tell your feet to skip to all the open spaces. When the drum stops, it's telling your feet to stop. Let's see if your feet can follow the drum. [Play an uneven, *long*-short, *long*-short rhythm. Check to see if children stop when the drum stops. Coach them to alternate their lead foot.] First, step and hop on one foot; then step and hop on the other.

1.1 Be sure your skipping takes you to open spaces so you can be all by yourself when the drum stops. Ready? *And*, 'Skip, and skip, and skip, and skip, and skip, and skip, and skip, and stop!' [Pause.] 'Look around . . . are there empty spaces that need to be filled?' [Repeat several times, helping children find open spaces away from others. Once the children are conscientious about safe spacing, challenge them to skip in different directions as they fill empty spaces—forward, backward, sideways.]

1.2 [Play three strong, short beats on the drum.] How did the drum sound or feel different this time? Yes! The three beats were loud, quick, and even. Can you stamp your feet to the three quick beats? '[Tap.] *Stamp*, [tap] *stamp*, [tap], *stamp*!' Let's put our skipping and stamping together. Here we go, 'Skip, and skip, and skip, and skip . . . [seven skips]. Are you listening for the three quick beats? [Pause.] '[Tap] stamp, [tap] stamp, [tap] stamp!' [Repeat several times, pausing to prepare the children for the three quick beats.]

1.3 Let's see if you are listening so well you don't need me to tell you when the three quick beats are coming. [Play "Seven Jumps," measures 1 to 10.] Ready to go! 'Skip, two, three, four, five, six, seven, and pause. [*Tap, tap, tap*.]' [Observe for *stamp, stamp, stamp*!] There are seven skips (measures 1 to 7), a pause (measure 8), and three stamps (quarter notes in measures 9 and 10)]. [Repeat once or twice.]

1.4 The stamping part could be more exciting! *Stamp* your feet three times, turn around, now *stamp* three more times, turn around the other way (measures 9 to 16). Try to make your stamping strong and quick! [Play three strong drumbeats for stamping and talk children through the turn.]

1.5 Make your skipping light. See if you can skip on the balls of your feet so your heels never touch the floor. [Softly tap the drum or play music, measures 1 to 8. Encourage forward body lean. Comment on how quietly the children's feet are touching the floor.] Why it is so quiet, you must be skipping on cotton clouds!

1.6 As you skip, swing one arm up and then the other. Look to see if your opposite arm swings forward as your knee lifts high. 'Up, and up, and up!' [The opposition of arms and legs usually develops without intervention. Remember to provide many, and varied, opportunities for free, spontaneous skipping to music and rhythmic patterns (both uneven and even). Select or design tasks to encourage a more advanced skipping pattern.]

1.7 Let's put our skipping, stamping, and turning all together in a dance. Start with a nice, strong shape. Follow what the music tells your feet to do. Ready? *And* go, 'Skip, two, three, four, five, six, seven, and pause [measures 1 through 8]; *stamp, stamp, stamp,* turn once around, *stamp, stamp, stamp,* turn around the other way [measures 9 through 16].' [Repeat cues and sequence many times.]

2.0 Everyone make a very strong shape when you hear one loud drumbeat. See if you can hold your shape until you hear another loud beat. [Beat the drum once, challenging children to hold their shapes for seven counts, then signal them to release their shapes. Repeat many times, encouraging children to make different shapes they can hold for different lengths of time. Listen to the music "Seven Jumps" (measures 17, 18, and 19 plus) to develop a feeling for the lengths of seven different holding patterns (sustained notes).]

2.1 Be sure your base is big enough to hold your shape very still. [Let children experiment holding balances on large and small bases of support.] What body parts did you find hard [or easy] to use for a base? [Knees, hands, heads, toes. Encourage bases that children can change easily and that help them hold a still shape.]

2.2 The bigger your base, the easier it is for you to hold a still, strong balance. Find different bases that help you hold very still and make you look very strong. [Children can work independently or you can call, "Change to a new base." Have children show different bases of support and let others in the class try them.]

2.3 [Terrence], show us your strong shape. Look—no wiggles at all and every muscle is very tight. Let's all try [Terrence's] still shape. No wiggles. [Lift different children slightly off the floor, commenting on how firmly and still they hold their shape. They love this! Be sure to lift carefully and give each child a turn sometime during the class.]

2.4 Tighten your tummy muscles to hold your balance very still. What other muscles can you tighten? [Seat, arm, leg muscles.]

2.5 See if you can balance or hold a shape at different levels. Some of your shapes will be high, some low, and some in the middle. Try to hold each shape for eight counts. Practice on your own, changing your shape and level when I say, 'Change.' [After awhile, vary this task by holding shapes for different lengths of time (e.g., two counts, five counts, and so on).]

2.6 [Play "Seven Jumps" music, measures 17 through 19.] Listen for the first, long sound [note]. Make a shape with your whole body and try to hold very still until the sound changes. Each time you hear or feel a different sound, make another shape and hold that shape very still. [Play an excerpt of seven sustained notes to give children practice in making and holding shapes for different durations. Repeat two or three times.]

2.7 Let's put our whole dance together and see if you can remember to skip in different directions, stamp on the three quick beats, and change shapes on the long sounds. Ready? *And* go. [Play music and give cues for measures 1 to 16—see learning experience 1.7.] Listen for the sustained [long] notes and be ready to balance.

3.0 Let's dance with a partner. Join hands with someone near. Come to the center circle if you need help finding a partner. Skip along together to the music, trying to stay next to each other. You will both have to take the same size skipping steps and go the same speed. [Play music.]

3.1 [Practice 3.1 to 3.3 to drumbeats, then music.] You might like to change your dance and clap your partner's hands on the three quick beats [notes]. Face each other. One of you hold hands up in front of you [show palms]. Clap your partner's hands three times. Be ready for the clapping after you take seven skips.

3.2 You may like to add a turn after the three claps. [Partners demonstrate.] 'Clap, clap, clap, turn once around, and clap, clap, clap, turn the other way around.'

3.3 We still have to practice the shape part of our dance. How can you and your partner make body shapes at different levels? One shape high and one shape low. Keep changing shapes and levels. Quickly decide who will start high and who will start low.

ASSESSMENT: PARTNER OBSERVATION

Watch your partner to see if each shape is held very still. How many shapes can you and your partner make and hold still at different levels? (Children tell or show the number of different shapes held.)

3.4 Some of you made five, six, or seven different body shapes and held each balance still. Let's put the whole dance together with the music. Ready to go? [Wait during introduction.] 'A-skip, two, three, four, five, six, seven, pause, eight; *stamp, stamp, stamp*, turn around once, four; *stamp, stamp, stamp*, turn around the other way, four. Hold a strong shape!' [Repeat from the beginning, skipping to the music.] If you like, clap instead of stamp.

3.5 Make your skips light, your stamps [or claps] strong, your shapes very still, and you will be the best first grade dancers in the world! [Give children plenty of time to practice. Call fewer cues ("skip," "stamp," "turn," or "balance") for each action.]

4.0 Quickly get into groups of seven and sit down in a circle. [Have children count off one to seven or put a sticker with one of seven numbers on each child's shirt. Check if everyone knows their number.] Decide what shape everyone in your group will hold. Number ones, raise your hands. When you hear the first long [sustained] note, number ones will show the shape they chose. Number twos, raise your hands. On the second held note, number twos will show their shape. [Continue seven times until all seven groups have shared their shapes. Encourage children to show their own unique shapes.]

4.1 Let's try the dance from the very beginning. Skip when you hear the skipping music. Keep your circle big and round by skipping clockwise—like the hands of a clock going around. [Play music.] Ready to go? 'A-skip, two, three, four, five, six, seven, pause, eight; *stamp, stamp, stamp*, turn once around [eight counts]; *stamp, stamp, stamp*, turn around the other way [eight counts]. Quickly, number ones [first long note], hold your shapes [eight counts]. Now number twos [second long note], hold your shapes [eight counts]. The dance starts all over again with everybody skipping and circling to the music. [With each repetition of the dance, add one more sustained note and one more shape until all seven groups are holding their shapes. Enjoy the entire dance!]

4.2 Now, here's a special challenge for all the groups. Listen closely. Number ones show wide shapes; twos make thin shapes; threes, twisted shapes; fours, round shapes; fives, angular shapes; sixes, very low shapes; and sevens, very high shapes! [Children will want to help name different shapes to hold.]

5.0 [You may want to try the following version of the traditional "Seven Jumps," a Danish folkdance filled with stunts and surprises. Dance "Seven Jumps" in a large, single circle, all hands joined. The dance begins with seven step-hops (skips) to the left and a jump-*stamp* (measures 1 through 8). Repeat seven step-hops and a jump-*stamp* to the right (measures 9 through 16). The circle formation is difficult for young children to maintain. As an alternative, they could join hands with a partner and skip freely about the room, following your balancing actions on the held notes. Play follow the leader with children copying each shape.] On the first sustained [long] note, everyone drops their hands, places them on their hips, and raises their right knees to balance. Everyone stamp their right feet to the ground on the second note and quickly rejoin hands. Skip to the chorus again [repeat measures 1 through 16]. We will follow the same balancing actions throughout the dance, adding a new holding or balancing action each time on the sustained note. For the second balance, place your hands on your hips and raise your left knee to balance. For the third balance, get down on the floor on your right knee. Get down on your left knee for the fourth balancing action. On the fifth balance, you get down on both knees, place your right elbow on the floor, and put your chin in your cupped hand. Do the same balance on the left elbow for the sixth sustained note. For action seven, you push the body forward to a front-lying position, touching your forehead to your cupped hands on the floor. [Have children practice each balance as you describe them. Note: Children may have a hard time holding all of the balances, but they will enjoy doing this dance tremendously. Repeat it two or three times or revisit this unit later in the school year. Encourage tight muscles and lifting up through the chest, even during low balances. Enjoy dancing with the children!]

Unit 4

Body Shapes and Movement Through Space

3 or 4 lessons

FOCUS Changing body shapes and the size of movement through extensions in space

MOTOR CONTENT

Selected from Theme 1—Introduction to the Body and Theme 3—Introduction to Space

Body

Body actions—extension and contraction
Locomotor activities—traveling and pausing
Body shapes—variety of shapes

Space

Extensions—small, large; near to, far from
Directions—up, down

OBJECTIVES

In this unit, children will (or should be willing to try to) meet these objectives:

- Create big body shapes and movements by stretching and extending body parts out into space (reflects National Standard in Dance 1a).
- Create small body shapes and movements by bending and contracting body parts in toward the body's center (reflects National Standard in Dance 1a).
- Understand movement is large or small, depending on the amount of space used as the body moves.
- Feel the body shape getting larger as body parts move away from each other and the body's center and smaller when body parts move closer to each other and to the body's center.
- Listen and respond appropriately to a variety of percussion instruments as well as verbal and nonverbal cues.
- Share ideas with others while creating and performing simple dance phrases, varying the amount of space used (reflects National Standard in Dance 2d).

EQUIPMENT AND MATERIALS

Percussion instrument(s) to produce sudden and sustained sounds: a drum, tambourine, wood or tone block, rhythm sticks, or rap stick (for sudden sounds); a gong or cymbal hit with a padded stick, triangle, or tinsha (for sustained sounds). *Optional music:* Selection A—Quiet music to accompany slow, light growing and stretching movement, such as Grieg: *Peer Gynt Suite,* "Morning, Act 4" or Bartok: For Children, "Vol. II no. 31 and Vol. III no. 15"; Selection B—Music with variations in intensity to contrast light and strong movement, such as: Rossini-Respighi: *La Boutique Fantasque,* "Can-Can"; Selection C—Sousa: "Semper Fidelis"; and Selection D—Brahms: "Hungarian Dances, Nos. 5 and 6." (See Resources).

LEARNING EXPERIENCES

1.0 [Softly tap a triangle or other resonant rhythm instrument.] Let's begin in very small, curled-up shapes close to the floor. As I tap the triangle, very slowly stretch and grow into a bigger shape. '[Tap:] Begin to grow . . . [tap] . . . grow up and out . . . [tap] become larger . . . . Now, when you are great *big,* slowly shrink . . . [tap] . . . back to the ground . . . [tap] . . . in your teeny, tiny shape.' [Repeat verbal cues many times while tapping the triangle. Children enjoy making little and big shapes with their bodies. Let them improvise dance movements to music or to a variety of percussion sounds to enhance their understandings of size and dimension. If taught in the spring, integrate these dance experiences with classroom activities on growth and change and with work in the visual arts.]

1.1 Can you feel you are filling up and using more and more space as you grow big? As you become smaller, you hardly need any space at all. Open your body to reach out into space with your arms and legs as you grow big. Close your body tightly and pull body parts near you to make little shapes. Work hard to change how much space you use. [Use verbal cues, sound accompaniment in 1.0, or music Selection A (see equipment list).]

1.2 This time really stretch out all your body parts. See if you can use even more space. A big, huge, enormous shape! Now, get teeny tiny—as small as you can. [Talk students through small shapes to big shapes and back to small continuously several times.]

Children brainstorm and collaborate to create a mural painting about how things grow and develop.

1.3 Your face, especially your eyes, can help show you are getting bigger or smaller. As you grow into a huge shape, let your eyes and face look far out into space. Your shape will look bigger! When you shrink, drop your eyes [head] and look into the middle of your teeny shape. Ready? *And*, '[Tap, tap:] Grow big and look out . . . [tap, tap] shrink smaller, look into your little shape.' [Repeat many times.]

1.4 Each time I tap the drum loudly, shoot your body parts far out into space and make a large shape. Then *zip!* Quickly shrink, pull body parts in, and look inside your tiny shape. Here we go: '[Tap loudly.] Big shape! [Tap softly.] Small shape! [Tap loudly.] Look out! [Tap softly.] Look in!' [Repeat many times. Change their bases of support often for greater variety in sudden movements. Beat the drum loudly for large shapes and tap softly for small shapes.]

1.5 With each loud sound, make one big movement that sweeps the air all around you. Up high! Down low! Sweep and stir up the air! Try to make each movement as large as the sound is loud. Use up a lot of space. [Accompany with drum, wood block, or the like, varying the intensity. Remind children to care for others by moving safely into open spaces.]

1.6 This time, make small, tiny movements. Use a different body part with each tap of the drum [or triangle]. Here we go: '[Tap:] . . . A little movement . . . [tap] . . . another small movement . . . [tap] . . . move tiny with a different body part.' [Play soft taps close together, then stagger the frequency to see if children are moving to the sounds.]

1.7 Let's dance without listening to a drum. Begin in very tiny, little shapes. The two of you will very slowly and carefully grow into larger, bigger shapes. Keep filling up all the space around you with big, stretched-out shapes, then shrink back into teeny, tiny shapes. Find a partner and begin. [Allow children time to work without accompaniment. Their movements and pauses will create natural rhythmic phrases.]

1.8 Think about how things grow and change. How can the two of you grow together into one big shape and then shrink back together into one teeny, tiny shape? [Accompany as in 1.0 or use music Selections B and C. When using recorded music, increase volume for growing shapes; decrease volume for shrinking shapes.]

1.9 Can you and your partner move fast to change shapes? Jump up and shoot your body parts out into space to make big shapes. Quickly shrink into tiny shapes. [Repeat. Then explore slow ways of changing shapes. Use percussion, if you wish.]

1.10 Let's make up a movement sentence of opposites. 'Open fast to make a big shape! Now close *slowly*. Open! *Close*.' [Accompany with percussion, repeating several times. Encourage partners to explore contrasts and feel different lengths of movement phrases, strong and light accents, and fast and slow qualities.]

2.0 See how you can travel through all the empty spaces, taking big steps and jumps on the loud taps and small steps and jumps on the soft taps. Here we go: '[*Tap, tap, tap:*] Great big traveling movements. [Tap, tap, tap, tap, tap.] Travel with little steps and jumps.' [Repeat cues many times, varying the intensity and number of taps.]

2.1 When you push off into the air, straighten your knees and your toes. This makes your legs look very long and helps you jump higher and take bigger steps. [Continue drum beat. See 2.0.]

Open fast to make a big shape!

2.2 Let's see if we can make big and small movements with our whole body. Travel and stretch your body parts out *far*. Use lots of space for each big movement. Ready? *And*, '[*Ta-dum, ta-dum, ta-dum, ta-dum*:] Push out, stretch up, make big body movements . . . [da-de, da-de, da-de, da-de] . . . so small, you hardly even travel.' [Talk children through the task, varying the intensity of the drum. Vocalizing "ta-dum" and "da-de," or your own words or sounds, helps to establish the rhythmic pattern and accent of alternating big and small movement.]

2.3 Travel quickly, looking for and moving into empty spaces. Suddenly, push off into a huge jump or spin around with tiny, little jumps, depending on what the drum tells you to do. Listen and move! '[Tap, tap, tap, loud *tap*!] Travel, travel, travel—a big *jump*!' [Alternate volume by clicking the rim of the drum to indicate small, quick, light jumps.]

2.4 [Play music.] How does this music make you feel? With a partner, explore different ways to travel and dance in place with big and small movements. Think about your partner's shapes [see 1.8] and how you could add moments of stillness to your dance. [Variation without music: Ask children to think of an idea or story about something that grew very big or very small. Encourage them to tell their idea or story with big and small movements.]

2.5 Let's share our big and small dances. We are looking for how much or how little space you use. Really show us the difference between big and small movements. [Groups of three to eight children may perform at one time.]

3.0 This time, the drum [or music] will tell you when to make big and small movements. [Play music Selection B or C. Adjust the volume as in 1.8.] Travel with big, huge movements when the music is louder. When you hear soft music, stop traveling and make small, little movements right where you are. [Increase volume for about two to four measures; 8 to 16 beats.] Here we go: 'Travel . . . travel . . . *great big movement* . . . [softer music] . . . now little movements right where you are.' [Repeat sequence many times.]

3.1 Let's try the opposite. Travel with very tiny movements, barely stirring the air as you go [quiet music]. You almost look invisible. Then make huge, *enormous movements* right where you are in your own place [louder music]. Really take up a lot of space as you stretch and extend your body parts far away from each other.

3.2 [Divide class in half.] Group one, travel with large movement when the music is loud and stop. Group two, travel with small movement when the music is soft and stop. Listen closely. Move only when it is your turn. Here we go: 'Group one, big traveling . . . traveling . . . [16 beats] and hold; now group two . . . travel with small steps . . . [16 beats] and hold.' [Repeat, changing roles.]

3.3 Now both groups will move at the same time. Group one, move 16 counts with small movements. Group two, move 16 counts with large movements. Then, change the size of your movements for the next 16 counts. Here we go: 'Group one is small, group two is big [count 16 beats]; now group one is big and group two is small [count 16 beats].' [Accompany with music Selection B or C, giving cues.]

3.4 After moving in two separate groups, everyone move 16 counts with large movements, then 16 counts with small movements. Here we go: 'Group one, small movements; group two, large movements [count 16 beats]; now everyone travel with large movements [count 16 beats]; and now everyone make small movements [count 16 beats].'

3.5 Let's have half of each group come and watch as the other half performs. I will talk you through the dance as the music plays. Remember your movement may travel or be right on the spot. Make the size of your movement clear to the audience while traveling and while moving in place. Fill up the space or take only a tiny bit of space. [Accompany task and talk children through the dance sequence outlined in 3.4.]

Unit 5

Traveling, Pausing, and Changing Speed

3 or 4 lessons

FOCUS Traveling and pausing, changing speed and responding to musical phrases

MOTOR CONTENT

Selected from Theme 1—Introduction to the Body and Theme 2—Introduction to Weight and Time

Body

Locomotor activities—variety of running, stepping, jumping
Nonlocomotor activities—curling, stretching, rising, sinking
Actions of body parts—apply force (pressing)

Effort

Speed—fast, slow; sudden, sustained
Force—strong, light; firm, fine

OBJECTIVES

In this unit, children will (or should be willing to try to) meet these objectives:

- Explore and demonstrate a variety of locomotor and nonlocomotor activities to fast and slow musical phrases (reflects National Standards in Dance 1a, 1b).
- Create their own fast and slow dance phrases to music, accurately repeating movements and showing clear changes in speed and force (reflects National Standard in Dance 2d).
- Understand the tempo in music and movement of their bodies may vary from fast to slow and that the suggested music is divided into fast and slow sections called phrases.
- Demonstrate the ability to define and maintain personal space while exploring movement standing in place (reflects National Standard in Dance 1d).
- Work safely by looking for and traveling to empty spaces and work cooperatively by listening and responding appropriately to verbal and nonverbal directions.
- Take an active role in class discussions about interpretations of and reactions to their dances (reflects National Standard in Dance 3b).

EQUIPMENT AND MATERIALS

Tambourine or drum; triangle or other resonant rhythm instrument. Recording of folk dance "Lott Ist Todt" (*see* piano arrangement below). Alternatively, use a classical music selection with variations in tempo, alternating quick with slow movement, such as: Selection A—Bartok: *For Children,* Vol. III, nos. 1 and 2, or Brahms: The Best of Brahms, "Hungarian Dance No. 5" (See Resources).

Lott Ist Todt

LEARNING EXPERIENCES

1.0 As I tap the tambourine [or drum], look for and travel into the empty spaces. Let the tambourine tell you how to move. Stop quickly when I say, 'And stop.' Here we go: 'Travel . . . travel . . . travel . . . looking for empty spaces . . . your own places . . . and stop.' [Tap the tambourine at a moderately quick, steady pace, talking students through this task many times.]

1.1 Listen to the tambourine as you travel and try to take only one step per beat. The tambourine will tell you how fast to move. [Tap a variety of even and uneven rhythms at a moderate tempo.]

1.2 This time, I'm going to play the tambourine very slowly. How will you move? Yes! Slowly, also. Ready? And, '*Travel.*' [Greatly exaggerate the pronunciation of "travel." Tap a slow, steady beat or rub the tambourine or drum skin with the palm of your hand.]

1.3 [Restricting the space prevents children from going too fast. Have children move in one-half or one-third of the area.] Let's try moving safely and quickly now. The tambourine is telling you how fast to travel. Listen and move through those empty spaces. Off you go.

1.4 I will tap the tambourine at different tempos, sometimes fast, other times slowly. Listen to the changes in speed as you travel and try hard to move at the same tempo as the tambourine. Ready? *Begin*: [Fast taps with fingertips.] 'Travel, travel, travel, travel.' [Slowly rub tambourine skin with palm.] '*Travel, travel.*'

1.5 Try to change the speed of your traveling as soon as you hear the tambourine change. Tell your muscles to be ready to speed up or slow down.

1.6 [After a few phrases, have groups of children demonstrate how accurately they can change speeds.] Let's watch how [Ramon] and his group are able to follow the tambourine by changing the speed of their travel. Watch their quick, light traveling [fast tempo] become slow and strong [slow tempo]. Their muscles are working all the time!

1.7 [Familiarize yourself with the musical selections.] Phrases are musical sentences. They tell us how to move just like the tambourine. Listen for changes in the musical phrases as you travel. If the music slows down, you slow down. If the music speeds up, you move fast. [Play your choice of musical selections.]

1.8 Remember to take more time between your steps if the music is slow. What do you need to do if the music is fast? Right! Speed up your steps and take less time between each movement. [Music.]

1.9 Let's perform our fast and slow traveling dances. The music will tell you when to move fast or slow. Those of us watching in the audience are very interested in seeing how the speed of your traveling changes with the tempo of the music. [Rotate groups so all children have an opportunity to perform and observe.]

2.0 [Accompany with slow beat on triangle as you give the task.] Right where you are, without moving your feet, begin to move your body very slowly as I tap the triangle. Stretch as far as you can all around you without moving off your spot. Think about taking all the time in the world to move. Slowly stretch or reach as far as you can to all the spaces around you.

2.1 With each tap of the triangle, move just one body part. '[Tap:] Allow one body part to rise, two, three; now [tap] sink, two, three; [tap] lift another body part to the ceiling, two, three; now [tap] lower it, two, three; [tap] and stretch a body part high, two, three; [tap] and bend it low, two, three. Move one body part at a time.'

2.2 As I play slow taps on the triangle, *slowly* change the shape of your body with each tap. Remember we are working on making one new shape for each tap. Here we go: '[Tap:] Shape. [Tap.] New shape. [Tap.] Can you change your shape again? [Tap.] And a new one. [Tap.] Make each shape look different.'

2.3 This time, as I tap the tambourine, shoot up into the air with quick jumps. Think of filling the space above your head with fast movement. Bend your knees and push off quickly—explode into the air! Remember your nice, soft landings. [Student demonstrates.]

2.4 Staying in your own space, move quickly when I tap the tambourine and *slowly* as I shake the tambourine. Listen to the different sounds and change how you move when the tambourine tells you. Here we go: '[Shake:] Very *slowly* move your body parts . . . all around you . . . nice *big* stretches up to the ceiling . . . down to the floor . . . out into space.' Now quickly change your body shape each time you hear a tap. [Tap, tap, tap, tap]; [shake] once again, *slowly* move.' [Repeat, alternating tempo.]

2.5 [Accompany with music.] Remember that a musical phrase is like a sentence telling you something important. The music is telling you when to move fast and when to move slowly. Listen and, without traveling, move to the music right where you are.

Explode into the air!

2.6 Some of you may be able to design your own pattern or phrase of jumps, which you can remember to do when the fast music plays. Or create a phrase of slow movement to do when the slow music plays. [Allow children time to create fast and slow dance phrases without, then with, the music.]

2.7 [Divide the class into two groups.] Group one will dance very quickly, and group two will dance very slowly. Listen to the music and move only when your fast or slow music plays. Hold very still when it is the other group's turn to dance. [Play music selected in 2.6. Exchange roles so all children have an opportunity to experience fast or slow extremes in tempo.]

3.0 [Accompany with music.] Let's travel quickly through space when the musical phrases are fast. Move very slowly on the spot during the slow phrases. Remember to move quietly so you can hear changes in the music.[Review some movement possibilities.]

3.1 The musical phrases are telling us when to move fast and when to move slowly. Think of how you can change the speed of your movement. Show me differences between fast and slow movement by taking more or less time between each movement.

3.2 This time, see if you can move on the spot very quickly when you hear the fast music and travel slowly during the slow music

AEROBIC FITNESS

Walking is a great exercise for everyone's heart. Maybe someone else at home needs exercise, too. Take someone for a 20-minute walk.

3.3 Let's get into small groups [mixed groups of four to six children]. Find your group and sit down in a circle with a big, empty space in the middle. When you hear the slow musical phrases, stand up and begin to move forward into the middle of your circle. When you hear the faster music, quickly travel away from the center back to your starting places. Ready? Begin. [Play music and cue children by saying, "Slowly into the center," and, "Quickly back out."]

3.4 During the slow music, imagine you are rolling or pushing something very *big* and very, very *heavy*. When you hear the fast music, quickly travel back to your places to show us that you are finished with your big job! Listen carefully. The music will tell you when to change.

3.5 Let's dance together again and see if we can move lightly on our feet. And oh! No noise with our mouths. [Reduce volume of music.] Make sure you can still hear the music.

3.6 Work hard to make the differences in speed and muscle tension very clear. Travel by moving very slowly with strong muscles with lots of time between each step. Then travel quickly and lightly with many short steps. Take care to make your fast feet safe.

3.7 Remember that you are discovering and showing differences between slow, strong movement and quick, light movement as you travel and move on the spot. Try to change your speed exactly when the music changes—feel the change coming and make it happen in your body! [Continue music.] First listen to the music, then we'll move to the music.

3.8 Let's watch our dances. When you move slowly, we [the audience] should be able to tell how big and heavy your object is because you are moving with such strength and concentration. When you travel quickly, share your excitement by showing us light, crisp steps—steps that sparkle and crackle! [Accompany with music and allow sufficient time for all groups to perform.]

Imagine pushing something very big and heavy. Push with your hands, arms, hip, legs, back, and side. Make your object look bigger. Push harder.

Second Grade Games

Passing With the Feet

4 to 6 lessons

FOCUS Dribbling and passing the ball in different directions with the feet

MOTOR CONTENT

Selected from Theme 1—Introduction to Basic Body and Manipulative Control and Theme 2—Introduction to Space

Body

Locomotor activities—traveling to receive or intercept passes
Manipulative activities—refining dribbling, passing, and trapping a ball with different surfaces of the feet

Space

Directions—sending the ball forward, sideways, and backward
Pathways—changes in the pathways of the ball and the child

OBJECTIVES

In this unit, children will (or should be willing to try to) meet these objectives:

- Dribble, change direction of the ball, and pass it with the inside or outside surface of either foot or with the heel (reflects National Standard in Physical Education 1).
- Trap, collect, and control the ball with the sole, the instep, and the inside or outside of either foot (reflects National Standard in Physical Education 1).
- Push the ball with the inside or outside surface of the foot or tap it with the heel to change the direction of the ball (reflects National Standard in Physical Education 1).
- Explain that if they keep their weight balanced on the balls of their feet when dribbling or preparing to receive a pass they can change directions quickly (reflects National Standard in Physical Education 2).
- Accept responsibility for improving the dribbling, passing, and trapping skills of both feet (reflects National Standard in Physical Education 5).
- Share the ball with others to give everyone equal opportunity to practice and enjoy skills (reflects National Standards in Physical Education 5, 7).
- Participate in moderate physical activity for sustained periods of time (reflects National Standards in Physical Education 3, 4).

EQUIPMENT AND MATERIALS

One soccer ball for each child, cones (or plastic jugs, beanbags, or the like) to scatter about the teaching area.

LEARNING EXPERIENCES

1.0 See how you can dribble the ball with your feet into all the spaces about the room without letting your ball touch anyone or anything. When you hear the signal to stop, remember to stop the ball only with your feet.

1.1 Keep the ball close to your feet. Push it lightly with the inside of your feet and try to keep up with your ball.

1.2 Show everyone you have control of your ball. Keep changing the pathway of your ball. Push it sideways with the outside of either foot and, sometimes, even try to send it backward with your heel.

1.3 Keep your feet close to the ball as you dribble about the room and try to stay up on the balls of your feet. Staying up on the balls of your feet will help keep you balanced and ready to change the direction of the ball quickly.

1.4 Listen as you practice dribbling with soft, gentle touches with the inside, outside, or heel of either foot. When I clap my hands, sharply change the pathway of your ball.

1.5 As you dribble the ball about the room, frequently pass your ball against a wall near you, collect your ball [take the speed off the ball], and dribble a moment. Then pass the ball against the wall again. Keep dribbling and passing the ball to different parts of the wall. As you travel, take care not to interfere with another ball or dribbler.

2.0 Each time I clap my hands, see if you can make your ball change pathways as you dribble, always keeping your ball close to your feet.

2.1 Try to make your change in pathway very sudden by pulling or pushing the ball into a different direction with the inside or outside of your foot.

Show everyone you can control your ball.

Make sure both feet get many turns so that they can each practice controlling the ball.

2.2 On your own, dribble close to someone and then suddenly avoid your classmate by pushing or pulling the ball sideways or by tapping the ball backward with your heel. Then dribble off and find another person to dodge.

2.3 You have been traveling about the entire space. Now try to stay in your own very small working space and practice pushing the ball forward, backward, and sideways. Don't let the ball get away from your small space. Push it gently in different directions. Stay up on the balls of your feet so you can move your feet quickly to keep your ball in your own little space.

2.4 Be sure you are constantly changing your dribbling foot. Good soccer players change their dribbling foot often. Give both feet plenty of practice so you feel good dribbling with either foot. Make both feet work. Don't let one foot be lazy.

3.0 In a moment, each of you will get a cone [bleach bottle or the like] and place it in a space away from other cones and away from the wall. Then we will see how suddenly you can change the direction of your ball every time you come to a new cone as you dribble about the room. Remember to place your cone away from other cones and the wall. Get a cone and begin.

3.1 As you dribble, take full responsibility for your ball. Keep your head up with your eyes looking out ahead of you as you dribble. Keep control of your ball and try hard to avoid others.

3.2 Show everyone you are in complete control of your ball. Dribble the ball close to a cone and quickly pull or push it sideways or backward to keep it from hitting the cone. Then dribble quickly and safely off to a new cone.

3.3 You are doing a great job of alternating feet as you dribble. Now make sure you are giving both feet a workout when you get close to the cone. Be careful. You may be giving one foot more practice in pushing or pulling the ball sideways or backward. Make your feet share the work fairly.

4.0 This time, let's try practicing sending straight passes to a partner so your receiver's feet hardly have to travel from their spot to collect or stop the ball before sending it back to you.

4.1 While you are waiting for the pass, be sure your weight is balanced on the balls of both of your feet. Being balanced on both feet makes it easier for you to move quickly to get in line with the pass so the ball rolls right straight to you.

4.2 Work on making that passing surface of your foot swing straight out and point toward your partner. This will help you make accurate passes straight to your partner.

4.3 When receiving a pass, quickly adjust your feet to line up the front of your body with the ball. Then point the toes of your receiving foot down close to the ground in front of the ball and bring your foot back toward you just as the ball contacts your foot. This drawing back of the foot helps to slow the ball down and keeps the ball from bouncing away from you. [Help a child demonstrate.]

4.4 Passers, aim your passes at a spot to one side of your partner. Swing your passing foot right out to the spot where you are aiming. Receivers, be ready to travel to get the front of your body in line with the ball. Have the toes of your stopping foot pointed down low, waiting in front of the ball, ready to draw your foot back toward you the moment the ball touches your foot.

4.5 Receivers, begin to change the part of your foot you use to stop the ball. You can stop the ball with your sole, the inside, and the outside of your feet. Try to use all different parts of your foot. The more different surfaces of your feet you use, the more skillful you will be at stopping the ball.

4.6 Before you pass, check to see if you have the passing surface of your foot facing the direction you want the ball to go. Remember to make that passing surface of your foot swing right out toward the exact spot where you want the pass to go. Passers and receivers, don't forget to give both feet equal chances to practice.

4.7 For awhile, act like there is someone in front of you trying to take the ball away from you and you have to pass the ball backward. After you stop the ball, turn around and, using the heel of your foot to pass the ball, see if you can pass the ball backward straight to your partner.

4.8 Let's see how many completed passes you can make without touching the ball with your hands. Great—how many did you get? Try hard and see if you can make at least three more passes the next time.

5.0 Get into groups of three with one ball away from other groups. Let's watch one group. Two stand up and take the ball. Show us how the two of you can pass the ball back and forth with your feet as you both travel forward down the floor in your lane. So far, that's easy, isn't it? Guess we better make it harder. The third person in your group is going to be a player on a different team who stands facing the two passers and tries to intercept their pass [steal the ball]. When she intercepts the ball, the passer becomes the defender [the one who intercepts (steals) the ball]. Each group decide who gets to be the first defender and start your game.

5.1 Defenders—you who are trying to intercept the pass, don't try too hard to take the ball away. At first, give the passer room to reposition [get back in a good position] after passing.

5.2 Passers, as soon as you pass the ball, run ahead to a spot away from the defender to be free to receive a pass. Protect the ball: Don't reposition [go] near the defender.

5.3 I am going to put one rule into this game. Once the receiver touches the ball with a foot, the pass is completed and the defender (the one trying to get the ball) must wait to intercept the ball when it is passed again.

5.4 Remember, when soccer players dribble and pass the ball, they aren't allowed to touch the ball with their hands. What do you think should happen in your game when someone touches the ball with their hands? [They likely will say something to the effect of, "When a passer touches the ball with a hand, the passer must change places with the defensive player."]

5.5 Let's have the defensive players on each lane switch lanes so we can practice passing and intercepting passes with different players. As you start your game again, receivers, try to dribble the ball a time or two before you pass the ball.

5.6 Some of you may feel you need another rule in your game. If you do, sit down in your lane for a moment and discuss your new rule, then get up and add it to your game. Does it make your game better?

5.7 Let's share some of the new rules. Which groups put in a new rule? [Have children discuss and or demonstrate their small group games. This sharing encourages children to self-assess: Which rules work well? Do all players have an equal opportunity to practice skills and enjoy movement challenges?]

5.8 Passers, face forward as you reposition [move] to receive a pass.

5.9 Receivers, try not to be too close to the passer as you run down your lane. Act like you have just half of the lane that is yours and stay in your own part.

ASSESSING FOOT DRIBBLING				
Class list	Pushes with various parts of the feet in dribbling. (scale, date)	Changes direction using either foot. (scale, date)	Dribbles to open spaces keeping ball near the feet. (scale, date)	Stops or collects the ball with various parts of either foot. (scale, date)
M. Green	4 8/30 5 9/16	4 8/30 4 9/16	3 8/30 4 9/16	5 8/30 5 9/16
J. Sabastian	3 8/30 4 9/16	2 8/30 3 9/16	4 8/30 4 9/16	2 8/30 3 9/16

Scale: 5 = *Very consistent (90% or more)*   4 = *Consistent*   3 = *Getting the idea*
2 = *It's new; some success*   1 = *Unsuccessful*

Catching With One Foot Stationary

2 to 3 lessons

FOCUS Reaching to catch while keeping one foot stationary

MOTOR CONTENT

Selected from Theme 1—Introduction to Basic Body and Manipulative Control and Theme 2—Introduction to Space

Body

Manipulative activities—tossing and catching beanbags and balls of various sizes

Space

Areas—personal and general, tossing in spaces near to and away from the catcher
Directions—extending forward, backward, sideways to catch

OBJECTIVES

In this unit, children will (or should be willing to try to) meet these objectives:

- Toss a beanbag (or ball) to spaces about the catcher to give the catcher practice in reaching to catch (reflects National Standard in Physical Education 1).
- Extend their reach when catching by keeping one foot stationary and taking a long step with the other foot toward the ball, bending the front knee as they extend their arms and hands to catch (reflects National Standard in Physical Education 1).
- Understand that reaching the throwing hand out toward the intended target when they release the beanbag (or ball) helps direct the beanbag (or ball) (reflects National Standards in Physical Education 2).
- Know that to extend their reaches when catching they must step out toward the beanbag (or ball) with one foot and bend the knee of the forward leg (reflects National Standard in Physical Education 2).
- Help each other develop catching and tossing skills by trying to make every toss go to a space to the side or the front of the receiver (reflects National Standard in Physical Education 1, 5).
- Willingly participates and accepts challenges in team play (2 vs 2) [reflects National Standard in Physical Education 7).

EQUIPMENT AND MATERIALS

One beanbag, yarn ball, tennis ball, or 6 to 10-inch lightweight ball for every two children; markers such as floor tape, polyspots, hoops or ropes.

LEARNING EXPERIENCES

1.0 Everyone, see if you can toss the beanbag so your partner can catch it without moving their feet to catch it. Get a partner, one beanbag, a working space, and begin.

1.1 I can't believe how many of you knew that your tossing hand should be pointing right to your catcher's hoop when you want them to catch the beanbag without moving their feet.

1.2 Count to see how many catches you and your partner can make without having to move your feet. Remember, tossers, if you are tossing with enough power and reaching your tossing hand right toward your catchers, the catchers should not have to move their feet to catch.

1.3 Let's change partners and help each other remember to reach right out with the tossing hand toward the catcher.

1.4 See if you and your new partner can catch as many as you did with your first partner. Remember that you have to start all over if either of you move your feet when catching.

2.0 Now you know that you can make the beanbag go right to your catcher. Let's see if you can intentionally make your catcher reach to catch. Toss the beanbag softer so it doesn't quite get to your partner. Catchers, try to reach and stretch to catch the beanbag, keeping one foot glued to the floor.

2.1 Tossers, think! Where will your tossing hand point to make your partner reach to catch? Can someone tell where it should point? Great—point your tossing hand to a spot to the side of your catcher where you want the beanbag to drop.

2.2 Catchers, remember you are trying to catch the beanbag with one foot glued to the floor. To be successful at reaching to catch, you have to be ready to step out with one foot toward the beanbag and really make those arms and hands reach out to catch.

2.3 Tossers, watch your catcher's feet. If both feet are moving, it's probably because you are tossing the beanbag too far away from your partner. Aim your toss a little closer to your partner the next time.

3.0 When you are the catcher, as you keep one foot glued to the floor, see if you can step way out toward the beanbag with your other foot as you catch. Stepping toward the beanbag with one foot makes it possible for you to reach and catch beanbags that are much farther away.

3.1 As you toss, watch your catcher's feet. Toss the beanbag far enough to the side of your partner to make your catcher move one large step to reach and catch the beanbag.

3.2 Catchers, think! How do you decide which foot to use to make that step to the beanbag? Right! Use your foot nearest to the spot where the beanbag will fall.

3.3 When you are the tosser, toss the beanbag first to one side of your partner and then the other side so you give each other practice in stepping to both sides to catch.

3.4 Catchers, as you take your step, keeping one foot glued to the floor, shift [move] your weight out toward the foot you stepped out on and by bending that knee toward the beanbag you can reach farther. [Have a child demonstrate.]

3.5 Tossers, how can you make your catcher change the foot that is glued to the floor each time you toss the beanbag? Right! Change which side you throw near to each time.

3.6 When you are the catcher, step with the foot nearest the beanbag and keep your other foot glued to the floor.

4.0 [Changing the size, shape, weight, or other features of the equipment changes the challenge. Based on your observations, either give the students the option of changing equipment or select it yourself.] Let's see if we can be accurate tossers and really stretch to catch when we work with different equipment.

4.1 Be patient as you try new equipment. It may take a few tosses and catches for both of you to experience before learning how far you each can stretch and still catch the [larger ball]. What changes are you noticing? Right! You need to use two hands to catch this ball.

4.2 Make your tosses a bit more gentle if your partner needs time to get used to this ball.

4.3 Keep stepping out on one foot and keep the other glued to the floor. Really stretch to catch.

4.4 Find two others and challenge them to see who can make the most successful stretched catches in two minutes. The catch counts only if the catcher stretches to catch.

5.0 [Masking tape is a safe way to define the bases. You may also use tape to have everyone throwing the same distance or let the teams determine how far apart to put their bases to create their own challenges and accommodate individual differences. When all of the class is playing the game, time them for two minutes. If only a part of the class is to experience the task, limit the number of tosses to 20 and have one child sitting out count the tosses as they are thrown and have another child count the number of completed stretched catches. Rotate responsibilities.] Let's play "Stretch and Catch." Listen to all of the instructions before getting organized. You will need two bases placed about 6 to 10 steps apart and one ball or beanbag for a group of four. Divide your group of four into two teams of two players each. One team will compete first, trying to see how many completed stretching catches they can make out of ten tosses when the catcher's foot is on the base as the ball [beanbag] is caught. The other team of two will score, by counting out loud each time the catching team stretches and catches the ball while one foot is still on the base. If you catch and you don't hear the scorers count, you know you must not have stretched to catch or your foot was off the base when you caught the ball. Change places after ten tosses so both teams get practice in competing and scoring several times.

5.1 Catchers, get your weight on the balls of your feet, ready to step in any direction.

5.2 Tossers, you have to work on sending your tosses into the spaces out away from catchers to make them stretch to catch. Be careful not to toss too far. Remember they have to still keep a foot on the base.

5.3 Catchers, it is up to you to reach and stretch, keeping one foot on the base. Step away from the base on the foot nearest to the spot where you see the ball heading.

Stepping and reaching to catch.

5.4 Catchers, be ready to take a big step and bend that knee to help you stretch farther.

6.0 All partners count your own successful stretched catches, keeping one foot on your tape. Let's see how many you can make in 45 seconds. I'll time you.

6.1 Select a different kind of ball or a beanbag and see if the two of you can catch it as many times as you did the big ball.

	ASSESSING THROWING AND CATCHING			
Class list	**Throws so that catcher has to step and reach to catch.** (scale, date)	**Continues throwing arm toward the intended target area.** (scale, date)	**Catcher steps with the leg nearest the object and bends that knee.** (scale, date)	**Reaches toward ball to catch with hands only.** (scale, date)
C. Gail	4 1/14	4 1/14	4 1/21	4 1/21
B. Dunn	4 1/14	4 1/14	3 1/21	2 1/21
O. Limon	4 1/17	5 1/17	5 1/24	5 1/24

Scale: 5 = Almost always   4 = Most of the time   3 = Getting the idea; about half of the time   2 = It's new; some success; about 1/3 of the time   1 = Unsuccessful most of the time

Unit 3 — Dribbling With Either Hand

3 to 5 lessons

FOCUS — Dribbling a large ball with either hand while traveling in different directions

MOTOR CONTENT

Selected from Theme 1—Introduction to Basic Body and Manipulative Control, Theme 2—Introduction to Space, and Theme 3—Introduction to Movement Quality (Effort)

Body

Manipulative activities—dribbling a ball with either hand while traveling and when stationary

Effort

Speed—accelerating and decelerating when dribbling the ball

Space

Directions—dribbling a ball forward, backward, and sideways with either hand while moving into empty spaces

OBJECTIVES

In this unit, children will (or should be willing to try to) meet these objectives:

- Dribble a ball with either hand while accelerating, decelerating, and changing directions (reflects National Standard in Physical Education 1).
- Know and apply the concepts of *accelerating* and *decelerating* (reflects National Standard in Physical Education 2).
- Understand that they need to push the ball farther ahead of them the faster they travel (reflects National Standard in Physical Education 2).
- Devote every minute of class time to working on improving their dribbling skills (reflects National Standards in Physical Education 5 6).
- Be considerate of others while dribbling, to create and maintain a safe working environment (reflects National Standards in Physical Education 5, 6).
- Sustain moderate to vigorous activity for longer periods of time in class, recess, and at home (reflects National Standards in Physical Education 3, 4).

EQUIPMENT AND MATERIALS

One 7-8-inch ball for each child, cones to scatter about the floor; poster in big block letters: ACCELERATE = SPEED UP! DECELERATE = SLOW DOWN!

LEARNING EXPERIENCES

1.0 Let's see how many people remember how to dribble the ball with one hand without bumping into anyone. Be ready to stop when I clap two times. We have enough balls for everyone. Show how polite you can be to each other as you get your ball and begin dribbling about the room.

1.1 You have remembered how to dribble! I don't see anyone slapping the ball with a flat hand. You are all dribbling the ball by pushing it with your whole hand. Try again and see if you can push the ball forcefully enough to make it come back up to your waist every time you dribble.

1.2 Let your hand ride the ball up and push it back down as you dribble. [Wait until the children have developed a regard for safety of themselves and others before suggesting increasing their speed.] Some of you might be able to travel a little faster—but be careful. Look where you are going and stop quickly if you come close to another person.

1.3 If your ball is getting away from you, try to slow down until you can keep the ball with you. As you begin to dribble, always try to look for an open space.

1.4 Spread your fingers over the ball as you dribble so the pads of your fingers and the palm of your hand are pushing the ball. You want to develop a "feel" for the ball in your fingers and palm so you know where the ball is at all times without looking at it.

1.5 Try not to let the ball come up higher than your waist as you dribble. You can move faster if you don't bounce it too high.

1.6 See if you can change hands as you dribble in your own space.

1.7 Try to dribble the ball about the room changing hands. Pretend that someone is coming to take the ball away and switch it to the other hand.

2.0 Start out dribbling the ball slowly and see if you can speed up and then slow down. Keep changing your speed, keeping the ball close to you the whole time you are dribbling. [Post action words accelerating and decelerating.]

2.1 When you speed up, it is called *accelerating*. Let's all say our new word—*accelerating*. It means to change speed by getting faster and faster. See if you can accelerate safely into the open spaces and then slow down.

2.2 Don't start at your top speed. Remember, accelerate means to speed up, so some of you need to start slower so you can go faster and faster and then slow down. [Start and stop the children frequently so they can practice accelerating. Make sure they understand that you want them to increase their speed gradually—not just dribble fast.]

2.3 If *accelerate* means to get faster and faster, who thinks they know what *decelerate* means? Sure, it means to get slower and slower. Safely start dribbling and practice slowing your speed down while you keep dribbling. [Having a poster or large cards for the children to see and read these words provides additional meaning to the lesson.]

2.4 As you dribble about the room, when you see an open space, accelerate into it and decelerate while you look for another open space.

3.0 See if you can dribble the ball in one direction and then change and go in another direction.

3.1 Dribble and look at me, always keeping the front of your body facing me as you dribble. Change your direction each time I raise my hand. Sometimes you will be dribbling forward, backward, or sideways.

3.2 This is going to be tricky. You are going to have to watch, think, and dribble all at the same time. When I point to myself, travel forward; if I push my palm toward you, dribble backward; if I point one arm to the side, travel sideways in the direction I am pointing. If I point the other arm to the opposite side, travel sideways in that direction. Let's spread out and stand so you all are facing me, and keep your eyes on me.

3.3 As you dribble sideways, try to make your feet slide or gallop. Choose the one that is the most comfortable for you, trying to make the movement very smooth.

3.4 Think a moment. Which hand does the dribbling when you dribble sideways, letting the right side of your body lead? Good, the right hand—the hand on the leading side. As you dribble sideways, change your direction by sometimes letting the left side of your body lead and sometimes the right side. Make sure you dribble with the hand on the leading side of your body.

3.5 Work hard on dribbling sideways and backward.

3.6 On your own mix up your directions again. Go forward, backward, and sideways to the left and to the right. Make sure you are letting the sides of your body lead when you travel sideways and the back of your body lead when you travel backward. Take care always to try to look where you are going so you don't bump into anyone.

4.0 Let's play follow the leader and see if you can follow a partner who is dribbling and copy their changes in direction. Work with the person who is closest to you. Decide who will be the leader, who will be the follower, and begin. [Change leaders frequently.]

4.1 Followers, stay behind your leader and carefully watch what direction they are going and the hand they're dribbling with. Be ready to change your direction and your dribbling hand each time you see your leader change. Take turns being the leader and the follower. [Monitor the change in leaders.]

4.2 Leaders, change your directions slowly so your partner can follow you easily.

4.3 Some leaders are dribbling a long way in one direction before they go in another direction. If your partner is a good copier, see if you can travel short distances before changing your direction.

5.0 Working all by yourself, see if you can accelerate and decelerate often as you dribble the ball all about the gym. When you plan to accelerate, always look for an open space to keep the activity safe for everyone.

5.1 Try to dribble the ball about waist high as you accelerate and a little lower as you decelerate. Pushing the ball farther out in front of you makes you travel faster to keep up with the ball. Dribbling lower makes it possible for you to change your direction quicker. Remember to push the ball with your whole hand all the while you are dribbling fast or slow or high or low.

5.2 Look at the space where you are going and not at the ball. You have to look for and move into open spaces as you dribble.

5.3 [Set up cones all about the floor.] See if you can accelerate as you dribble toward a new cone and decelerate as you get near to the cone. Keep finding new cones.

5.4 Be careful not to be a one-handed dribbler. Keep changing your dribbling hand each time you come to a new cone. Make your hands take turns.

5.5 This time, as you dribble from cone to cone, see how quickly you can change directions as you come to each new cone.

6.0 Let's play a game of 'dribble tag' while we stay in our own playing areas. The object of the game is for everyone to keep dribbling their ball while a tagger tries to tag you. Get into groups of five or six. Walk off your playing areas and then sit down in your own area. One person in each group raise your hand; this person will be the tagger to start the game. [Demonstrate with one group.] When you are tagged softly on the back, you will become the tagger. [Some groups may choose to have the tagger dribble as they attempt to tag. If this is too difficult, suggest the tagger put the ball away.]

6.1 Stop and check the boundaries of your space. Make sure your space does not overlap the space of others. Then start your game again.

6.2 Take a bit more care. You can keep from getting tagged if you really plan your time to accelerate and decelerate better and stay ready to quickly change your direction and your dribbling hand.

6.3 Now, let's make the game harder. Instead of tagging another player, those of you who are the tagger, see if you can touch one of the bouncing balls of the other players as you keep *your* ball bouncing. [When groups show competency in dribbling, have the the tagger dribble a ball, too, as she tries to touch the ball of another player.]

6.4 [Let the class share their games.] Everyone sit in your own working space. Let's have [name two or three groups] stand up and share their dribbling games in their own spaces. Observers, look for the changes in directions and the changes in the dribbling hands. [As each set of groups demonstrates, you may have the observers focus on different aspects of the unit content.] This time, watch the height of the bouncing ball. Does the ball go lower or higher as the dribbler travels faster? Now, watch for acceleration and deceleration by the dodger and the tagger. How does the change in speed help the tagger or the dodger? [Comment on the content of the day's lesson, such as how the groups are sharing the space or the pushing action of the hands of the dribblers.] See how well everyone is sharing the space? You really should be proud of how safely you are playing and how considerate of each other you are when tagging.

6.5 Play 'dribble tag' or your own dribbling game during recess or at home this week. Record in your journal the days of the week and number of minutes you play each day. [Repeat for 2-3 weeks.]

ASSESSING HAND DRIBBLING					
Class list	**Pushes and rides the ball during dribble.** (scale, date)	**Uses either hand to dribble.** (scale, date)	**Uses pads of fingers and avoids palm dribbling.** (scale, date)	**Accelerates and decelerates with control.** (scale, date)	**Dribbles in 3 directions with control.** (scale, date)
B. Burke	4 1/16	3 1/16	4 1/16	3 1/23	2 1/23

Scale: 5 = *Always or almost always*   4 = *Consistently; 2/3 or more of the time; needs additional practice on own*   3 = *Somewhat; about 1/3 of the time; needs instruction and additional practice*   2 = *Sometimes or seldom; may need special instruction*   1 = *Never; needs a modification or a new task*

Tapping With the Dominant Hand

5 to 6 lessons

FOCUS Tapping a bouncing ball with the dominant hand

MOTOR CONTENT

Selected from Theme 1—Introduction to Basic Body and Manipulative Control and Theme 2—Introduction to Space

Body

Manipulative activity—tapping a bouncing ball with the dominant hand

Space

Directions—traveling in different directions to tap the ball

OBJECTIVES

In this unit, children will (or should be willing to try to) meet these objectives:

- Increase the number of consecutive taps they can make by focusing on the ball and repositioning quickly in front of the ball (reflects National Standards in Physical Education 1, 5).
- Know that they must send the ball into empty spaces away from the receiver when trying to make their partner travel to tap the ball and that tapping the ball only with the dominant hand helps develop skill in repositioning to play the ball (reflects National Standard in Physical Education 2).
- Control the power and path of the ball when tapping underhand, accepting some of the responsibility for improving their own and others' skills (reflects National Standards in Physical Education 1, 5).
- Apply skills and knowledge acquired in this unit to manage their own tapping games both at recess and at home (reflects National Standards in Physical Education 3, 6).

EQUIPMENT AND MATERIALS

One 8.5- to 10-inch vinyl ball, ropes or cones, rolled newspaper wands, wooden or plastic blocks (all items for every two children).

LEARNING EXPERIENCES

[Change partners during each class to give all the children several chances to develop the ability to accept and adjust to different personalities and skill levels.]

1.0 Today, let's see how many times you can tap the ball back and forth to a partner, letting the ball bounce once each time before you tap it. Stand facing each other about 6 or 10 steps apart with your back toward the side wall. You will need one ball for two people. See how quietly you can find a partner, get a ball, and begin.

1.1 When you are the first to tap the ball, drop the ball in front of you and let it bounce before you tap it to your partner.

1.2 What do we need to do with our tapping hand to make the ball bounce right in front of the receiver? That's right! You must reach out with your tapping hand toward your receiver, just as you did when tossing a ball to get the ball to go straight and bounce in front of your partner.

1.3 Always tap the ball with your writing hand. Tapping it with the same hand every time makes you practice moving quickly to get your whole body in line with the ball.

1.4 Good partners help each other by trying to control the power of their taps. Each time you tap the ball, concentrate on giving your partner more chances to practice returning the ball by tapping it just hard enough to land right in front of your partner.

1.5 Are you all finding out that it is sometimes hard to control the power of your tap and the direction of the ball? Maybe your receiver can help you make the ball bounce right in front of them by moving their feet to get in line with the ball.

1.6 It's fun for both partners when you can keep the ball going back and forth without missing. I've noticed that both partners are pointing the tapping hand right to their partner and hustling to get to the ball if it doesn't come right to them. Some of you may like to count how many times the two of you can tap the ball back and forth, letting it bounce once before you tap it back.

1.7 Tappers, try to direct the ball more carefully by following through with your tapping hand right toward the spot where you want the ball to land. See if you can send the ball so that it bounces right in front of your partner so they do not have to travel to return the ball. This will help everyone develop more control of the ball, and the two of you will make more taps before either of you miss.

2.0 Some of you are switching hands to tap the ball. Work on repositioning your body to tap the ball, using the same hand for every tap. Get ready to move to get your body in front of the ball so you can tap with your writing hand—your *dominant* hand.

2.1 Tappers, begin to make the ball bounce on purpose in the empty spaces about the receiver so everyone has to practice traveling three or four steps to line up their bodies with the ball to return it.

2.2 Receivers, on what part of your feet do you want your weight to be so you are ready to move quickly? Yes! Everyone try getting your weight forward on the balls of your feet—not on your heels, to help you move to the ball more quickly.

2.3 Each time you tap the ball, return quickly to the middle of your space with your weight forward so you are ready to move in any direction to return the ball. We call this our 'ready position.'

2.4 Let's find out how many times you and your partner can tap the ball making each other travel to tap the ball. Sit down with partners next to you. Now one set of partners stand up. The standing team is going to concentrate on sending the ball into empty spaces to make the receiver travel to return the ball. If you are sitting, watch the feet of the receivers and count out loud each time a receiver has to travel to the ball to send it back. The teams will change places when a ball is not returned or when a receiver fails to [does not] travel before returning the ball. [Changing roles several times can give them practice in assessing traveling to return a ball. Analyzing the performances of others often helps children better understand the skill you are trying to teach.]

2.5 Partners, see if you can break your own record. Remember to make your receiver travel to return the ball, letting the ball bounce each time.

3.0 This time, your partner is not on your team. You are both trying to make each other miss by sending the ball away from the receiver to make him travel in different directions to return the ball. Make it bounce close enough so it's possible for your partner to return it.

3.1 Some of you may like to get a rope or a wooden block and rolled up newspaper to tap the ball over. Place the rope [wooden block, newspaper] between the two of you.

3.2 Where should your hand point when you are trying to make your partner travel to return the ball?

3.3 As you send the ball back to your partner, watch where the ball lands in relation to your receiver. Now, try to direct the ball to land where your partner will have to travel forward to return it.

3.4 See how quickly you can return to your home spot after you return the ball.

3.5 Tappers, change the force of your tap on purpose to make the receiver move forward or backward to return the ball. Take care not to tap it too hard so you both can stay in your own working space.

3.6 Let's play a cooperative game of 'Hand Tennis' by working together to see how many times the two of you can send the ball back and forth, letting the ball bounce before returning it.

4.0 [Some pairs may be ready to work in groups of four, putting one ball away and practicing sharing space and turns with their partners as they send the ball across the "net" or rope.] Let's play a game called 'Hand Tennis.' Decide if you can play this one against one or two against two. In this game, the sender(s) gets a point any time a receiver returns the ball without letting it bounce first. Players in each game decide how many points are needed to win the game. Some of you may want to use cones or ropes for nets or boundary lines.

4.1 Stop and think a moment. What might we be doing that helps our opponent score a point? Sometimes we tap the ball right to the opponent while they always make us travel. Let's really try hard to send the ball to an empty space instead of to the tapper.

4.2 Remember to make your tapping hand flat and reach out to the spot where you want the ball to land each time you tap the ball.

4.3 Sit down and discuss if you need another rule for your game. [You might choose to require tapping only with the dominant hand for awhile to reemphasize repositioning.]

4.4 Some of you might like to challenge another group and play two against two.

4.5 Those of you playing two against two need to be sure each of you on the same side of the net is getting about the same amount of practice. To help all of you share equally in the practice, try to send the ball back near the person who did not send it to you.

4.6 You people really have developed some good tapping skills, and you have done a fine job of working with many classmates as teammates and opponents. Sit down. Let's take a moment to share our games and our skill in tapping to make the receivers travel to tap the ball. [As the children share their games, comment on how they move quickly to get to the ball, how some are placing the ball to make it hard for the receiver to return it, the different rules each group has made, and how the tapper is following through to the spot they intend the ball to go.]

ASSESSING TAPPING A BALL

End of unit closure: Ask what action words describe their performance in this unit (written responses preferable). More words should describe strengths, but at least one word needs to describe what needs improvement. A compilation of the class or grade lists can serve as a guide to future lessons. You could post lists in the gym or even use them for a writing, art, or media project.

Unit 5

Throwing and Catching

4 to 5 lessons

FOCUS Throwing and catching fly balls and grounders

MOTOR CONTENT

Selected from Theme 1—Introduction to Basic Body and Manipulative Control and Theme 3—Introduction to Movement Quality (Effort)

Body

Manipulative activities—throwing and catching fly balls and grounders

Effort

Speed—returning the ball quickly after the catch

OBJECTIVES

In this unit, children will (or should be willing to try to) meet these objectives:

- Throw and catch fly balls and grounders and return the ball quickly with accuracy after they catch it, giving classmates as many turns as possible (reflects National Standard in Physical Education 1).
- Know that bringing the ball back in the line of flight at the moment the ball contacts their hands helps to spread the force of the ball over a longer period of time, helping to keep it from rebounding out of their hands (reflects National Standard in Physical Education 2).
- Learn that to throw the ball high in the air, the throwing hand needs to be traveling upward upon release and, to throw a grounder, the throwing hand needs to be pointing downward upon release (reflects National Standard in Physical Education 2).

EQUIPMENT AND MATERIALS

One small, soft ball for *every* one to two children (use sponge, yarn, or any other small, soft ball that will not intimidate catchers.) *Optional:* Rope.

LEARNING EXPERIENCES

1.0 Today, let's see if you can throw your ball to the wall so it comes back to you along the floor with very little bouncing. Get one ball, find a space away from others about 10 to 15 steps from the wall, and begin. [Make sure the children have enough space in between each other to throw the ball safely. You may also teach this unit outside or inside with the children working in partners instead of against a wall.]

1.1 One of the first rules in catching a grounder [a rolling ball] is to move to get directly in front of the ball with your hands low to the ground, your palms facing the ball, and your little fingers close together. Work hard to travel and get in front of the ball. Do not let the ball get past you.

1.2 As you prepare to receive a rolling ball, get the foot on your nonthrowing side out in front of the other to help you return the throw quickly. Standing with your feet apart often lets the ball roll through your legs.

1.3 Bend your knees to help you get both hands close to the floor and your little fingers close to each other to catch the rolling ball.

1.4 Let's try to throw the ball overhand to make the ball come back faster. Release the ball when your throwing hand is pointed down. This will help you hit the wall close to the floor.

1.5 To throw harder, step forward on the foot opposite your throwing hand as you throw the ball.

1.6 Really have quick feet if the ball is not coming straight back to you, but be careful of others. Run and get in the path of the ball with your palms up and hands low.

1.7 Aim your release at a low spot on the wall. Make your hand follow through toward your target. [Putting pieces of masking tape on the wall near the floor may help some children aim their releases downward.]

1.8 Some of you may want to try 'charging' the ball. Run up and collect the ball before it stops rolling, then return quickly to your throwing spot. If the ball is coming back very fast, you won't have time to run very far.

1.9 The moment you collect the ball, throw it quickly back to the wall. See how fast you can get rid of your ball.

2.0 Let's try rolling and collecting ground balls with a partner. Partners stand facing each other. Think a moment. Should we throw as hard to our partner as we were to the wall? No, we have to ease up a bit because our partner is going to try to collect the ball.

2.1 Roll the ball underhand, making your hand reach toward your partner so the ball rolls straight to your partner.

2.2 Catchers, be in the ready position as you wait for the ball. You need to be on the balls of your feet, knees bent, and hands low in front of you, ready to move to collect the ball.

2.3 Good partners try to roll exactly where they want the ball to go. Release the ball when your hand is straight out in line with your partner. This will make the ball roll straight to your partner.

2.4 Catchers, remember, the first thing you must think about when collecting a ground ball is to move to get your body and hands directly in front of the ball.

2.5 When collecting a grounder, keep your little fingers close together, palms facing the ball. Bend your knees to get lower to catch a ball coming low.

2.6 Let's see if you can throw the ball to the side of your partners so they will have to be ready to run in front of the ball to collect it.

2.7 When you catch, try to have one foot ahead of the other instead of side by side. Getting the foot forward opposite your throwing hand gets you ready to throw quickly.

2.8 Catchers, watch the ball carefully. Don't wait for the ball to come to you. Run up quickly to get it.

2.9 Keep your eyes focused on the ball. Let's count how many catches you can make without missing.

2.10 Go back to the ready position with your weight on the balls of your feet as soon as you throw the ball. The ready position prepares you to move quickly in any direction to catch a ball. Remember, your hands should be low to the ground with your knees bent and eyes focused on the ball.

3.0 Practice your overhand throw. Throw your ball up high on the wall and try to catch it with two hands. Select a ball you feel you can throw and catch, a place to work, and begin. [Pointing out an existing line high on the wall or some other easily identifiable mark helps to encourage children to aim high. Children can also throw to partners over a rope stretched 8- to 10-feet high between two standards.]

3.1 Because you want to throw the ball high, be sure when you release the ball to make your throwing hand point high in the air toward your target as you release the ball.

3.2 Remember to step forward on the foot opposite your throwing hand as you throw the ball high on the wall.

3.3 When you catch a ball above your waist, point your fingers upward, palms facing the ball, with your thumbs close together. [Have a child demonstrate. Caution the children to make sure they are not pointing their fingers directly at the ball so the ball can hit the ends of their fingers.]

3.4 Release the ball when your throwing hand is high above your head, pointing to your high spot on the wall. Pointing your hand will help send the ball to your target.

3.5 Good catchers always make their hands 'give' in line with the ball as they catch the ball. Giving as you catch helps to keep the ball from bouncing out of your hands. [Demonstrate the "giving" action with the hands by bringing them toward you along the line of flight.]

3.6 After you throw, keep your eyes focused on the ball, moving quickly to get under the ball to catch it when it bounces off the wall.

3.7 Hit the wall as high as you can without making it difficult to catch. Then, the minute you catch it, throw it back again.

3.8 Count how many times you can throw the ball overhand up high against the wall and catch or collect it without it getting by you.

4.0 Let's show we are good, accurate throwers when we practice throwing high fly balls back and forth to a partner. Get a partner, one ball for the two of you, and begin.

4.1 It's great to see so many remembering to step forward on the opposite foot to throw the ball. Everyone try to finish your throw with most of your weight on the foot opposite your throwing arm [your front foot].

4.2 To throw the ball higher, lean back as you prepare to throw, aiming your release at a spot higher above the head of your receiver. Take care to judge how hard to throw the ball. See if you can send it high and make the ball come down right to your partner.

4.3 Catchers, watch the ball and move to about where it is going to drop. Catch the ball and return it quickly.

4.4 Still throwing the ball high, begin to aim your throw to make your catcher travel a step or two in different directions to catch the ball. Be caring as you throw. Don't make your catcher run into the space of other players.

4.5 To throw the ball higher into the air, release the ball as your hand is traveling upward. Throwing the ball higher gives the catcher more time to get to the spot where the ball will drop. Keep practicing your high overhand throw, remembering to keep your ball in your own working space.

4.6 Catch the ball when it is high. Focus your eyes on the ball from the time it leaves the hand of the thrower until it is in your hands.

5.0 Let's see if we can mix up our flies [explain term, if necessary] and grounders. Catchers be ready for either kind of throw.

5.1 Catchers, to help you get ready for either kind of throw, watch the arm and hand of the thrower. You can tell by the thrower's hand if the ball is going to be a fly or a grounder. If you see the throwing hand open up, pointing high in the air, you know the ball will be a high fly. If the hand is pointing down, you will be getting a grounder.

5.2 You may like to play a game where you score points for catching fly balls and grounders. Decide with your partner the points scored for catching a fly ball and for fielding [explain term, if necessary] a grounder.

5.3 [Some may be ready to work in groups of four or six. You may make this decision or let the children choose to enlarge their groups. If more than two are playing, however, emphasize giving everyone equal opportunities to practice throwing and catching.]

ASSESSING OVERHAND THROWING—TRUNK ACTION

Name _____   Rater _____

Rating Criteria: Steps 1-3 are based on a validated developmental sequence for "Trunk Action in Throwing and Striking for Force" with Step 3 representing a more advanced pattern.

				Step 1 No trunk action or forward-backward movement (arm may pull trunk into a passive rotation, but there is no twist-up before throwing).	Step 2 Spinal or block rotation (spine and pelvis rotate away from intended flight, then begin forward rotation, acting as a unit or "block").	Step 3 Differentiated rotation (child twists away from intended flight, then begins forward rotation with pelvis while upper spine still twists away).
Date	Grade	Games unit	Task			
10/97	Pre-K	#5	3.0			
9/98	K	#5	2.0			
10/00	Gr. 2	#5				

Adapted from "Developing Children—Their Changing Movement" by M.A. Roberton and L.E. Halverson (In B.J. Logsdon, et al., *Physical Education for Children*, 1984, p. 66). *Note*: Videotape analysis may be necessary to see step 3 of "trunk action." Additionally, use videotape analysis to assess "arm action components" (backswing, upper arm, and forearm) and use direct observation/video analysis to assess "action of the feet." See Roberton and Halverson, 1984, pp. 68-74 above or K.M. Haywood, *Laboratory Manual for Life Span Motor Development*, 1993, Human Kinetics, Champaign, IL.

Bouncing a Ball and Traveling at Different Levels

3 to 4 lessons

Bouncing a ball forcefully and traveling under or over it at different levels

MOTOR CONTENT

Selected from Theme 1—Introduction to Basic Body and Manipulative Control, Theme 2—Introduction to Space, and Theme 3—Introduction to Movement Quality (Effort)

Body

Manipulative activities—bouncing a large ball

Effort

Speed—moving quickly
Force—strong

Space

Levels—high, medium, low

OBJECTIVES

In this unit, children will (or should be willing to try to) meet these objectives:

- Increase the power of their bounces by jumping to take the ball higher, keeping their backs straight and forcefully throwing the ball down on the floor.
- Change their levels as they travel quickly many times under or over a bouncing ball as the height of the bounce diminishes (reflects National Standard in Physical Education 1).
- Increase the number of trips they make under and over the bouncing ball by decreasing the distance they travel away from the ball and moving quickly while focusing on the ball (reflects National Standards in Physical Education 1, 7).
- Understand the ball will go straight up and land in their own space if they bounce the ball straight down and, if bounced on the floor at an angle, it will bounce away from their space (reflects National Standard in Physical Education 2).
- Know that the ball will bounce higher if they get more speed and body action (reflects National Standard in Physical Education 2).

- Keep the ball in their own space, accepting responsibility for not interfering with others (reflects National Standard in Physical Education 5).

EQUIPMENT AND MATERIALS

One 8.5-inch rubber playground ball for each child, receptacles for the balls.

LEARNING EXPERIENCES

1.0 Today, see how you can bounce your ball in front of you away from others and the walls, making it bounce straight up so you can catch it without making your feet travel away from your space. Remember, there is a ball for everyone. Being careful of others, get a ball, find your own working space, and begin.

1.1 Think before you bounce your ball. When you want to make the ball bounce straight up in your own space, do you throw the ball so it lands close to you or far away? Right—you throw it close to you. [You or a child demonstrate where to bounce the ball to have it rebound straight up. Then demonstrate where on the floor you should send the ball to cause it to bounce away from your space.]

1.2 Watch where you bounce the ball. If you bounce the ball too far away from you, you will have to travel into someone else's space to chase your ball.

1.3 Keep your back straight up and down like the wall as you bounce the ball. Don't lean your head over the ball because the ball bounces up fast and it could hurt if it hits your chin or nose.

1.4 If your feet have to take more than a step or two before you go under your ball, you are not bouncing it straight down in your own space and it will get away from you.

1.5 Count how many times you can bounce the ball higher than your head, catching it without having to travel to catch it.

2.0 Show how high you can make the ball bounce and then catch it.

2.1 To help you bounce the ball higher, take your hands and the ball way up high and send that ball very fast and hard straight down on a spot close in front of you.

2.2 [Name a child who has been jumping to take the ball high with both hands in preparation to bounce the ball.] Let's watch [Dudley]. What does he do to make his throw bigger and stronger? He jumps! Others of you who haven't tried jumping to help you take your hands higher and get more force might like to try it. Remember, the higher you jump, the more force you can create to bounce the ball higher.

2.3 See if you can bounce your ball straight up very high and catch it without taking more than two steps.

2.4 Let's see who can bounce their ball the highest. Get into groups of three or four and have a contest.

3.0 Some of you are ready for something harder, which may be even a bit more fun. This time, after you bounce the ball straight up high, don't catch it. Let it continue to bounce. Then see how you can travel quickly back and forth under the ball not letting any part of your body touch it.

3.1 As you travel quickly, keep changing your level, traveling lower and lower to get under the bouncing ball.

3.2 Some of you are traveling too far away from the ball after you go under it. This extra traveling takes time. If you don't travel so far, you probably can go under the ball more times.

3.3 Try to keep your eyes looking at the ball even when you are traveling lower so you know where the ball is and how low to go to keep the ball from touching you.

3.4 Jump to create more power to bounce the ball higher. The higher your ball bounces on the first bounce, the more times your ball will bounce, and the more times you will be able to go back and forth under the ball.

3.5 You have to bend those knees to get low. I've seen some of you even roll once or twice under the ball when it gets really low. [Have a child demonstrate.]

3.6 Let's count how many trips you can make under the ball. You can count your own trips or, if you like, find someone and take turns being the counter.

4.0 Have you noticed the ball continues to bounce several times after it is too low even for you to roll [travel] under it? Can you think of something you could do when the ball is bouncing low? Keep counting the trips you make and try to do something as the ball bounces low.

4.1 Great! Many of you traveled under the ball as long as you could and then you started jumping over the ball until it stopped bouncing. Let's all try to add jumping over the ball when it starts to bounce too low to get under it.

4.2 Don't forget to keep your eyes on the ball as long as you can.

Watch the ball with your eyes as you travel under the ball.

4.3 Watch the distance you are traveling away from the ball as you go over or under the ball. Remember the farther you travel from the ball, the fewer times you can go under or over it.

4.4 Let's have this half of the class sit down. The rest of you, give your best performance and really work on seeing how many times you can go under and over the ball especially when it is bouncing low. Can you see someone doing something you haven't tried before? [Change roles.]

4.5 I bet you saw something when you were watching that you would like to try that will give you more trips. Try it, and then we will count our trips.

4.6 Now let's all get ready to bounce our balls at the same time and see how many trips we can make under and over the ball. Ready? [Pause.] And bounce!

4.7 Now, let's see how many of you can break your own record. [Allow extra time for children to share their accomplishments with a partner and teach their favorite ways. Encourage continued practice at recess or at home. Students may record the days of the week (or number of times) they practice in a week.]

ASSESSING MOVEMENT IN RELATION TO A MOVING OBJECT							
Bounces ball to send it straight up.	(date)	Avoids touching ball during movement.	(date)	Quickly changes direction in moving under and over the bouncing ball.	(date)	Changes levels to go under and over the ball.	(date)
J. Keller	10/2	C. Church	10/4	P. Snyder	10/4	L. Love	10/2
S. Kronbach	10/2			K. Starr	10/4		

For each item, write the names of children needing additional instruction and practice to be proficient.

Punting and Kicking

3 to 5 lessons

Punting and kicking a ball high and far

MOTOR CONTENT

Selected from Theme 1—Introduction to Basic Body and Manipulative Control, Theme 2—Introduction to Space, and Theme 3—Introduction to Movement Quality (Effort)

Body

Manipulative activities—punting and kicking a stationary ball, catching and collecting aerial and rolling balls

Effort

Force—strong

Space

Levels—high and low
Pathways—along the ground and in the air

OBJECTIVES

In this unit, children will (or should be willing to try to) meet these objectives:

- Improve the ability to kick a stationary ball, increasing the distance, kicking it in a straighter pathway, and trying to "loft it" by getting the tops of toes and foot under the ball (reflects National Standard in Physical Education 2).
- Identify three important characteristics of punting and use those as (partner) coaching cues (reflects National Standard in Physical Education 2).
- Observe the performance of others and name the part(s) of the foot making contact with the ball and which foot lands first after punting when the kicker takes both feet off the ground (reflects National Standard in Physical Education 2).
- Know that the speed of the kicking foot and the distance the foot travels before the ball is contacted develops the force they need to kick effectively (reflects National Standard in Physical Education 2).
- Know that extending their arms out away from their body after they release the ball when punting helps to maintain balance (reflects National Standard in Physical Education 2).
- Work hard to improve their punting, kicking, and catching skills and help to create a learning environment that is challenging and enjoyable for all (reflects National Standards in Physical Education 5, 6).

- Resolve conflicts during game play by adding or changing rules (reflects National Standard in Physical Education 6.)

EQUIPMENT AND MATERIALS

One 8.5-inch playground ball for every two students, four to six traffic cones or other devices to mark the boundaries of the working space outdoors.

LEARNING EXPERIENCES

1.0 Let's see how many of you can put the ball down on the ground and kick it hard to a receiver. The kicker will stand in line with the traffic cones on the wide side of the kicking area, and the receiver will stand across from him. Find a partner and take one ball for the two of you. Find your working space and begin.

1.1 Work hard to try to kick the ball straight, making your kicking foot swing out straight toward your receiver.

1.2 Receivers, keep your eyes focused on the ball and try to move quickly to get in line with the ball so you can collect or catch it. Then put the ball down and see if you can kick the ball straight back to your partner.

1.3 If you are kicking your ball straight, try kicking the ball a little harder. I am going to come around and ask you what you are trying to do to kick your ball harder.

1.4 Some of you said you are running a few steps toward the ball as you prepare to kick it. If you haven't tried this, you might want to run and see if you can kick the ball harder.

1.5 [Anthony] said he tried to swing his kicking leg and foot faster to get more speed in his kick. If you try swinging your kicking leg and foot faster, some of you may find you, too, can get more distance when you kick.

1.6 Try to get the toes of your kicking foot under the ball as you kick it so you can feel the top of your shoe contacting the ball.

2.0 To prepare to kick when the ball is on the ground, take a big step forward and place your supporting foot close to the side of the ball. Then swing the kicking leg really fast as you kick the ball. [Help a child demonstrate.] The bigger the step you make when placing the supporting foot next to the ball, the bigger the swing you can make with your kicking foot. The big step and swing help to add power and distance to your kick.

2.1 If you are having trouble placing your supporting foot to the side of your ball as you prepare to kick, don't run to kick the ball. Just stand far enough away to take just one big step as you place the foot and kick the ball. [Have a child demonstrate.]

Contact the ball with the top of your foot, keeping your toes down underneath.

2.2 Some of you are having trouble keeping your balance as you kick. Try holding your arms out to your sides and see if this helps you balance.

2.3 To help you put even more power into your kick, try to straighten your knee as you swing your kicking leg forward and upward.

2.4 When you are the receiver, pay close attention to the path of the ball. Does the ball come to you along the ground or do you get to try to catch a fly ball? Be ready to run up or to get to the ball quickly.

2.5 Kickers, work hard to see if you can get your toes and the top of your foot under the ball when you kick. This way, your receiver gets to practice catching the ball when it is in the air.

2.6 When you feel you made a good, hard kick straight to your partner, the next time you get the ball, put it down on the ground, take a few steps away from the ball and run to kick the ball. See if running as you kick helps you to make the ball go even farther.

3.0 [At first, you may choose to give these experiences on punting to individual children who are successful in creating power by taking a big step onto the supporting foot in preparation for kicking the ball. Soon, however, most children will be eager to try the punt.] Remember the big step you took before you kicked the ball? This time, hold the ball out in front of you with both hands and, as you take your big step, see if you can drop the ball and swing your free leg forward, kicking the ball before it touches the ground. We call this a *punt*. [Have a child demonstrate.] Partners, be ready to travel to try to catch the ball on a fly. Return to your place after you get the ball and punt the ball back to your partner.

3.1 When you punt, you might have to toss the ball slightly out in front of you as you step so you can make contact with the ball with the top of your foot. [Getting the ball to fall just right in punting is not easy for some. Encourage these children to lift the ball in front of them about shoulder height before dropping it to give them more time to swing the kicking leg.]

3.2 Think a moment. What can you do to help you keep your balance after you punt? [Extend arms out to the sides as the kicking foot swings forward.] Watch the arms of the people next to you while they punt. See if you can find something for your neighbors to do to improve their balance. Keep checking each other's balance, offering suggestions for improving balance. [You may want to go around and ask children what clue they are giving to improve balance.]

3.3 You are all being helpful to each other in making suggestions for improving. It's great! We have a teacher for everyone in the class when you all give helpful suggestions to each other. This time, see if you can watch your neighbor's feet right after the ball is punted. Tell your neighbor which foot lands first—the kicking foot or the other foot. [They will get more distance if they lift off from the supporting foot and land on this nonkicking foot before the kicking foot touches the ground. This is an advanced level of skill that most may not achieve.]

3.4 See how many times you can get the ball to go up high when punting. Think. Step. Drop—and kick! Get the top of your foot under the ball. Kick it with your shoe laces.

3.5 Receivers, move to get your body directly in front of the ball. Some of you may catch the ball more frequently if you bend your elbows and bring the ball in toward your chest.

3.6 Kickers, extend your ankle and point your toes to flatten out the kicking surface on the top of your foot. This can help to make the ball travel farther away from you when you punt.

3.7 Remember to swing the kicking leg fast and straighten the knee as you punt.

3.8 You may want to experiment in tossing [dropping] the ball a little farther out in front of you so you have to take a bigger step. This will increase the space the kicking leg uses in punting, maybe giving your kicking leg more speed, which will make your punt go farther.

3.9 Receivers, watch your kicker and the ball. Try to get to each ball quickly. Be ready to run up and charge a grounder or move under the ball to catch a fly. You really look sharp when you display the same enthusiasm [excitement] for improving your catching skills as you are showing in your kicking.

4.0 You and your partner might like to count to see how many times you can collect or catch each other's punt without letting the ball get past you. Start over when you miss.

4.1 Do you and your partner want to challenge two others in class to see which team can catch the most flies and grounders without having the ball get past you? If so, find two others and stand across from them and begin.

4.2 Some of you might like to get into groups of four or six and make up a different punting game. Decide how you are going to play your game, find a space, and get started.

4.3 Let's watch some of these new games for a moment. [Let the different groups show their games and discuss the rules they invented.]

4.4 You may choose to play your own game or some of you might like to try one of the games you just saw.

ASSESSING PUNTING					
Class list	Drops ball from shoulder height to spot swinging foot will contact the ball. (scale, date)	Balances support leg well after longer, final step. (scale, date)	Swings kicking leg freely in line with dropped ball. (scale, date)	Contacts under the ball with instep. (scale, date)	Continues kicking leg forward and upward. (scale, date)
Adams, M.	4 9/2 2 9/11	3 9/7 3 9/9	3 9/7 2 9/9	3 9/11 2 9/13	3 9/11 3 9/13
Bard, C.					

Scale: 4 = *Yes* 3 = *Most of the time* 2 = *Some of the time or partially* 1 = *Seldom or never*

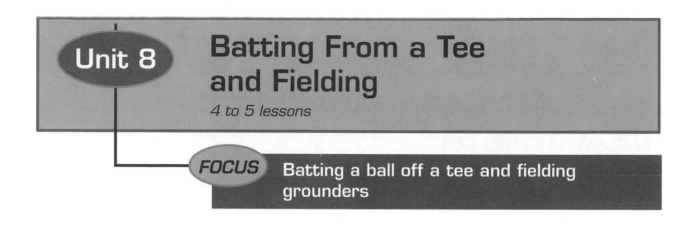

Unit 8

Batting From a Tee and Fielding

4 to 5 lessons

FOCUS Batting a ball off a tee and fielding grounders

MOTOR CONTENT

Selected from Theme 1—Introduction to Basic Body and Manipulative Control and Theme 3—Introduction to Movement Quality (Effort)

Body

Manipulative activities—batting a small ball off a tee, fielding a rolling ball or grounder, and throwing the ball back to the catcher

Effort

Speed—fast, quick
Force—strong

OBJECTIVES

In this unit, children will (or should be willing to try to) meet these objectives:

- Bat the ball off a tee by standing about one step away from the tee looking at the back of the ball, pointing their toes toward the plate, taking a step forward on their front foot as they swing the bat, and extending their arms as they swing the bat (reflects National Standard in Physical Education 1).
- Know that when collecting a rolling ball they must get their bodies and hands in front of the ball with their palms facing the ball, little fingers pointed down and close together, and their knees bent (reflects National Standard in Physical Education 2).
- Develop an alert "with it" attitude as they work, keeping their eyes on the ball and being on the balls of their feet ready to run to retrieve the ball (reflects National Standard in Physical Education 2).
- Change places quickly within their groups after the batter has had five chances to hit, giving everyone in their group a chance to bat, catch, and field the ball (reflects National Standard in Physical Education 5).
- Be patient with other batters in the class who hit balls into their working space, politely tossing the ball back (reflects National Standard in Physical Education 6).

EQUIPMENT AND MATERIALS

One batting tee; one plastic bat; one whiffle ball, foam ball, or large vinyl ball (all items for each group of two or three students). (You can improvise batting tees by placing plastic golf tubes inside traffic cones or standing traffic cones on boxes or wastepaper baskets.)

LEARNING EXPERIENCES

[Caution: Place all left-handed children in the groups at the right top or bottom left of the class formation as shown in the diagram below. When standing to hit the ball, they then face the other batters and can be more careful so that their swinging bat will not interfere with anyone in another group. Caution all children to hold on to their bats when swinging at the ball. Batter places the bat near the tee when changing from batter to fielder. Use yarn or sponge balls if the unit must be taught inside because the plastic whiffle balls can travel very fast and frighten children if they are hit by one. Have the two lines of hitters far enough apart so the catcher of one group will not back into the catchers of another group. Space the batters in the same line far enough apart so the batters do not interfere with each other or endanger the catchers.]

F = Fielder   B = Batter
C = Catcher   LB = Left-handed batter

F	F	F	F	F
B	B	B	B	LB
C	C	C	C	C
C	C	C	C	C
LB	B	B	B	B
F	F	F	F	F

Sample arrangement of fielders, batters, and catchers.

1.0 Today we are going to work on batting the ball off the batting tee to a fielder. There will be three people in each group. Each person will have five turns to bat, and then all three of you will change places. This group stand up and show how to change positions. The catcher places the ball on the tee and takes three big steps back so she never gets hit by the swinging bat. The batter hits the ball five times and the fielder catches or fields the ball and throws it back to the catcher who puts the ball back on the tee. After five hits, the batter lays the bat near the tee and goes out to become the fielder. The catcher will become the batter and the fielder will move to become the catcher. Get into groups of three. One person get a bat, the other two get the tee and the ball, go to a station, and begin.

1.1 Catchers, remember to keep three big steps away from that swinging bat.

1.2 Batters, don't crowd the base. Stand so the hitting (thickest) part of the bat passes over the tee. Point your toes toward the batting tee—not at the fielder.

1.3 Swing the bat level with the ground [demonstrate] by reaching your arms out away from your body as you swing the bat. Your elbows should straighten out and not be bent as you hit the ball.

1.4 Fielders, run the instant the batter hits to line up your body with the ball. Remember, to collect a rolling ball, get little fingers side by side with fingers pointing down and palms facing the ball.

1.5 Fielders, don't hold the ball—throw it quickly back to the catcher.

1.6 Catchers, be alert and run to get in front of the tee the minute the ball is batted so you'll be ready to catch the ball the fielder throws to you. Reaching your hands up ready to catch the throw gives the fielder a target to throw at.

1.7 Let's watch [Lindsey's] group and see how the catcher stays three steps away from the batter. Batters, always make sure there is no one behind you before taking your swing. You should be able to see your catcher three steps away to your side. As you swing the bat, step toward the fielder with the foot nearest the fielder.

1.8 Batters, don't crowd the tee. Be sure the hitting part of the bat passes over the tee.

1.9 Catchers, watch the batter and make sure the front of the batter faces the tee not the fielder. Be sure to tell them to change the position of their feet and point their toes toward the tee—not out toward the fielder.

2.0 Let's all try to think what our jobs are at each of these positions. Batters need to watch out for others and swing the bat level with the ground. Fielders need to run toward the ball and get their hands down in front of the ball so it can roll right into them if it is a grounder. Catchers are always going to move three steps away from the swinging bat, ready to step in front of the tee to catch the throw from the fielder after the ball is hit and quickly put the ball back on the tee.

2.1 Batters, be your own coach and tell yourself what to do. Say, 'Check your feet, eyes on the ball, step, and swing!' Keep saying this out loud each time you swing.

2.2 Remember to hold the bat up. Don't let it rest on your shoulder. Look at the center of the ball, keeping your eyes on it all during your swing.

2.3 Fielders, hustle a little faster to the ball. Remember to bend your knees to get your hands near the ground and keep your palms facing forward with your little fingers side by side to catch the ball with both hands.

2.4 Catchers, hold your hands out in front of you to show the fielders a target. Fielders, as you throw, try to point your throwing hand at the target your catcher makes with the hands.

2.5 Fielders, run quickly to meet the ball. Don't wait for it. Try to get it back to your catcher quickly.

Fielders run quickly to meet the ball.

2.6 Everyone should be on the balls of their feet and alert to what is happening everywhere in your game. Let's be hustlers.

3.0 [Look for groups who are successful hitters and who get the ball quickly back to the catcher.] Place a base out between the batter and the fielder. Now the batter runs and touches the base and tries to get back and touch home base before the catcher gets the ball. Be sure to lay your bat down before you run to the base and return home quickly. Fielders are to run to collect the ball and throw it back to the catcher. Players, change positions after the batter hits the ball and runs to the bases three times. [Batter becomes the fielder, fielder becomes the catcher, and the catcher bats next.]

3.1 Fielders, keep your weight forward on the balls of your feet so you can run quickly to get the ball and send it back to the catcher.

3.2 Everyone look alert. Show with your body and eyes that your mind is in the game and you are ready to play your position. Batters, after you hit the ball, remember to lay the bat down before running. Don't ever throw the bat.

3.3 Catchers, watch the ball as your fielder throws it. Be ready to line up your body with the ball, getting under the ball so you can catch it. Let's watch this half of the class and see if you can tell me what you see that tells you the fielders are really ready to play. [Observers should be able to note that the fielders are on the balls of their feet, ready to field the ball; knees are bent, arms hanging loose in front; their fingers are pointed down to catch grounders.]

3.4 Batters be ready to show your hustle as you bat the ball off the tee. Lay the bat down and quickly run to the base. Make your feet fly in straight pathways to the base and back to homeplate before the catcher gets the ball.

3.5 Now we have many hustling fielders. Let's watch a catcher. Can you tell me things you must do to be a good catcher? Be sure to take your three steps back from the swinging bat for safety and then concentrate on getting in front of the tee to catch the throw from the fielder the moment the batter lays the bat down and starts to run for the base.

4.0 We have been practicing hustling and being alert in a game. Since we watched the fielders the last time, let's watch the catchers this time. See if you can pick out some of the things they have learned to do to be safe, alert catchers in a game. [Stand three steps back from the batter; move quickly in front of the tee the moment the batter lays the bat down; give the fielder a good target to throw to; quickly return the ball to the tee.]

ASSESSING BATTING

Have a volunteer stand facing the batter and videotape each child swinging two or three times from the front and from the side. This video can be valuable to the teacher for evaluating present batting performance, for comparison with later data, and to the child for self-assessment. It would be ideal to have a separate videotape for each child for ease in future videotaping of the same skill.

Second Grade Gymnastics

Unit 1

Changing Levels, Directions, and Supporting Body Parts While Traveling

4 to 5 lessons

FOCUS Traveling in a variety of ways

MOTOR CONTENT

Selected from Theme 1—Introduction to the Body and Theme 2—Introduction to Space

Body

Locomotor activities—personally designed ways of traveling
Body parts—changing the body part supporting the body

Space

Levels—changing
Directions—changing

OBJECTIVES

In this unit, children will (or should be willing to try to) meet these objectives:

- Work to develop greater versatility in their gymnastic ability by (1) selecting different body parts to support their weight as they travel, (2) executing a movement in different directions, and (3) either starting and finishing at different levels or changing the level while performing an activity (reflects National Standard in Physical Education 1).
- Learn that short, slow series of movements are easier for others to observe and copy than long, fast series of movements (reflects National Standard in Physical Education 2).
- Accept responsibility for attempting their best work when working alone or with a partner (reflects National Standard in Physical Education 5).

EQUIPMENT AND MATERIALS

One mat for each four children, and one handleless jump rope for each child.

LEARNING EXPERIENCES

1.0 [If the mats are 4 by 6 feet or larger, two children can work at a mat at the same time, each close to an end, traveling straight across the width of the mat.] Each time you cross the mat [or rope], let's see if you can try very hard to

STRENGTH

To be skillful in gymnastics, you need good, strong hands. Help make yours strong when you're at home by placing your hands flat on the floor and pushing hard against the floor as you take your hips and legs into the air and control the landing of your feet. Try this several times, taking your hips over your hands only as high as you can control your push-off and the landing on your feet.

travel in a different way. There should be no more than [four] at any mat [one at any rope]. Be careful of others and start your turn when the person sharing your space is off the mat. Find a place and begin.

1.1 While you are waiting to take your next turn, take a moment and try to think of different body parts you can place on the mat [floor, ground (if outside)] first to start your traveling.

1.2 Great! I've seen people placing their hands down first, some the lower leg, even a shoulder. I see so many different body parts being used as I look at the whole class. Each of you see if you can start your traveling with a new body part each time you go across the mat [rope].

1.3 Watch the body part the person in front of you places first on the mat. Try to make the part you touch first to the mat very different than theirs.

1.4 Sometimes it's fun to try things you see others do. As you wait your turn, take a moment to watch people at work at other places. Find someone starting the movement on a body part you haven't used as your starting body part and see if you can copy their work. Let's all be very careful to do our best gymnastic work because someone may be watching, and they need only good examples to copy.

2.0 Now let only your hands and feet touch the mat [floor, ground] and see how many different ways you can find to travel. Take care not to start your turn before the person you are sharing the space with is finished.

2.1 You can create more ways of traveling if you think about your tummy and change where it points as you travel. Sometimes make it point toward a wall [fence, if outside], sometimes to the floor, or sometimes to the ceiling [sky], but only let your hands and feet touch the mat.

2.2 Think about your hands as you prepare them to support you. If the palms and fingers are nice and flat on the floor when you take your weight on them, you can make them push harder to help hold you up.

2.3 Some of you are letting your arms collapse as soon as you try to make them support you. You must make your arms very strong to help them support your weight. Remember, only you can control your muscles. Tighten your arm and shoulder muscles and try to avoid bending your elbows as you press against the mat with your hands. This will help you control your body and not let body parts fall.

2.4 Keep changing the level you take your feet as you travel across the mat [rope]. See if you can control them when you send them way up and when you take them a bit lower.

2.5 Leaders are to try to show at least two different levels with your feet as you travel down the mat. Be careful just to let your hands and feet touch. Watch carefully the level of your leader's feet. See if you can copy the changes in levels your leader makes. Do your best work so your copiers have only good examples to copy. Each group choose a leader and begin. [If the children have been moving across the width of the mat to allow two to work at the same time, you may want to have the leader travel down the length of the mat to create more working space.]

2.6 As you think of your own way to travel on your hands and feet, see if you can change your direction at least once.

2.7 Try to mix up your starting direction. If you started out traveling forward on your last turn, see if you can start your next trip sideways or backward. Thinking gymnasts can start their work from any direction and change their direction.

3.0 Select one special way of traveling in gymnastics and see how many times you can change directions as you perform that same movement as you travel down the mat one time.

3.1 As you travel and change directions, try to make your movement continuous. Don't stop as you change directions. Make it smooth.

3.2 Show you care about the quality of your performance, making every trip down the mat represent your very best work. Try not to collapse. Keep thinking, 'Only I can make my arms strong.' Coach yourself to give yourself confidence to do a good job.

3.3 Plan ahead. Tell the person behind you [next to them, if working on individual mats] the directions in which you are going to travel before you start your turn. Watch carefully to see if the performers travel in the directions they told you before they started.

3.4 Sometimes it is easy to change your level before you change your direction. For example, start at a low level and do a forward roll. Change to a high level by jumping up and turning in the air. Then change to a low level and go immediately into a sideways roll or a backward roll.

3.5 Try to make the jump and turn in the air come right after you finish your forward roll and go immediately into a sideways or backward roll. No stops except to finish.

3.6 See if you can combine one kind of roll with two other ways of traveling, trying not to stop before you hold a still position to finish.

3.7 If you can, show a definite change in level as you combine your two ways of traveling.

3.8 Those who think they can, try to combine two ways of traveling, showing a change in levels and a change in direction.

4.0 One person is going to be the leader, the other is going to try to copy exactly whatever the leader does. Let's see which copier has the best set of eyes and the best memory. Leaders, combine a very short series of movements, showing your very best work. Copiers, watch carefully and copy exactly what you see. If the copiers don't copy it exactly, leaders, repeat your series again and give them another chance to watch it and copy it. Try to choose a partner who has about the same gymnastic skill as you and begin.

4.1 Copiers, watch carefully everything your partners do. What body parts do they use to support their weight? What is the order of their movements? What directions do they travel in? Remember, your job is to watch and then copy.

4.2 Leaders, listen carefully. If your copier repeated the movements exactly, perform your original series and, without stopping, add one or two new things to your series. Copiers, let's see who's up to the challenge of copying a longer series. Try to copy exactly every part of this longer series. [Change roles several times.]

4.3 Leaders, are you finding out that sometimes it is hard to think of something to add? Can anyone tell us the things we have been working on to help us add variety to our gymnastic movements? Sure, you have been working on traveling on different body parts, changing levels, and changing directions. Remember these things we have worked on to help give you variety. If you haven't included a change in direction or a change in level, add these. You can also travel on different body parts when you need to make your series longer.

Copy your leader's movements exactly.

4.4 Let's have a seat and watch [Lisa and David]. [Lisa], do your movement series, and [David], you repeat it. Notice how hard [David] is working to copy [Lisa's] series exactly. [Lisa] knows [David] has difficulty with cartwheels and, even though she loves to do them, she hasn't included one in her series. That is really being a sensitive partner. Each of you try to select things to do you know your partner can copy.

4.5 Copiers, you be the leaders now and remember to include several different ways of traveling. Try to show variety in your series. Those of you who have been the leader, you are going to find out it is hard to copy, so watch carefully and be ready to repeat exactly the series your partner performs.

(Each time learning experiences are selected from 4.0 to 4.5 the teacher may need to remind the children that a short, slow series of movements is easier to perform than a fast, long series. Also, it may be advisable for the teacher to observe the pairing of the children carefully to see if those who are working together are sensitive to the skill level of their partner. Apparatus can be included at anytime during the lessons at the discretion of the teacher. In some cases, the children might be given the option to include it.)

Backward Roll

4 to 5 lessons

FOCUS Developing the backward roll

MOTOR CONTENT

Selected from Theme 1—Introduction to the Body and Theme 2—Introduction to Space

Body

Locomotor activities—rolling backward, sideward, and forward; stepping, jumping, and step-like actions to mount and dismount apparatus

Space

Directions—changing and maintaining directions (forward, backward, up, down)

OBJECTIVES

In this unit, children will (or should be willing to try to) meet these objectives:

- Be consistent in establishing their starting positions for the backward roll by squatting with back toward the mat, lifting hands up to the sides of the head, pointing thumbs toward the head, and tucking the head and chest tightly to the knees (reflects National Standard in Physical Education 2).
- Perform the backward roll from a squat position by lowering the seat and rolling onto the back, placing palms flat on the mat, pushing equally with both hands, letting the toes reach back over the head to touch the floor, and keeping tucked (reflects National Standards in Physical Education 1, 2).
- Develop a sequence involving mounting and dismounting apparatus, facing in different directions and performing forward and backward rolls in a straight line (reflects National Standards in Physical Education 1, 2).
- Recognize that pushing forcefully against the mat with both hands creates space between the mat and the head needed to roll backward comfortably (reflects National Standard in Physical Education 2).
- Work quietly, standing away from the performer, mats, and apparatus to help create a safe learning environment (reflects National Standard in Physical Education 5).

EQUIPMENT AND MATERIALS

One tumbling mat for every four to six children, a selection of basic low apparatus appropriate for mounting and dismounting, such as benches, boxes, stools, and balance beams.

LEARNING EXPERIENCES

1.0 [Two or three children can roll across the mat at the same time.] Think about making your muscles tight to show sharp, straight lines with your arms, legs, and your body as you practice your very best rolls.

1.1 [Children waiting a turn tend to crowd next to the mat.] Show you care for the safety of yourself and others by standing two or three steps away from the person in front of you when waiting for a turn.

1.2 No matter what type of roll you are doing, concentrate on placing your palms flat on the mat, then push firmly against it. Flat hands and a good strong push help you prepare to support your weight with your arms as you roll.

1.3 Let's work on firming up your body shape every moment during your performance. Start by standing up tall. When you start your roll, tuck your tummy close to your knees and tighten all of your muscles to make your whole body feel round and strong. Keep this same firm, round feeling as you roll.

1.4 Pop up after you roll and hold a tall, stretched, still position, fingers reaching to the ceiling at the end of your roll.

1.5 Without losing the round, firm feeling as you roll, see if you can change your roll. [Practice, then let children demonstrate.]

1.6 What did you do to change your roll? [Changed the direction of the roll, changed its speed, or changed their starting position.] Keep these ideas in mind and, each time you roll, change something to make your roll different.

2.0 I have observed that some of you are trying to include a backward roll. To start the backward roll, you must first back up to the mat, squat down, and get your weight balanced on the balls of both feet. Second, tuck your head and tummy close to your knees and legs, then raise your hands over your shoulders with flat palms up and fingers stretched with the thumb of each hand near an ear. Third, staying tucked, rock back on your heels, then your seat and back, staying in a tight ball. Repeat this rocking several times. [Have a child demonstrate each step. Never push a child doing a backward roll.]

Ready position for a roll.

FLEXIBILITY

To help you become more flexible for doing the backward roll, practice rounding your back and rocking back and forth until you can touch the floor over your head with your toes. Do not rock all the way over unless you place your palms flat on the floor next to your head with your thumbs pointing toward your ears. Push with your hands and straighten your elbows to give your head room to move without hurting your neck. Do this 10 times each night so your back muscles and spine will become more flexible.

2.1 Squat with your back toward your mat, roll on your back, and push with your hands, letting your feet go straight over your head and trying to land just on your feet, not your shins.

2.2 Some of you will be able to roll straighter if you have stronger hands and arms. Positioning your thumbs by your head helps place your palms flat on the mat to get a strong push.

2.3 Keep your knees close to your head as you roll. Let your legs go back over your head with your toes reaching back toward the floor as you push hard with your hands. Land on your feet and stand up.

2.4 When you stand just before and after you roll, stand very tall, making the space between your belt and shoulders as long and tall as you can. Memorize this stretched posture and try to create it each time you want a top-notch performance.

2.5 Many of you are doing a great job of getting into a squat position with your thumbs up near your ears. Now let's watch [Timmy's] head and knees. He really keeps them tucked as he rolls.

2.6 Everyone try to remember to round your back and keep your knees and chest tucked tightly together as you roll.

2.7 [Especially when working with an individual child, you can say "push" just as the hands of the child touch the mat. Pushing at the same time as extending the elbows is critical to creating the space needed between the shoulders and the mat, freeing the head to complete the roll without putting undue strain on the neck.] When you feel your palms touch the mat as you roll backward, push your hands really hard against the mat and straighten your elbows to see if you can end up in a squat position.

2.8 If you end up in a squat position after doing a backward roll, you get an extra treat. You can roll forward across the mat back to your starting position. Try to start and finish your performance with that tall, stretched feeling in your upper torso [chest and shoulders].

3.0 [You may choose to introduce this earlier to some individuals or to the class.] Some of you will be surprised to find that standing with your legs apart is an easier starting position for the backward roll than a squatting position. Those who want to try the backward straddle roll stand up close to the mat with your heels touching the mat and spread your legs wide apart with your hands up and thumbs pointing to the sides of your head. Without letting your knees bend any time during the roll, try to drop softly back onto your seat and without stopping, go into a backward roll and end with your legs still wide apart. [Help a child demonstrate.]

3.1 If you are practicing the backward straddle roll, push hard with those hands and try to straighten the elbows to give your head some easy space to slip through.

3.2 See if you can do a backward roll, pop-up, and go immediately into a forward roll ending with a pop-up at the same place you started your first roll.

3.3 Try doing a forward roll with your legs crossed. Then stand up, keeping your legs crossed and twist forward on the balls of your feet, turning toward your front foot. When you twist toward the front foot, you will finish facing your starting place, so do another forward roll to take you back. [You may choose to have them cross their legs while standing and practice this twist when waiting a turn.]

3.4 Do your very best forward roll, pop-up, and go immediately into a backward roll back to your place.

4.0 Remember to stand back and not crowd the performer. This time, each of you is to roll three times. First, select and perform one roll and remember exactly how you did it. The second time, take the same roll but change your speed on purpose [intentionally]. The third time you roll, see if you can change your starting position. Be planning your three rolls as you wait.

4.1 Try to make every roll as perfect as you can, then go quickly into your next roll.

4.2 Try to complete your three rolls with as few extra movements as possible. Think about where your feet are as you are rolling and prepare them for your next roll so you don't make any unplanned movements.

4.3 At your mat, play follow the leader. Leaders, use your tall, stretched posture to start, then link three or four of your best rolls together, trying to make your bodies firm and each roll very sharp and crisp. Followers, watch your leader's performance carefully. One at a time, each of you try to produce photocopies of the leader's rolls. Change leaders so everyone gets several chances at being the machine that produces the exact copies.

5.0 Let's add a piece of apparatus to your mat. You may choose how you mount and dismount the apparatus, but all landings must be on your feet on a mat. Remember to practice that lifted, stretched feeling, showing it when you mount and dismount your apparatus. As you dismount, always land with your feet about hip-width apart, trying to bend your knees and hips, keeping your back straight up and down like the wall. This will help you make softer landings.

5.1 Some of you might like to face different directions to dismount, still landing on your feet. [Add mats at all points of dismount to extend length of working space.]

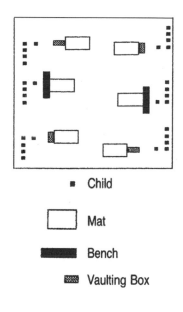

• Child

☐ Mat

▬ Bench

▨ Vaulting Box

5.2 If you land facing forward, try following your soft landing with a forward roll. If you land backward, try your backward roll. If you dismount sideways, you could keep traveling in the same direction as you dismount by doing a cartwheel.

5.3 Decide on the direction of your dismount before you take your turn. Plan ahead so you know which direction you have to travel in after you land. You will find it easier to travel in the same direction as your dismount.

5.4 Select your favorite way of mounting and dismounting and several different ways of rolling, including one forward and one backward roll, and put them together in a little sequence. Remember to start your gymnastic sequence [routine] with the top of your body stretched nice and tall and finish the sequence by holding that same posture very still.

5.5 Keep practicing, trying to make each part of your sequence planned. Don't let one little movement get into your sequence that is unplanned.

5.6 Let's share this lovely lifted feeling and the sequence you have developed. Two groups will perform at one time. Observers, look carefully to see how sharp and crisp the performers look when they remember to lift that space between their belts and their shoulders.

5.7 Some of you may enjoy trying to copy the sequence someone else has made. You may have seen a roll you hadn't included in your sequence or you might want to improve that stretched feeling and sharpen your performance.

Unit 3 — Balancing, Rolling, and Step-Like Actions

4 to 5 lessons

FOCUS Combining balancing, rolling, and stepping

MOTOR CONTENT

Selected from Theme 1—Introduction to the Body and Theme 2—Introduction to Space

Body

Locomotor activities—rolling and step-like actions
Nonlocomotor activities—balancing

Space

Levels—varying levels (high, medium, low)
Directions—varying (forward, backward, sideward, up, down)

OBJECTIVES

In this unit, children will (or should be willing to try to) meet these objectives:

- Show distinct changes in levels and directions when combining rolling and step-like activities (reflects National Standard in Physical Education 1).
- Place body parts over the base of support when balancing and when bringing them back down to the floor, avoiding collapsing or falling (reflects National Standard in Physical Education 1).
- Understand that they can perform step-like actions on a variety of body parts by lifting and transferring weight to a nonadjacent body part while maintaining contact with the floor (reflects National Standard in Physical Education 2).
- Recognize that they can use changes in levels and directions to develop variety in gymnastics and apply this idea to sustain moderate levels of gymnastic activity throughout class time (reflects National Standards in Physical Education 2, 4).
- Work to refine personal responses, striving to achieve greater constant tension in the body (reflects National Standards in Physical Education 2, 5).
- Recognize differences and similarities in other's gymnastic ability and show respect when observing, copying, or extending movement ideas (reflects National Standard in Physical Education 6).

EQUIPMENT AND MATERIALS

One tumbling mat and a bench or low box for every four to six children.

LEARNING EXPERIENCES

1.0 Remember that you can do step-like actions by lifting your weight from one body part to another? That makes step-like actions just like walking, except in gymnastics, we step with many different body parts. Staying in your own space, work on inventing step-like actions by stepping with many different body parts. Find a space on the floor all by yourself and begin.

1.1 In gymnastics, you want to try to step with body parts you do not usually think about when you are walking. Try to think about walking on body parts such as your lower leg, your forearms, your hands, and your seat.

1.2 See if you can walk on a combination of different body parts. Don't pick just one kind of body part and keep walking with it.

1.3 We can walk for a long, long time without falling when we walk on our feet because we carefully keep shifting our weight from one foot to the other and because we place each foot down carefully before we make that foot support us. Each time you start to step with a different body part you usually don't use for walking, try to place it carefully on the floor, making it strong enough to support you.

1.4 Thinking about walking, see if you can step with different body parts continuously for 30 seconds. I will time you. When I say 'stop,' either hold the position you are in when you hear stop or quickly go into a position you can hold very still.

2.0 Let's see how you can make step-like actions on different body parts take you onto, along, and off a bench. We can't just walk on our feet. [The children can help place the benches. Give them very precise instructions and careful monitoring to lift, carry, and place them safely. Sometimes it is best to have one group of six demonstrate for the class how to carry a bench.] Let's watch these six get ready to carry the bench, three people on each side of the bench. Keeping their backs straight up and down like the wall, they bend their knees and face the bench to grasp the bench with both hands. Then, keeping their backs and elbows straight, they straighten their knees to lift the bench. Now, carefully walking forward, not sideways, they walk to the spot where they want the bench to sit, and then, again bending just their knees, keeping their backs and arms straight, they place the bench on the floor. No one should let go of the bench until the bench is on the floor.

2.1 Keep making different body parts take your weight. Don't step with the same one or two body parts during your entire trip down the bench.

2.2 As you travel, carefully see if you can step onto and off the bench onto different body parts.

2.3 Take care when you step onto a different body part and place it on the bench or floor. Remember, you must prepare that body part to take your weight. Make the stepping body part nice and strong so it can support you and keep you from collapsing and falling.

2.4 Carefully watch the body parts the person in front of you uses for stepping. See if you can copy each step with exactly the same body part.

2.5 Watch the body parts the person in front of you uses for stepping and this time, see if you can step with a different combination of body parts.

3.0 See if you can do one of your very best rolls, trying to keep your body tightly tucked as you roll. [Place the mats in any formation you desire or allow the children to randomly arrange them. When they are carrying mats, however, instruct the children to work together quietly to lift and carry heavy or large mats—never dragging the mats.]

MUSCULAR, STRENGTH, AND ENDURANCE

Try this at home. With a partner, hold different balances until you both count to 20 or say the alphabet together. Use two, three, four, or five body parts to support you. Try to hold some balances that challenge you to remain still for the whole time by stretching free body parts as far from your support parts as you can.

3.1 No matter what kind of roll you do, think about creating and maintaining muscle tension to make nice, firm legs, arms, and bodies. Make straight lines with your legs. Begin to show really strong muscle tension.

3.2 This time, try a roll, then change your direction, and roll again.

3.3 Try not to stop in between your two rolls.

3.4 If you do a backward roll, remember to keep your chin on your chest to make your back round, push with strong arms, hands flat against the mat, stretch your legs and toes back over your head, and land on your feet.

4.0 If you have been successful in tucking your head and getting a straight push with your hands, try starting your roll from a different level.

4.1 See if you can do two rolls starting each at a different level. First, bend your knees and roll at a low level. Then, do your second roll at a medium level with your knees straight.

4.2 As you combine your rolls starting from different levels, work hard to keep your muscles tight and do your rolls crisply. Try not to feel *squooshie* or flabby when you are working on gymnastics. Feel very strong and tight.

5.0 Now see if you can select a level and roll in any direction, then go immediately into a balance. Hold your balance very still while you say your name to yourself and then carefully come out of your balance and stand up nice and tall.

5.1 Try to get your balance in your mind before you begin to roll. Work on moving smoothly from your roll right into a balance.

5.2 [Analyze the roll and the balance of two or three students performing different rolls and balances.] Let's watch [Santos]. Notice how he starts his forward roll at a medium level with his knees straight. [Pause.] Watch his hands when they reach forward after he finishes his roll. [Pause.] He places his hands carefully down on the mat, then his forehead, and goes immediately up into a headstand. [Select other balances if most of the class cannot do headstands.] See, he didn't do one extra movement between the roll and his headstand. All of you go back and try to go from your roll to your balance without doing one extra movement.

5.3 Those of you who have been able to roll and go into a balance eliminating the extra movements, see if you can follow your roll with step-like actions instead of a balance.

5.4 Try to make your roll go in one direction and your step-like actions take you in a different direction.

5.5 If you are really thinking, you can change your level and direction at the same time.

6.0 Let's try to develop greater variety in our gymnastics by skillfully changing our levels and directions as we combine rolls with step-like actions. Be sure there are no more than four [five or six] at any working place and begin quietly.

6.1 Make the floor a part of your gymnastic working space. Begin to show changes in direction, doing step-like actions on the floor as you leave the bench and as you leave the mat.

6.2 As you travel down or on and off the bench, try to make different body parts do stepping movements to take you to the mat.

6.3 Try to start your rolls from different levels. You have to think to make your work different. We seem to find it easier to keep repeating the same thing each time. Some of you may want to start your roll from a standing position. [Arrange additional mats if available.]

6.4 Because we are working on the floor, bench, and mat and on changing directions, we should be able to have more than one of us working at an area at the same time. Before you start, each of you find a space to begin to work and see if you can all be working at one time on changing your directions and levels as you roll and do step-like actions. If your movement takes you close to another person, carefully change your direction for a moment. [You may need to help some groups with their spacing. In addition, you may need to have the children stop work, "freezing" right where they are, and have them notice their spacing to keep a safe working environment.]

6.5 [Stop the class and have different groups share their progress, intermittently with practice until all groups have shared.]

6.6 Let's see which group can be in continuous movement for one minute. Try to make each stepping action or roll planned and show clear changes in levels and directions. [Repeat, timing learning activity for longer periods of time.]

6.7 [Some groups may be able to change direction so skillfully that they can be successful in adding occasional balances.] If you are able to change directions without making unplanned movements, you may like to add a balance somewhere in your routine. Be very careful of others. Always be ready to change direction when you see someone ahead of you.

Make appropriate use of:	Yes	No
1. levels and directions	
2. changes of speed	
3. general/personal space	

Is able to:	Yes	No
1. use hands and feet	
2. roll on body surfaces	
3. fall and recover	
4. combine two or more movements	

Uses the following equipment:	Yes	No
1. climbing rope	
2. vaulting box	
3. high balance beam	
4. low balance beam	
5. parallel bars	
6. small apparatus	

Demonstrates awareness of:	Yes	No
1. body alignment	
2. balance/off balance	
3. turning and twisting	
4. body shape	
5. flight	
6. traveling/stopping	
7. landing	

Demonstrates appropriate form for:	Yes	No
1. running	
2. jumping	
3. hopping	
4. skipping	
5. galloping	

Comments:

_____

_____

_____

_____

Student name _____

Date _____

_____
Physical Education Teacher

*Used by permission of A. Hudgens, Elementary Physical Education Teacher, Charlotte-Mecklenberg Schools, Charlotte, N.C. Revised and reprinted from Logsdon, B., K. Barrett, M. Ammons, M. Broer, L. Halverson, R. McGee, and M.A. Roberton. 1984. Physical education for children: A focus on the teaching process. 2nd ed. Philadelphia: Lea & Febiger, p. 419.

Unit 4

Making Body Shapes On and Off Apparatus

4 to 5 lessons

Creating different body shapes while balancing on and traveling off or over apparatus

MOTOR CONTENT

Selected from Theme 1—Introduction to the Body and Theme 4—Introduction to Relationships of Body Parts

Body

Locomotor activities—traveling on and off apparatus
Nonlocomotor activities—balancing

Relationships

Body parts—intentionally add variety by changing the relationships of body parts while in the air or while balancing

OBJECTIVES

In this unit, children will (or should be willing to try to) meet these objectives:

- Create different shapes with their bodies while in the air or while balancing by intentionally changing the relationships of body parts (reflects National Standards in Physical Education 1, 2).
- Learn that they can add variety to their movements by changing the relationships of different body parts and by forming different body shapes (reflects National Standards in Physical Education 1, 2).
- Understand that bending with their ankles, knees, and hips helps to cushion their landings (reflects National Standard in Physical Education 2).
- Accept personal responsibility for the safety of themselves and others by waiting until the area is clear to start their approach to the apparatus and demonstrate respect and courteous manners when taking turns (reflects National Standards in Physical Education 5, 6, 7).
- Take pride in creating different shapes with their bodies by fully stretching, bending, or twisting (reflects National Standard in Physical Education 7).

EQUIPMENT AND MATERIALS

Mats, benches, vaulting boxes.

LEARNING EXPERIENCES

1.0 Carefully, in your own working space, see how you can jump high into the air and land right on your takeoff spot.

1.1 As you jump, really stretch and reach as high as you can with both arms.

1.2 Each time you jump, try to make a different shape with your body while it is in the air. Remember to land on your takeoff spot.

1.3 Gymnasts really care about their bodies. Let's show we are gymnasts. Stretch those legs and ankles while you are in the air and then bend at your ankles, knees, and hips to help you land softly.

1.4 Listen to the sound you make as you land. Show control—make your landings quiet and soft.

1.5 What is the difference between a twist and a turn? Let's try a twist. Keep your eyes focused on one spot and make your hips, shoulders and other body parts face different directions as you jump and land. Don't let your eyes look at a different spot. Can you feel your body twisting like a pretzel?

1.6 This time, let's try a turn. Do your eyes stay focused on the same spot? No. In a turn, your whole body moves around at the same time. In a twist some parts turn while others stay still.

Can you twist your body like a pretzel?

1.7 Face someone, and the two of you name the different shapes you can make with your bodies. One partner jump, make a nice shape in the air, and end with a soft landing. Now carefully copy the shape your partner made exactly. Take turns being the copier.

2.0 Think of a balance that you can hold for five seconds. Take your balance and hold it still, counting slowly to five. Now, with nice muscle tension and control, carefully bring the body parts down and stand up tall.

2.1 Each time after you stand up tall, take a different balance. Hold it. Carefully come out of it and stand tall. Take pride in holding your balance and coming out of it carefully.

2.2 Try not to collapse. Tighten those muscles and be as strong as you can when holding your balance, coming out of it, and while standing tall.

2.3 After you are in your balance, see if you can change the shape of your body by moving your free body parts [body parts not supporting you]. [Pause.] Now, carefully come out of your balance, stand tall, then take a different balance, change the position of your free body parts, and stand tall. Continue working and thinking of new balances.

2.4 Let's share our ideas. This half sit down and let's look for different body parts used as bases of support, shapes being made, and how people are controlling their movement to stand up tall and not fall. [Repeat later, after 2.5, letting other half show.] Keep trying new balances, changing the relationship of your free body parts. You can bring them close together, far apart, both to one side, take some up, some down, or some forward. After you change their relationship, come out of each balance carefully and stand tall to show your performance is ended. Don't collapse! Keep that muscle tension so you are in control when changing relationships and coming out of the balance.

2.5 You can add variety to your performance by making some of your changes in relationships slow and others very fast. Remember to make these changes without losing your balance.

3.0 See how you can arrive softly on the apparatus and make a high dismount off the apparatus. Try to land softly, absorbing the force of your landing by keeping your back straight like a wall and giving with [bending] your ankles, knees, and hips. Hold your landing and stand tall.

3.1 Remember to be careful and give the person in front of you time to hold their landing and get out of the way before you take your turn. Each time you take your turn, try to make your jump off the apparatus take you higher by reaching up with your arms and pushing up from the apparatus with your feet. Make your feet land close to the apparatus, then stand tall and still for a moment.

3.2 Those of you who feel you are really getting nice and high off the [apparatus] might like to see, as you dismount, if you can keep your eyes focused on one spot, twist while you are in the air, and then land on your feet. Remember, if you are twisting you won't take your eyes off the spot you chose to watch.

3.3 When you land after you have twisted in the air, try hard to keep your back straight up and down like the wall. Don't drop your head and lean forward. Keeping your back straight will help keep your body weight over your feet so you can hold your balance as you land.

3.4 Each time you dismount from the apparatus, try to make different shapes while you are in the air. Change the relationships of some of your body parts. Make each shape different. Remember to have a nice, soft landing and hold still when you land.

3.5 Really try to *stick* your landings. Don't let your feet move when you land. Try to stick right on the spot which your feet touch first.

4.0 After you land on your feet, carefully go into a balance on different body parts, hold it, then come out of it carefully, and stand tall. Keep it safe for everyone. Let the person in front of you leave the mat before you begin.

4.1 Plan your balance before you arrive on the apparatus. See how few movements it can take you to go into that balance after you dismount.

4.2 Some of you might like to add a roll after you land to take you into your balance. But only take balances that you can really control and hold.

4.3 After you take your balance, hold your whole body still, change the relationship of the free body parts two or three times, then carefully come out of your balance, and stand tall.

5.0 [Set up arrangements of apparatus that provide the children with two or three different places to mount, dismount, and balance.] Each time you come to a new place to dismount, take care to wait for the person ahead of you to leave so you have a clear space to land. Really try to make your shape in the air look different from the one before. Each time you balance, make a different balance and see if the relationships you create with those free body parts can be different.

5.1 Think about the shapes you are making in the air. Be sure you are making your shape as clear to an observer as you can.

5.2 Act like you have an audience and begin to select and perfect some of your favorite ways to mount, dismount, and balance.

5.3 Let's give a gymnastic show for each other. This half of the class sit down on the floor away from the apparatus and look at these Olympic gymnasts who have just arrived at [school]. Watch carefully, and I would imagine you might see something new and challenging you would like to try.

5.4 Now, I am not sure what country these gymnasts represent, but I am sure their country is proud of them. Would you please give your performance? Gymnasts who are observing, see if you can see something you would like to try. Gymnasts are always looking for and adding new things to their routines.

5.5 Try to remember one thing you saw someone do and try to perfect it. It may have been a new balance, a new roll, or maybe a different shape.

SELF-ASSESSMENT IN GYMNASTICS

At the end of the unit (perhaps as homework) children write what they do best, what they have improved the most, and what they need to practice to improve even more. Use their personal assessment to improve their performances.

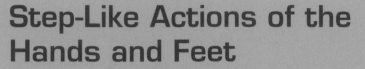

Unit 5

Step-Like Actions of the Hands and Feet

4 to 5 lessons

FOCUS Stepping with feet and hands

MOTOR CONTENT

Selected from Theme 1—Introduction to the Body, Theme 2—Introduction to Space, and Theme 3—Introduction to Time

Body

Locomotor activities—step-like actions on hands and feet, rolling

Effort

Time—changing speed

Space

Levels—changing
Directions—changing

OBJECTIVES

In this unit, children will (or should be willing to try to) meet these objectives:

- Select, practice, and improve their performances of personally chosen combinations of step-like actions or combinations previously identified (i.e., cartwheel) (reflects National Standards in Physical Education 1, 7).
- Work to develop the muscle tension needed to transfer or support their weight and to develop tight, clear lines with their bodies (reflects National Standards in Physical Education 1, 2).
- Recognize that step-like actions are performed by maintaining contact with the floor with at least one body part as their weight is lifted and transferred from one nonadjacent body part to another (reflects National Standard in Physical Education 2).
- Learn that muscle tension is needed to safely transfer their weight from one body part to another, to change speed or direction; and learn to recognize when they have altered their speed, direction, or base of support (reflects National Standard in Physical Education 2).
- Concentrate, creating a businesslike atmosphere, thereby encouraging improvement in everyone's gymnastic abilities (reflects National Standards in Physical Education 5, 7).

EQUIPMENT AND MATERIALS

One large (4- by 6-foot to 5- by 10-foot) mat for each four to six children. (Consider having some children select gymnastic movements they can do safely on the floor and rotate groups rather than make more than four or five share a mat.)

LEARNING EXPERIENCES

1.0 Today, let's see if you can select a gymnastic movement and have fun with it by safely performing your movement, using at least two different speeds. You will be working with [three] others at a mat. Stand at the side of the mat about three or four steps away to give each performer working space in front and at the end of the mat.

1.1 As you practice changing speed, try not to let yourself collapse. Take responsibility for making your muscles tight and strong to support you.

1.2 See if you can do your movement at one speed and, without stopping, carefully repeat it showing a definite change in your speed.

1.3 You might want to try to add a pop-up to give you a big change in level just before you change speed. Think of the pop-up as being part of one of your movements. Don't stop between your two movements. Make the momentum [speed] you get in your pop-up take you right into your second movement.

1.4 As you pop up, swing both arms high in front of you, up over your head, stretching your whole body from your toes to the tips of your fingers while you are in the air. Create and feel a big, straight feeling.

1.5 You're doing a great job of remembering to give each performer the space near the mat to use as they work. Select a gymnastic movement you haven't tried today and see how successful you can be in performing that movement at two different speeds. [Consider repeating tasks 1.1 through 1.4 after 1.5.]

1.6 Some of you might try adding a jump turn if you have been rolling. Others might want to try cartwheels, going to your left and to your right, changing directions instead of speed.

1.7 Select the performance you think you did best and polish it to make it ready to share. Be sure you include two different speeds or directions and a definite change in level before you stop.

1.8 [Ask two or three groups to share their changes in direction and speed until all groups have shown.] As we watch classmates share their changes in speed and or direction, notice how the pop-up between the two movements blends one movement into the other with no stop in between.

2.0 Do one of your favorite gymnastic movements. As you do it, concentrate on the changes in muscle tension you are creating to help you change speed, direction, or make those stretched pop-ups.

2.1 Each time you take your turn, see if you can experiment with a different form of traveling down the mat. Be sure your muscle tension helps you create a controlled performance posture all the time.

2.2 Begin to make step-like actions, stepping from one body part to another. Place each new body part carefully on the mat or floor as you step.

2.3 Think ahead. Create the muscle tension each stepping body part needs to support you.

2.4 Keep experimenting with making different body parts do your stepping.

2.5 Finish your stepping actions by holding your last step very still and steady.

3.0 This time, each of you do one forward roll and come to your feet, then quickly change and go right into a backward roll. Right at the moment you are stopping the forward roll and going into the backward roll, think about your muscle tension. See if you can feel muscles tightening to help you change direction.

3.1 Before you start your performance, pause a moment and get focused [concentrate] on your work. Think about the placement of your hands and the muscle effort you must create to keep from collapsing and to make a safe, sudden change of direction. Talk to your muscles to make them stronger.

3.2 The gymnasts next in line will be the first leaders. Leaders, select and perform a movement and, with strong muscles, reverse your [go in the opposite] direction and repeat your movement. Everyone else, watch your leaders and see if you can copy their movement exactly. [Change leaders, varying the challenge. You could have the new leader start in a different direction or use different step-like actions. Encourage firm, strong muscles to help change direction and to keep everyone from collapsing when shifting their weight to each new base of support.]

3.3 Try to copy your leader exactly with every part of your body doing exactly what the leader did. Keep focused [concentrate] on creating and easing up on muscle tension. See if you can feel your muscles working constantly to take your weight onto a new body part and to show definite changes in direction.

4.0 Practice linking 8 or 10 stepping actions together, then stop and hold a posture on or off the mat to give your work a finished look. Everyone waiting a turn, remember to stand at the side of the mat about two or three steps away to give each performer the floor space needed in front of and at the end of the mat to create longer sequences.

4.1 Many of you must be creating greater muscle tension because I see fewer people collapsing. Now, concentrate on adding step-like actions that take parts of your body way up high.

Several can share a mat safely even when linking several movements together.

4.2 Create straight lines above you with the body part you take high. Try hard to firm up your muscles to prepare each stepping body part to support your weight and to stretch the body parts in the air to make straight lines.

4.3 As you step with different kinds of body parts, see if you can make one definite change in level.

4.4 Keep changing the body parts doing your stepping. Some of you might enjoy trying to make a series of stepping actions only on your hands and feet.

4.5 Leaders, as you begin your next turn, start by standing alert and focusing your eyes straight ahead, stretching the part of your body between your belt and your shoulders to make it very long. Finish your series with this same stretched position.

5.0 Select several stepping actions you enjoy and keep practicing them in the same order. Name your stepping parts in order to the people behind you. Those waiting a turn, observe if the stepping actions were performed in the order the performer said they would perform them.

5.1 Sharpen your body lines each time you repeat your step-like actions in order. Firm up your muscles to make straighter and more planned lines with your body. See if this effort to sharpen body lines makes you feel more like a performer.

5.2 If any of you are doing cartwheels, be sure you place each hand flat on the floor as you step with it. You must prepare first one hand to support your weight, then the other hand, then one foot, and then the other foot.

5.3 Firm up the muscles in your arms, making them very straight and strong as your hips and feet go high in the air over your hands. Straighten each elbow so you can support your complete weight, first on one hand and then the other.

5.4 When you do step-like actions in gymnastics, always try to feel your muscles firm in the body part taking your weight. Make those muscles tight as you shift your weight from one stepping body part onto another.

5.5 For those doing the cartwheel, start with the whole front of your body facing one wall. Perform your cartwheel, making yourself end up still facing that same wall.

5.6 Try to link several of your stepping actions together without stopping. If you are feeling comfortable working on a cartwheel, try to perform two cartwheels carefully, one right after the other.

5.7 Think about what your legs look like when your hands are doing the stepping. In performing many stepping actions in gymnastics, your legs, ankles, and toes should be stretching for the ceiling when they are in the air—not drooping down like spaghetti.

6.0 Now practice your best step-like actions you can do several times. Make clear, stretched lines with your free body parts not doing the stepping. Follow your stepping actions by rolling carefully in any direction, popping up, and holding your landing in a nice, stretched standing position.

6.1 Everyone, firm up and keep your alert performance attitude throughout your whole series. Stretch tall and focus straight ahead, holding that tall position a moment when you end.

6.2 Some of you might like to try doing the roll first, then follow it with your step-like actions. Tighten your muscles so you look and feel like a gymnast all the way.

6.3 *Smooth* your sequence. Make it one, continuous movement until you hold your finishing pose. Eliminate all stops except your ending.

6.4 [Invite others in the building—visitors, secretary, principal, nurse, and so on, to come in and be an appreciative audience.] Gymnasts always like to share after they practice hard. This half of the class, come enjoy the show with me, and let's see if the performers look like gymnasts from the beginning of their performances to the very end. Performers, show tight, firm muscles and your very best step-like actions and rolls. Repeat your whole combination twice. Please hold each finish tall and very still. [Change roles.]

6.5 You can work on perfecting your own combination or you may choose to add something to it that you enjoyed seeing someone else do in their combination.

ASSESSING SECOND GRADE GYMNASTICS				
Class list	**Combines speed and level changes in movement.** (scale, date)	**Shows speed and direction changes.** (scale, date)	**Shifts weight smoothly in step-like or wheeling actions.** (scale, date)	**Focuses on controlling movement and improving performance.** (scale, date)
Hank Woolsey	4 9/18	4 9/18	3 9/18	3 9/18

Scale: 5 = *Very consistently; almost always*   4 = *Consistently; most of the time*   3 = *Getting the idea; about half the time*   2 = *It's new; some success; about 1/3 of the time*   1 = *Unsuccessful most of the time*

Second Grade Dance

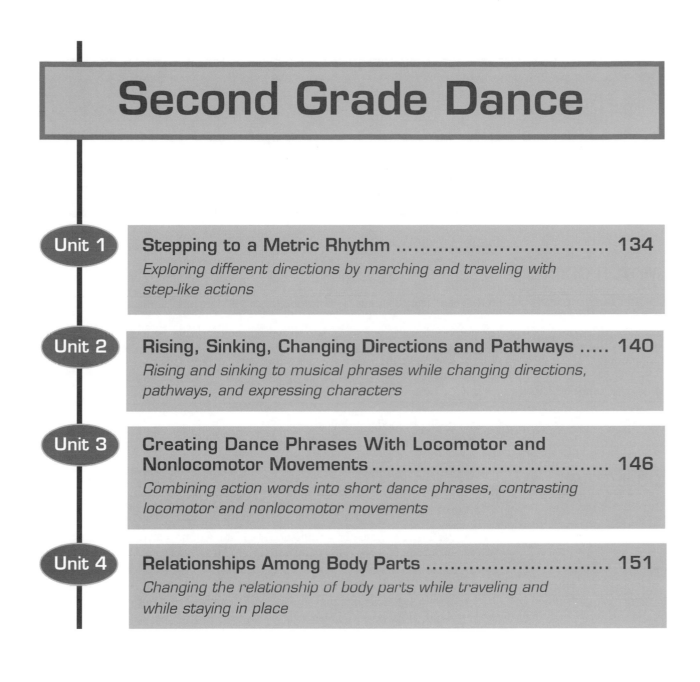

Unit 1

Stepping to a Metric Rhythm

3 or 4 lessons

FOCUS Exploring different directions by marching and traveling with step-like actions

MOTOR CONTENT

Selected from Theme 2—Introduction to Weight and Time and Theme 3—Introduction to Space

Effort

Time—stepping and step-like actions to a metric rhythm (a march)

Space

Levels—high, medium, low (deep)
Directions—forward, backward, sideways

OBJECTIVES

In this unit, children will (or should be willing to try to) meet these objectives:

- Perform a variety of stepping and step-like actions with different body parts at different levels (reflects National Standards in Dance 1b, 1d).
- Explore a variety of directions by traveling forward, backward, and sideways.
- Demonstrate accuracy in moving to a drumbeat and march music (reflects National Standard in Dance 1f).
- Understand that they can perform step-like actions on a variety of body parts by lifting and transferring weight to a nonadjacent body part while maintaining contact with the floor.
- Begin to develop the performance attitude of attentiveness, concentration, and focus necessary in dance (reflects National Standard in Dance 1g).

EQUIPMENT AND MATERIALS

Drum or other percussion instrument capable of producing a clear, strong sound. March music with a strong 2/4 meter, such as Selection A—"The Stars and Stripes Forever" by Sousa, Selection B—"March" from *The Nutcracker* by Tchaikovsky, Selection C—"Soldier's March" from the *Album for the Very Young* by Robert Schumann, Selection D—"March" from *The Comedians* by Kabalevsky, Selection E—"March" from *Soirees Musicales* by Rossini-Brittan. *Optional:* Musical accompaniment for learning experiences 2.0 to 2.8, Selection F—"Spider Dance" by David Karp or "Spiders" by James Bastien; Selection G—Ravel's *Bolero*.

LEARNING EXPERIENCES

1.0 [Tap a moderately steady pace on a drum.] Travel with marching steps, filling all the empty spaces. When you hear the drum stop and my words, 'And stop,' quickly hold a still position. Let's try it now. *And* go, 'Travel, travel—*and stop!*' And again, 'March, march, march—*and stop!*'

1.1 Each time you stop, feel all your muscles paying attention! Attentive muscles are alert, not floppy. [Continue playing even drumbeats, occasionally saying, "And stop."]

1.2 As we travel, work hard not to follow anyone else. Use those magic eyes to look for and march through empty spaces. Keep finding and filling open spaces.

1.3 As you travel, listen to your feet. Walk on quiet, spongy soles. We shouldn't hear anything but soft drumbeats. [Practice.] Let each step absorb your weight carefully and quietly.

1.4 Use all the available space. Stand up straight and tall and lift knees as you go. Feel your back lengthening upward to the sky. [Continue tapping even drumbeats, "1, 2, 1, 2."]

1.5 Tighten your muscles to stop quickly when you hear the signal, 'And stop!' [Repeat, "And stop!" signal several times to check attentiveness and concentration.] Stop on a dime—right where you are!

1.6 [Mark a circle or rectangle in center area for small steps; use all of the dance area for large steps.] Listen carefully to the drum. Soft drumbeats will tell you to travel with *small,* marching steps. Louder drumbeats will tell you to take large steps and use all of the available space.

Take bigger marching steps—use all the space!

1.7 As you travel, make your marching very tidy by lifting and placing one foot down, then the other. Feel the ball of your foot touch first, then your heel. Make very clear stepping actions by lifting and carefully placing your foot on the floor.

1.8 [Play lively march music with a moderate tempo.] Pat hands softly on your thighs . . . now clap . . . now pat, '1, 2, 1, 2.' Feel this beat with your feet and begin to travel by walking or stepping alongside a partner. You both will need to take the same size steps. [Challenge students with disabilities to move in their own ways and challenge those without disabilities to discover possibilities of moving along with those who have disabilities.]

1.9 *You* decide when to change your direction. Maybe go forward for four counts, then backward for four. March forward for eight counts, then sideways [right-left] for four. Try many different directions! Decide on a sequence you and your partner like and repeat it again and again. [Continue music, providing adequate time for developing and repeating sequences. Let half of the class share partner marches, then reverse roles.]

STUDENT SELF-ASSESSMENT

Provide students with ongoing opportunities to respond (verbally or in writing) by asking questions. For example,

- What were the two best things that happened while working with a partner or a group? (List examples of a positive working attitude, cooperation with others, sharing the leadership role, exchanging movement ideas, and so on.)

- What was the biggest problem you faced when creating or practicing movement sequences?

- Can you and your partner (or group) think of three goals to improve your performance? (Record goals in a journal as an individual, group, or class.)

2.0 Some of you may be able to step with other body parts besides your feet. What are some parts we can use safely? [Hand, knee, elbow, forearm.] This time, as you travel to open spaces, try to gently step with other body parts. [Alone or with a partner.]

2.1 Remember when we had spongy soles on our feet? Try that idea again—make all stepping body parts spongy. Gently place each part on the floor as you 'step . . . step . . . step . . . .' [Play slow to moderate, even drumbeats.]

2.2 Lift each body part up a bit before you place it on the floor. Lifting makes it a step instead of a slide or glide. Try stepping with your hand, knee, foot, side of the leg or arm, elbow, or seat. [Continue drumbeats.]

2.3 Let's make up a stepping dance that has 16 counts. Step with your feet for 8 counts, then step with other body parts for 8 counts. Here we go. [Tap a slow, steady 4/4 rhythm.] 'Foot, foot, foot, foot [to 8]; now another part, part, part, part [to 8].' [Repeat verbal cues several times.]

2.4 Look for and move into empty spaces. Travel with large marching steps on different body parts.

2.5 Listen to the alive, spooky quality of this music [play music selection F]. How does the music make you want to move? What kind of stepping actions can you show? On feet? On different body parts? Where can you go? Forward, backward, sideways? [Have children share ideas, then set off to work alone or with a partner.]

2.6 Remember to lift body parts up before placing them on the floor. Show careful, cautious stepping on different body parts. Imagine that each time you place a body part on the floor [ground], it leaves a print, trace, spot, or dot. What kind of mysterious floor patterns can you make?

2.7 As you step, try to stretch high, then low. Bend, stretch, and twist in different ways. Make your whole body work at each stepping action.

2.8 Select your favorite ways of stepping and create a movement phrase. Practice these stepping actions until you can repeat your phrase exactly the same way. Work toward large actions and smooth transitions. [Share dances, if you like. See photo, page 138.]

3.0 Marching on your feet, lift your chest high and look in the direction you are going. Travel to several different empty places in our dance area, keeping your chest facing forward. Whenever we stop, be ready to tell me exactly where your chest is looking. [Play lively march music, such as selections A through E.]

3.1 In what other direction can we travel? [Sideways.] Imagine looking first with one side of your body as you travel and then with the other. Travel sideways to the right or left.

3.2 When we travel backward, where do we need to focus our eyes so we don't get in anyone else's way? Right, look over a shoulder and look with your back. March backward *safely*.

3.3 As I tap the drum, I will name the direction for traveling. See if you can match your steps to the beat and listen for the next change in direction. [Announce the direction change on the first beat of every eight counts as you

Children's concept of *patterns* in repetition is illustrated in their imaginative crayon drawings. Second graders explore two-dimensional skills of *patterning* in art. You can integrate art and physical education with classroom studies of animals, insects, spiders, and nature. "Look around. What patterns can you identify in the classroom, gymnasium, home, outdoors? What patterns do we create on the floor as we step?"
Drawing by Brendan Drury, age 7.

Repetitions of directions, levels, or pathways traveled creates interesting "patterns" in space. Young children can achieve a body feeling for spatial patterns by exploring and repeating simple changes of direction, such as advancing forward to greet a partner, retreating backward to say good-bye, moving in different directions to open spaces, or crossing pathways by traveling sideways, right to left, toward others.

maintain a steady pace.] Ready? And, 'Forward, [count two to eight]; now sideways, [count two to eight]; backwards, [count two to eight].' [Repeat many times, then play march music softly, continuing directional cues, if needed.]

3.4 Let's make up a traveling dance that has changes of direction. As you travel with very important and careful stepping actions, show the audience how important your front is if you travel forward. Or how important your side is when traveling sideways or your back when traveling backward. Change your direction often. [Play lively march music.]

3.5 Lift your chest and head high. Look proud as you go! Show your very best posture.

4.0 Let's see if we can step with different body parts each time we change directions. Let's start out with forward marching on our feet. 'Forward, 2, 3, 4, place feet softly, 6, 7, 8; now sideways 2, 3, 4, step with knees, 6, 7, 8.' [Initially, suggest body parts to use.]

4.1 Every eight beats [taps], change your direction and select different body parts for your stepping actions. You have a lot to think about. The music will play as you travel. I will tap a drumbeat when it's time to change.

4.2 Some of you might travel for 16 beats before you change direction and your stepping body parts. This will give you more time to show how well you step with different body parts in different directions. [Tap a steady pace.]

4.3 As you change body parts, work hard to step softly. Tighten muscles so you place each body part carefully on the floor.

4.4 [Accompany initially with a drum, then play march music.] In this dance, we'll step with our feet for 16 counts; change direction and step with different body parts for 16 counts; repeat stepping with feet—but only for 8 counts; then change direction, stepping with different body parts for 8 counts. As you travel, I'll tell you when to change body parts and direction. [Conclude by challenging children to change every four counts.]

5.0 Let's create a marching dance on foot that shows the audience at least three changes of direction and a salute [demonstrate]. Every time you change direction, march to face a different classmate. How many people will you salute? Yes, three altogether. [Play march music softly and talk students through the sequence.]

5.1 As you march changing directions, show us how important your movement is with your face and entire body. Pull in your abdomen [stomach] and lift through the chest, chin up, eyes wide open and smiling as you meet others. [March music.]

5.2 Some of you may want to make up a marching dance with another person. Work together to decide when to change directions. End with a big salute to your partner as a thank you! Find a person with whom you can work safely and quietly and begin. [Let students choose march music with a moderate or fast tempo. Rotate among partners, asking questions and reinforcing quality movement responses.]

5.3 [Invite half of the class to share their dances, then reverse roles.] Audience, observe for partners who move with the beat and show fantastic focus when changing directions. You should not have to guess where partners are going next—their eyes and body facing will clearly show the way!

Unit 2

Rising, Sinking, Changing Directions and Pathways

4 or 5 lessons

FOCUS

Rising and sinking to musical phrases while changing directions, pathways, and expressing characters

MOTOR CONTENT

Selected from Theme 1—Introduction to the Body and Theme 3—Introduction to Space

Body

Locomotor activities—walking, running, hopping, skipping
Nonlocomotor activities—rising and sinking

Space

Levels—high, low (deep)
Directions—up, down, forward, backward, sideways
Pathways—floor (straight, zigzag, circling)

OBJECTIVES

In this unit, children will (or should be willing to try to) meet these objectives:

- Demonstrate rising and sinking actions while traveling in different directions and changing pathways (reflects National Standards in Dance 1a, 1b).
- Move to drum rhythms and musical phrases of four- and eight-beat durations (reflects National Standard in Dance 1f).
- Create a small group dance in time with the music by improvising rising and sinking actions while traveling forward and backward in straight and curved pathways (reflects National Standards in Dance 1e, 2b).
- Understand they can slow down or speed up their rising and sinking actions by tightening or releasing muscular tension to control the force of gravity.
- Change the mood of their dances by varying locomotor and nonlocomotor movement to invent and portray different characters (reflects National Standard in Dance 2c).

EQUIPMENT AND MATERIALS

Drum or tambourine; musical Selection A—"Seven Steps" or other piano arrangement, Selection B—"Bingo." (Substitute other 4/4 music with a moderate walking tempo or challenge children with 2/4 music using slow running steps.)

LEARNING EXPERIENCES

1.0 [Designate a small dance area to sustain a group focus, encouraging cooperation.] Find your own space and sit down, ready to listen. Together, let's all move one hand. Slowly lift a hand up above your head and carefully let it fall. Lift it up and let it fall again. Imagine you are in a slow-motion movie. Keep lifting one hand with me, then letting it slowly, gently fall. Feel your hand rising and falling. [Repeat, alternating hands.]

Focus on the body part that is rising and sinking. Watch it go high and sink low.

1.1 Slowly lift a different body part up and let it sink or drift down all the way to the floor. [Observe and name body parts used.] Again and again, make each part rise slowly, then let it sink.

1.2 Let's change speeds. Lift a body part quickly and let it sink fast. Fast, but quiet sinking. Be careful not to let the body part drop on the floor. Tighten your muscles a bit to make the body part rise and sink at the speed you want. Explore many ways one body part can rise and sink fast . . . change . . . try a different body part . . . another body part . . . change again . . . on your own, keep changing body parts.

1.3 Focus on the body part that is rising and sinking. Watch it go high and sink low. Don't watch me. Keep your eyes glued on your moving body part.

1.4 In your own space, rise and sink with the sounds of the drum and my voice. Ready? 'Rise, 2, 3, 4, 5, 6, 7, hold; sink, 2, 3, 4, 5, 6, 7, hold.' [Tap a moderate to quick, even beat, softly repeating cues and counts. After three or four times, omit verbal cues and accent beat one. See if children change the direction of their rising and sinking on the accented beats.]

1.5 [Familiarize yourself with the fast, steady walking tempo and phrasing of music A or the moderate tempo of B. You'll introduce the music in 1.7. For now, tap a steady, even walking rhythm, accenting the first beat of the eight-beat phrase. Tap slowly at first while children combine walking with rising and sinking; then gradually increase up to tempo of the music.] Let's walk with the beat while you rise and sink. Crouch down in a low position close to the floor. *Ready?* 'Rise, walk, walk, walk, walk, walk, walk, hold; *sink,* walk, walk, walk, walk, walk, walk, hold.'

1.6 In this dance, it is very important to listen to the drum and to change your rising and sinking with the strong, loud beat. If you are counting to yourself, that change comes right with beat number one. Try it again, making your rising action last seven beats and hold on count eight. Then make your sinking action last seven beats and hold on eight.

1.7 Let's spread away from each other to the outer edges of our dance space. Everybody face the center circle and crouch down low, ready to begin. [Join in this informal circle dance.] Take small steps forward. Gradually, 'Rise, walk, walk, walk, walk, walk, walk, hold; back out—sink, walk, walk, walk, walk, walk, walk, hold.' [Tap a quick, walking tempo in eight-beat phrases, accenting the first beat. Say, "Rise" or "Sink" alternately on the first beat of each phrase. Repeat until up to tempo with the music, then add music.]

1.8 With the music and drumbeat, move into and back out of the center circle, looking up and out into space as you rise and looking down low as you sink.

1.9 Listen carefully to the music. You will hear the length of the phrases change. Some phrases are eight beats long, others are four. On the longer [eight-beat] phrases, you will rise and sink as you move forward and backward, in and out, of the center. Everyone take your low starting position away from, but still facing, the center. [Put on music selection A or B and quickly rejoin the group in a large, informal circle formation. Dance with the children and count and cue.] Ready? 'Forward [walk rising], 2, 3, 4, 5, 6, 7, hold; backward [walk sinking], 3, 4, 5, 6, 7, hold; forward, 2, 3, hold, backward, 2, 3, hold; forward [walk rising], 2, 3, 4, 5, 6, 7, hold; forward, 2, 3, hold, backward, 2, 3, hold; forward [walk rising], 2, 3, 4, 5, 6, 7, hold.' [Repeat the entire sequence two or three times with cues, then ask the children to try it without cues. When using music selection B, substitute "sinking and rising in place" during the last five measures. Call out "B" (sink); "I" (rise); "N" (sink); "G" (rise); "O" (jump).]

2.0 Walk over and face someone. Now, turn and walk over to face someone else. Again, leave that person and walk up to another person. This person will be your partner. Let's make a large double circle facing clockwise. [See diagram below.] The two of you stand side by side and take your low starting position. Be ready to rise with the music. [Play music and give cues.] 'Forward [walk rising], 2, 3, 4, 5, 6, 7, hold; backward [walk sinking], 2, 3, 4, 5, 6, 7, hold; forward 2, 3, hold, backward 2, 3, hold . . . and stop!' [Stop music.]

2.1 After you walk forward and back three steps, the two of you circle eight steps around. Try it. 'Circle, 2, 3, 4, 5, 6, 7, 8; now forward, 2, 3, 4, 5, 6, 7, 8.' [Count out and cue the whole sequence several times. Observe ways children choose to circle. Invite partners to demonstrate. Share and try out others' ideas.]

2.2 Let's add circling to our group dance! Remember, it comes after the three step phrases. From the beginning. Ready and, 'Forward, 2, 3, 4, 5, 6, 7, hold; backward, 2, 3, 4, 5, 6, 7, hold; forward, 2, 3, hold, backward, 2, 3, hold; circle, 2, 3, 4, 5, 6, 7, stop; forward, 2, 3, hold, backward, 2, 3, hold; circle, 2, 3, 4, 5, 6, 7, stop.' [Repeat sequence throughout the music. If using music selection B, remember to substitute rising and sinking in place during the last five measures. Children enjoy calling out letters for "Bingo."] 'B—sink, 2, 3; I—rise, 2, 3; N—sink; O—bend down and swing arms up to jump high into the air!'

2.3 All of us have learned an entire dance! I wonder what will happen if we change one small part of the dance to make it more challenging! Listen closely. On the words, 'Forward, 2, 3, hold, backward, 2, 3, hold,' let's make a zig and a zag in our pathway. Stand beside your partner. Zig by walking three steps diagonally forward [demonstrate], away from your partner, and hold [widening the space between you]. Now, zag by walking three steps diagonally forward toward each other again and hold. The two of you, zigging away diagonally and zagging to meet together, make a diamond pathway on the floor! [Practice several times without the music, always traveling forward in a clockwise direction to make diamond pathways.]

2.4 [With music.] Now, let's see if you can do the entire dance. Ready? 'Forward, 2, 3, 4, 5, 6, 7, hold; backward, 2, 3, 4, 5, 6, 7, hold; zig forward away [from partner], 2, 3, hold, zag forward toward [partner], 2, 3, hold; circle, 2, 3, 4, 5, 6, 7, stop; zig forward away, 2, 3, hold, zag forward toward, 2, 3, hold; circle, 2, 3, 4, 5, 6, 7, stop.' [Count or cue. If using music selection B, follow cues in 2.2.]

2.5 Think about walking with your best posture. Lift your chest and chin up high. Look up as you rise, lifting and stretching your arms to the sky. [Repeat entire dance.]

3.0 [Revisit this unit later in the school year and challenge children by substituting "running steps" for "walking steps" and "hops" for "holds." The following is an adaptation of the original "Seven Steps," an Austrian folkdance performed in German-speaking countries (Van Hagen, Dexter, and Williams 1951).] From the beginning, 'Run forward, 2, 3, 4, 5, 6, 7, hop; run backward, 2, 3, 4, 5, 6, 7, hop; zig forward [away from partner], 2, 3, hop, zag forward [toward partner], 2, 3, hop; skip in a circle, 2, 3, 4,

5, 6, 7, stop; zig forward, 2, 3, hop, zag forward, 2, 3, hop; circle, 2, 3, 4, 5, 6, 7, stop' [partner outside double circle moves up to meet a new partner].

3.1 When you zig away from your partner, begin with your outside foot. To zag toward each other, begin with your inside foot.

3.2 Vary your skipping [circling] by facing your partner holding hands or take a shoulder-waist position, as you circle around.

4.0 Join with another pair and sit down in your group of four, ready to listen [or have children work with a partner]. Think of a person, character, or object—either real or invented. Your group will perform your dance the way you think this person, character, or thing would dance it. Show us what you are thinking through your movement, not your voices. Get started as soon as you have your idea. [No music. Rotate to each group, observing progress. Offer suggestions for portrayals, if needed: ballerinas, clowns, campers, robots, space explorers, sports figures, entertainers, cartoon characters, sad people, happy people.] Discover many different ways to walk, run, hop, and skip while rising and sinking. How can you make your way of moving look special?

4.1 In dance, we can tell a story or something about a person, character, or object just by the way we move. We talk to the audience through our movement and expression [face and body]. We do this by *exaggeration*, which means we make our movement or expression *larger* than real life! For example, if you portray [show] 'sadness,' your whole body must show this feeling. Let's all try a simple 'walk, walk, walk, walk.' [Repeat, moving with the children]. Your chest, back, and arm movement must become big and heavy with sadness. Your legs and ankles must give and bend with each step because you are carrying the weight of the whole world.

4.2 How would you *exaggerate* movement to portray happiness? [Children demonstrate.] Yes! Your walking, running, or skipping steps would be bouncy and springy—alive with energy! Your rising might soar up to the sky and your sinking could drift down softly, resting only for a moment, ready to take off again! [Explore and invent new ways.]

4.3 As you work on your group dance, try to capture the feeling of your person, character, or thing. *Exaggerate* your walking or running steps and rising or sinking so the audience will clearly *see your movements* and *feel your expressions*. [Practice without, then with, the music.]

4.4 [Music.] As you work on your idea, be careful not to lose the musical phrases of your dance. Find ways to change directions or levels *every* four or eight counts. Move toward, away, above, or below your partner[s]. Move in front of your partner[s], behind, or side by side. You decide.

4.5 Let's sit down and share our dances. Children in the audience may want to guess what person, character, or object is performing the dance. [Children love performing on a stage or in a marked-off area of the room.]

4.6 [You may choose to have the children repeat learning experiences 4.0 to 4.5 another day without musical accompaniment, which would allow children to explore the concept of exaggeration more fully. They could make locomotor and nonlocomotor movements "larger" at different levels or while changing directions and pathways. Beginnings, pauses, and endings would come from the feeling of the movement phrase rather than the music. For example, a "sad dance" would likely have a slow beginning or ending and long pauses between some movements. A "happy dance" could begin or end suddenly and show many quick, pauses and flashes of movement!]

ASSESSMENT: DISCUSSION ON ATTITUDES AND PERCEPTIONS

After each group performs, allow time for guessing and brief supportive discussion, for example, "What did the movement tell us about the character?" How did this movement portrayal help us understand the story or feelings of the character?" "What was the mood of the dance?" "That's an idea we could explore more . . . " Informal conversations and dialogues can help teachers assess student's knowledge, understandings, and perceptions.

Unit 3

Creating Dance Phrases With Locomotor and Nonlocomotor Movements

4 or 5 lessons

FOCUS Combining action words into short dance phrases, contrasting locomotor and nonlocomotor movements

MOTOR CONTENT

Selected from Theme 1—Introduction to the Body, Theme 3—Introduction to Space, and Theme 4—The Flow of Movement

Body

Actions of body parts—applying force (pushing, pulling)
Locomotor activities—skipping, galloping, stepping, jumping
Nonlocomotor activities—balances, gestures, twisting, turning, spinning; curling, stretching, rising, sinking.

Effort

Time—sudden, sustained
Space—direct, indirect
Flow—bound, free

Space

Levels—high, medium, low (deep)
Extensions—small, large
Pathways—air, floor

OBJECTIVES

In this unit, children will (or should be willing to try to) meet these objectives:

- Combine action words into movement phrases accurately repeating their movements; then vary phrases by changing time, space, or flow qualities (reflects National Standard in Dance 2d).
- Begin to demonstrate kinesthetic awareness, concentration, and focus when combining and performing movement phrases (reflects National Standard in Dance 1g).
- Show a serious working attitude and performance posture.
- Identify three personal goals to improve themselves as dancers (reflects National Standard in Dance 6a).

EQUIPMENT AND MATERIALS

Drum or tambourine; action words printed on posterboard, a computer print-out, or projected on the wall (see p. 149); and 50 to 75 index cards for action words.

LEARNING EXPERIENCES

1.0 When I begin tapping my drum, *skip* about the room, filling all the empty spaces. Lift your knees high as you go and look for big, open spaces. [Tap a lively long-short, long-short, uneven rhythm. Always have children dance in bare feet or shoes—no socks.]

1.1 Still moving into empty spaces, try *galloping*. Great, you are covering the whole space and no one is near anyone else! Remember, to gallop, you keep one foot out in front, ahead of the other foot. [Beat an uneven rhythm and call changes of the lead foot *every* eight, six, or four steps.]

1.2 Let's change the action and travel at a different speed. [Beat a slow, even walking rhythm.] *Slowly* step with each drumbeat, moving away from others. Show careful, cautious stepping . . . afraid, frightened, or scared stepping. Look all around as you go—in front, behind, to the right-left [side to side].

1.3 Listen to the drum. Take one step with each beat. [Vary tempo to test response to the drumbeat.]

1.4 Slowly creep to a new space or follow someone if you like. Place each foot carefully. Stepping *slowly*.

1.5 Move your whole body up and down in a slow, careful way. Lift through the chest, lift up each arm. Stay alert and be ready to stop at any moment!

1.6 Now take a faster walk. [Tap quick, even beats.] Add some silly or excited steps. Join hands and walk with a friend if you like. Go for a merry walk! Or, walk alone and wave to others you pass by. What body parts can wave hello or good-bye?

1.7 As you walk quickly, move hands in small, squiggly ways . . . now draw *large*, curvy pathways in the air with your hands [head, elbows, shoulders, hips, and so on]. Try making curvy lines or pathways on the floor with your feet, weaving in and out of others as you pass by.

1.8 Alone this time, move quickly in one direction, then abruptly switch and run in another direction. It's a darting run! Listen for a loud drumbeat to tell you to switch. [Tap a quick 4/4 rhythm, accenting the fourth beat.] Ready and, '[Tap:] Run, [tap] run, [tap] run, [*tap*] change.' [Repeat many times.] Be careful of others.

1.9 As you dart from one place to the next, your feet are making zigzag patterns across the floor. Dust your feet with chalk. Off you go! Leave a zigzag trail or path wherever you go. [Divide class in half, taking turns darting in zigzag pathways.]

1.10 *Slow* down. Take a long walk and see what other imaginary lines your feet can draw along the floor. Explore all the surfaces of the feet—heels, toes, soles, sides.

1.11 This time, let's jump or leap across the floor when you hear the loud drumbeat. [Play an even 4/4 rhythm, accenting the fourth beat.] Ready and, 'Run, run, run, *jump*; run, run, run, *jump*.' [Repeat.] Listen to this phrase [tap four soft, then four *loud* beats]. Here we go: 'Walk, walk, walk, walk; *jump, jump, jump, jump*.' [Repeat. Have children invent their own combinations.]

1.12 Choose two or three traveling activities and put them into a short phrase. Say your words as you do them, especially when you switch to the second action word. [Repeat each phrase three or four times. For example, "creep slowly, run in a zigzag, and leap!"]

2.0 In your space, let's rise and sink slowly. Say each word as you do the action very *slowly*.

2.1 Try sinking very fast. This is called a fall or collapse and should only take one count. Make your whole body give way to gravity like a parachute landing softly—*whoosh*! Ready? [Pause to increase suspense, then beat drum *loudly*.] Collapse and *fall*! [Practice several times.] Drop and fall lightly all at once—*whoosh*!

2.2 In your own space, try twisting one way; then untwist and twist a new way! Another way?

2.3 Let your twist take you into a turn. If you speed up this turning action, what happens to your body? It spins, whirls, twirls around! See how many different body parts you can spin on [seat, back, front, feet, and so on]. How can you turn around on one foot . . . the other foot?

2.4 With both feet together, show small bounces or jumps. [Repeat, pausing to increase suspense.] Jump with one foot . . . now the other. Keep this hopping small and continuous. How long can you keep going? [Remind children to change feet when one foot gets tired. Encourage children to move forward while hopping, especially if they have difficulty hopping in place repeatedly.]

2.5 Take one body part and see if you can carefully touch or link it to another part. How else can body parts meet or greet each other? Go over, pass under, reach into spaces to touch, link, or grip. Now separate body parts, pulling *slowly* apart or pushing quickly away! Think of your body parts as magnets that attract and repel.

2.6 In your space, see if you can hold a frozen shape. Now hold a more difficult shape on a small or narrow part of the body. Balance carefully. [Explore different bases of support.] Tighten muscles to hold each shape firm. Try to balance for three slow counts before changing to a new balance. [Repeat many times.]

2.7 Choose a body part that you can shake. Shake it lightly. Shake it hard! Find a new body part that you can shake. [Repeat until all body parts are loosened up.]

2.8 Pretend that you have something special in your hand. Pull it close to you. Now you have to part with it. Throw it away! [Repeat.] Again, hide your treasure . . . pull it close, surrounding it with your whole body. Now open your body and throw your treasure into the air! Again, close! [Pause.] Open!

2.9 Take two actions you can do while staying in your own space and put them together into a short movement phrase. [Bend and stretch, push and pull, twist and turn, shake and freeze are great ideas!] Say your words as you do them. [Have some of the children share their movement phrases with the class.]

3.0 We have practiced locomotor words that travel and nonlocomotor words that stay in your spot. Today, let's put some of these actions together into longer sequences. I will say the words. You can repeat them after me. 'Rise, skip, turn, and sink.' [Children repeat words.] Now do each action as you repeat the words. [Combine action words from example on page 149 in a variety of ways to make up your own sequences.]

Locomotor	Nonlocomotor	
skip	rise	touch
gallop	sink	dab
slide	collapse	freeze
step	grow	balance
creep	push	pull
dart	turn	lay
leap	shake	bounce
jump	spin	burst
run	open	close

Action words.

3.1 Combine 'slide, spin, touch, and creep.' A movement sequence begins with an action [for example, slide] and ends with an action [for example, creep] or a still position. And there are movements in between.

3.2 Here's another movement sequence. 'Dart, balance, twist, and explode!' Say these words and then try them out. Watch where you are moving so you don't bump into anyone.

3.3 Are you ready for one more sequence? 'Pull, step, shake, and leap!' Give this a try, watching carefully where you leap.

3.4 I will print a movement sequence [word list printed on poster paper or projected on screen or wall]. Read the words carefully, then say and perform the actions on your own. [Repeat several times, then challenge children to create their own sequences from the action word list. Consult the classroom teacher to add movement words to this list.]

4.0 Join with one or two other children to make a small group. I'll give each group index cards with three or four action words written on them. Your group can make up a movement sequence from these words. Raise your hand if you need help reading the words or ask your reading partner [if different than movement partner].

4.1 Remember the order of your words and decide how you will perform each action—slowly or quickly, straight or curvy, flowing or carefully.

4.2 Mix up your action words. See if you can do them in a different order. How will you perform each word?

4.3 Who would like to show their movement sequence and let others guess what words are on your cards [paper]? Don't tell your words the first time. When others have guessed, do your movement sequence again and say the words. [Give all who wish an opportunity to share. This may be done as a class or within small groups.]

4.4 Exchange cards with a different group, reading action words to each other. Practice putting your new words into a movement sequence. [Provide adequate time for exploration, discussion, and repetition.] Why do some action sequences work better than others, or feel better while performing?

4.5 Using paper and pencil [or computer], write down several action words to tell a story. [Success with this task depends on maturity and past experiences of your class. Consult the classroom teacher who might reinforce movement vocabulary and concept development through this activity or another creative writing activity.] Bring your story to dance class and we'll practice creating and designing movement sequences.

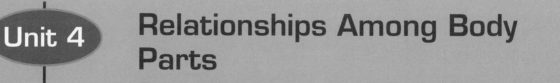

Relationships Among Body Parts

3 or 4 lessons

FOCUS | Changing the relationship of body parts while traveling and while staying in place

MOTOR CONTENT

Selected from Theme 1—Introduction to the Body, Theme 3—Introduction to Space, and Theme 5—Introduction to Relationships

Body

Locomotor—traveling (stepping, hopping, jumping, skipping, turning)

Relationships

Body parts—near to, far from, apart, together, meeting, parting, accompanied by music, percussion

OBJECTIVES

In this unit, children will (or should be willing to try to) meet these objectives:

- Change the relationship of body parts by bringing them near to each other (together or close to the body) or by taking them far from each other (apart or away from the body) (reflects National Standard in Dance 1a).
- Create a dance sequence, alone and with partner(s), combining traveling and pausing with body parts moving together and apart (reflects National Standards in Dance 2a, 2e).
- Understand that by changing the relationship of body parts, they create different body shapes and ways of traveling (reflects National Standard in Dance 2c).
- Accept responsibility for maintaining personal space while moving in place and while moving independently about the room, away from others (reflects National Standard in Dance 1d).
- Observe and perform confidently adaptations of folkdances (using resources in the local community); and describe their cultural or historical context (reflects National Standards in Dance 5a, 5b).

EQUIPMENT AND MATERIALS

Tambourine or other instrument capable of making percussive and sustained sounds (e.g., Mexican guiro, tone or wood block, rap stick, or claves [sharp percussion]); handle castanets, maracas, or shakers (sustained sounds); recording of "La Raspa," a New Mexican folkdance. *Optional:* Additional dance selections, such as Latin music or "Mexican Mixer," a traditional Mexican folkdance.

LEARNING EXPERIENCES

1.0 Let's begin by stretching our hands and feet apart in a very *wide* shape. Slowly bring your hands and feet together to make a new shape. As I tap the tambourine softly, slowly extend body parts apart. Here we go: '[Tap:] Apart, [tap] apart, [tap] apart, [tap] apart; [tap] now together, [tap] together, [tap] together.' [Repeat several times.]

1.1 Every time you separate your body parts, try hard to reach a full stretch. Show *wide* extensions that reach out. [Continue tapping and counting a 4/4 rhythm.]

1.2 From very long, narrow, stretched-out shapes, bend at your waist and bring your hands and feet near, or close together. [Repeat a few times.]

1.3 Begin in very small, curled shapes. Show how you can stretch way out from these compact body shapes. Stretch *all* your body parts. Way out! Now back to a tight, small shape. Keep trying these as I tap the tambourine. 'Stretch *wide*, 2, 3, keep going, 5, 6, 7, 8; and shrink back in, 2, 3, 4, 5, 6, 7, 8; [and so on].'

1.4 From a tight, curled-up shape, select two different body parts and stretch them far apart, then return to a compact shape. Keep showing two different body parts each time you stretch out. [Tap tambourine at a steady pace, repeating cues in 1.3 many times.]

1.5 Right where you are, change the relationship of your feet with each tap of my tambourine [even beats]. '[Tap:] Bring feet close together; [tap] take feet far apart. Meet and part, meet and part. Apart, together, meet and part.'

1.6 [Select a child using feet in a variety of ways, who is staying with the beat.] Everyone, name each relationship [Gary] makes with his feet: 'Apart, together, crossed, together.' Try to make your changes crystal clear so we can name the relationships you make with your feet. [Have children explore and invent movements. Then take turns demonstrating while a partner names relationships of the feet.] Teach your favorite pattern to your partner [or another set of partners]. See if you can change the relationship of your feet on every tap.

2.0 [Tap a steady tempo on the tambourine.] Travel about the room, changing the relationship of your feet with the beat. Step or jump on every beat!

2.1 Say out loud the relationship your feet are making with every tap of the tambourine.

2.2 See how each of you can make up and repeat a simple, short dance by changing the relationship of your feet as you travel. For example, 'Leap apart, apart, apart, and jump, landing with feet together.' Or, 'With feet together, jump, jump, jump, then a *big jump*, landing with feet apart!' [Encourage children to keep repeating their combinations or patterns.]

2.3 Every single time your feet land, try to touch the floor as softly as a cat. Make your ankles give as you land softly and bend your knees to absorb the shock of landing. [Steady beat.]

2.4 As you travel, change the relationship of your arms or other body parts. Can you reach wide with the arms, now bring them in close to your body? [Repeat.] 'Far away, near. Apart, close together.'] Now think of your own changes.

Watch your partners and give names to the changing relationships of their feet.

HOPSCOTCH

Besides dancing at home, you can practice hopping, jumping, and leaping by playing games of hopscotch. On a sidewalk or blacktop area where you are allowed, draw with chalk/stone various boxes or shapes. Include some changes of direction and holding still balances, too. You might like to try a hopscotch game from Bolivia, El Salvador, or Honduras (see Lankford, 1992 for instructions).

2.5 [Tap a steady jogging pace, accenting the first of eight beats, repeating cues several times.] As you travel, every time you hear the *loud* beat, change the relationship of your arms or feet. '*Change*, 2, 3, 4, 5, 6, 7, 8.'

2.6 I will tap a steady beat. Looking for and moving into empty spaces, show several of your favorite ways to take hands, arms, feet, or other body parts far apart and close together.

3.0 [Accompany by repeating two different sounds on the same instrument.] When you hear this sound [shake tambourine or scrape guiro], travel, keeping your feet close together. On the loud *tap*, freeze in a very *wide*, spread-out shape. Really separate all those body parts.

3.1 Show the audience a clear change in the relationship of your feet when traveling and while pausing. [Accompany as in 3.0.]

3.2 Make up a short dance combination by changing the relationship of your feet with every beat. Say the relationships you are creating out loud.

3.3 Design a short dance on the spot with body parts meeting and parting. Let's take four counts to separate body parts, then four counts to bring parts together. Some of you may want to choose different body parts with each phrase of four counts. [Keep accompaniment steady, tapping four beats to take body parts far apart, then four beats of shaking or scraping to bring body parts close together. Repeat, "Part, 2, 3, 4, meet, 2, 3, 4, (and so on)," to help children extend their actions over the full four beats.]

3.4 Listen carefully to the instrument and work hard to match your meeting and parting actions to the tempo. Take four full counts to complete each meeting or parting action.

3.5 [Tap a steady beat.] Travel throughout all empty spaces for 16 counts, then stop and, on the spot, change the relationship of your feet [or other body parts] for 4 counts. 'So we travel, [count to 16] and now change, change, change, change.' [Systematically observe children during learning experiences 3.0 to 3.5 and 4.0 to 4.4 and record performance levels.]

ASSESSING USE OF RELATIONSHIPS AND RHYTHM				
Class list	Moves in time to 4/4 rhythm.	Varies relationships of feet with each drum tap.	Changes relationships in time to accents.	Combines moving and holding in time to music patterns.
Alesia B.	3	1	3	3
Bryant C.	2	2	3	3

Scale: 5 = 90% or more   4 = 65-80%   3 = 40-60%   2 = 20-35%   5 = less than 10%

4.0 [Play "La Raspa" music. The first 16 counts make up the chorus followed by a 16-count verse. Have children listen for the definite change in music and raise their hand immediately after count 16 to signal the change. Repeat, listening again.] Let's try moving to the first 16 counts. [Accompany music by tapping a tambourine or guiro.] Ready? Eight counts to go: 'Wait, two, [count to eight]. And change [feet apart], change [feet together], change [feet apart], hold; change [feet together], change [feet apart], change [feet together], hold.' Repeat this 8-count phrase for a total of 16 counts. We'll call this the chorus or part A.

4.1 Now travel with light, lively steps and jumps all about the dance area. This is verse B and takes 16 counts. Try to cover as much space as you can safely . . . really enjoy all the open spaces!

4.2 Let's see if we can combine the chorus and verse. [Play music and repeat this simple version of "La Raspa." Emphasize clear changes of relationships with the feet [or other body parts] while dancing on the spot, and spontaneous steps and jumps while traveling. Once children become familiar with the chorus and first verse, move onto learning experience 4.3.]

4.3 Let's combine our chorus of 'feet apart and together' with different verses or ways of traveling. ["La Raspa" is a New Mexican dance originating from the Spanish colonial period and is performed in rondo form ABACADA. A is the chorus and B, C, and D are verses. Each verse is slightly different from the other and all are considerably different from A. The following adaptation of this folkdance emphasizes creative movement responses. To begin, divide class into three groups with everyone in their own space. Follow the rondo form outlined on page 155, beginning with all children taking feet apart and together for 16 counts.]

A   Chorus: *Whole class* dances in place, while you cue, *and* 'Apart, and together, and apart, and hold; and together, and apart, and hold.' Repeat this eight-count phrase four times (for 16 counts). Accompany with percussion [sharp taps] if you wish.

B   First verse: *Group one* travels about the dance area with steps, jumps, skips, turns, and the like to cover space with free-flowing movement. (16 counts. Shake or scrape instrument.) Groups two and three hold still.

A   Repeat chorus.

C   Second verse: *Group two* travels in their dance area with high-stepping hops, jumps, and leaps to sounds of the horn played in the music (16 counts). Groups one and three hold still.

A   Repeat chorus.

D   Third verse: *Group three* dances about freely, snapping or clicking fingers, clapping hands, slapping thighs, and so on (16 counts). Groups one and two hold still.

A   Repeat chorus.

Note: The music continues with a fourth verse, the chorus, a fifth verse; then, ends with three strong beats. Everyone dances to the last two verses, showing their own variations.

Children perform their own movement variations to mariachi music while others enjoy watching the dancing. Everyone has a turn to show their dance.

4.4 Repeat 4.3, asking children to create new or different movements for verses *B*, *C*, and *D* and their own surprise endings (with a partner or in small groups). They enjoy performing their dances, adding costume accessories, such as bright paper streamers or scarves in hand; wearing colorful bands, belts, or hats; or playing rhythm instruments, such as handle castanets, tambourines, maracas, or shakers.]

4.5 [Weave historical facts, traditions, stories, costumes, and art into this unit to extend unit objectives. Invite a parent or community member who is of South or Central American origin to demonstrate a traditional folkdance or to play a mariachi band instrument to which children can dance spontaneously. May 5 is Cinco de Mayo (Sin-koh day my-yoh), or Mexican Independence Day, celebrated by parades and festivities, highlighting the customs, national flag, foods, games, and dances of Mexico. Each Latin American country celebrates historical and cultural events through indigenous songs, folkdance, and plays, providing unique opportunities for student learning. Extend this unit in third to sixth grades by exploring authentic and traditional dances of Latin America.]

Appendixes

APPENDIX A: CONTENT STANDARDS IN PHYSICAL EDUCATION

A physically educated person

1. Demonstrates competency in many movement forms and proficiency in a few movement forms.

2. Applies movement concepts and principles to the learning and development of motor skills.

3. Exhibits a physically active lifestyle.

4. Achieves and maintains a health-enhancing level of physical fitness.

5. Demonstrates responsible personal and social behavior in physical activity settings.

6. Demonstrates understanding and respect for differences among people in physical activity settings.

7. Understands that physical activity provides opportunities for enjoyment, challenge, self-expression, and social interaction.

Reprinted from Moving into the future: National standards for physical education, 1995, with permission from the National Association for Sport and Physical Education (NASPE). Requests for permission to reprint can be sent to NASPE, 1900 Association Drive, Reston, VA 20191. [This source provides an introduction to the rationale underlying National Standards, descriptions of content standards, sample benchmarks, and assessment examples for Kindergarten through Grade 12.]

APPENDIX B: CONTENT STANDARDS IN DANCE (FOR CHILDREN IN GRADES K-4)

The National Standards for Arts Education are a statement of what every young American should know and be able to do in four arts disciplines—dance, music, theatre, and the visual arts (p. 131). Two different types of standards are used to guide assessment of student learning and program goals: (p. 18).

- Content standards specify what students should know and be able to do in the arts disciplines.
- Achievement standards specify understandings and levels of achievement that students are expected to attain in the competencies, for each of the arts, at the completion of grades 4, 8, and 12.

1. Content Standard: Identifying and demonstrating movement elements and skills in performing dance
2. Content Standard: Understanding choreographic principles, processes, and structures
3. Content Standard: Understanding dance as a way to create and communicate meaning
4. Content Standard: Applying and demonstrating critical and creative thinking skills in dance
5. Content Standard: Demonstrating and understanding dance in various cultures and historical periods
6. Content Standard: Making connections between dance and healthful living
7. Content Standard: Making connections between dance and other disciplines

Reprinted with permission of the National Dance Association from: Consortium of National Arts Education Associations (1994). *National Standards for Arts Education: What Every Young American Should Know and Be Able to Do in the Arts. Dance, Music, Theatre, Visual Arts*. Reston, VA: Music Educators National Conference, pp. 23-25. (For a rationale, description, and clarification of the National Standards in Dance, including Achievement Standards "a" through "h," write the National Dance Association, 1900 Association Drive, Reston, Virginia 20191).

References

The following references are from the Preface and the Introduction.

Barrett, K. R. (1984a). Educational dance. In B. J. Logsdon, K. R. Barrett, M. Ammons, M. R. Broer, L. E. Halverson, R. McGee & M. A. Roberton, *Physical education for children* (2nd ed., pp. 144-192). Philadelphia, PA: Lea & Febiger.

Barrett, K. R. (1984b). Educational games. In B. J. Logsdon, K. R. Barrett, M. Ammons, M. R. Broer, L. E. Halverson, R. McGee & M. A. Roberton, *Physical education for children* (2nd ed., pp. 193-240). Philadelphia, PA: Lea & Febiger.

Consortium of National Arts Education Associations. (1994). *National standards for arts education: What every young American should know and be able to do in the arts (dance, music, theater, visual arts).* Reston, VA: Music Educators National Conference (MENC). (Also see National Dance Association, 1994, below)

Logsdon, B. J. (1984a). Creating materials for teaching. In B. J. Logsdon, K. R. Barrett, M. Ammons, M.R. Broer, L. E. Halverson, R. McGee & M. A. Roberton, *Physical education for children* (2nd ed., pp. 422-454). Philadelphia, PA: Lea & Febiger.

Logsdon, B. (1984b). Educational gymnastics. In B. J. Logsdon, K. R. Barrett, M. Ammons, M. R. Broer, L. E. Halverson, R. McGee & M. A. Roberton, *Physical education for children* (2nd ed., pp. 241-294). Philadelphia, PA: Lea & Febiger.

Logsdon, B. J., & Barrett, K. R. (1984). Movement—the content of physical education. In B. J. Logsdon, K. R. Barrett, M. Ammons, M. R. Broer, L. E. Halverson, R. McGee & M. A. Roberton, *Physical education for children* (2nd ed., pp. 123-143). Philadelphia, PA: Lea & Febiger.

McGee, R. (1984). Evaluation of processes and products. In B. J.

Logsdon, K. R. Barrett, M. Ammons, M.R. Broer, L. E. Halverson, R. McGee & M. A. Roberton, *Physical education for children* (2nd ed., pp. 356-421). Philadelphia, PA: Lea & Febiger.

National Association for Sport and Physical Education (NASPE) Standards and Assessment Task Force. (1995). *Moving into the future: National physical education standards: A guide to content and assessment.* St. Louis: Mosby.

National Dance Association (NDA). (1994). *National standards for dance education.* Reston, VA: American Alliance for Health, Physical Education, Recreation & Dance (AAHPERD).

Preston-Dunlop, V. (1980). *A handbook for modern educational dance.* London: Macdonald and Evans. (Original work published 1963) (1990 ed. published, Boston: Plays)

Russell, J. (1975). *Creative dance in the primary school* (2nd ed.). London: Macdonald & Evans. (Original work published 1965)

Suggested Readings

The following sources relate to the Introduction.

Allison, P. (Ed.). (1994). *Echoes II: Influences in elementary physical education.* Reston, VA: American Alliance for Health, Physical Education, Recreation & Dance (AAHPERD).

Council on Physical Education for Children (COPEC). (1992). *Developmentally appropriate physical education practices for children.* [Position paper]. Reston, VA: National Association for Sport and Physical Education (NASPE).

Jewett, A. E., Bain, L.L., & Ennis, D. D. (1995). *The curriculum process in physical education.* Dubuque, IA: Brown and Benchmark.

Laban, R. (1975). *Modern educational dance* (3rd ed., revised by L. Ullman). Great Britain: The Chaucer Press, Ltd. (Original work published 1947, Macdonald & Evans) (1990 ed. published, Plymouth, UK: Northcoate House, distributed in U.S. by State Mutual Book and Periodical Service, 5th Ave. 17th Floor, New York, NY 10175 Tel 212 682 5844).

Melograno, V. J. (1996). *Designing the physical education curriculum* (3rd ed.). Champaign, IL: Human Kinetics.

National Association for Sport and Physical Education (NASPE) Motor Development Task Force. (1994). *Looking at physical education from a developmental perspective: A guide to teaching.* [Position paper]. Reston, VA: NASPE & American Alliance for Physical Education, Recreation & Dance (AAHPERD).

Silverman, S. J., & Ennis, C. D. (1996). *Student learning in physical education: Applying research to enhance instruction.* Champaign, IL: Human Kinetics.

RESOURCES FOR UNIT PLANS

Suggested Readings

Belka, D. (1994). *Teaching children games: Becoming a master teacher.* Champaign, IL: Human Kinetics.

Bennett, J. P., & Riemer, P. C. (1995). *Rhythmic activities and dance.* Champaign, IL: Human Kinetics.

Boorman, J. (1969). *Creative dance in the first three grades.* New York, NY: David McKay.

Boorman, J. (1973). *Dance and language experiences with children.* Don Mills, Ontario: Longman Canada Limited.

Buschner, C. A. (1994). *Teaching children movement concepts and skills.* Champaign, IL: Human Kinetics.

Clements, R. (1995). *My neighborhood movement challenges: Narratives, games, and stunts for ages three through eight years.* Reston, VA: American Alliance for Health, Physical Education, Recreation & Dance (AAHPERD).

Diamondstein, G. (1971). *Children dance in the classroom.* New York: The Macmillan Company.

Diem, L. (1986). *The important early years.* Reston, VA: American Alliance of Health, Physical Education, Recreation and Dance.

Doolittle, S.A., & K.T. Girard. (1991). A dynamic approach to teaching games in elementary physical education. *Journal of Physical Education, Recreation & Dance 62* (4).

Engel, B. S. (1995). *Considering children's art: Why and how to value their works.* Washington, DC: National Association for the Education of Young Children (NAEYC).

Franck, M., G. Graham, H. Lawson, T. Loughery, R. Ritson, M. Sanborn, & V. Seefeldt. (1991). *Outcomes of quality physical education programs.* Reston, VA: National Association for Sport and Physical Education (NASPE).

Graham, G. (1992). *Teaching children physical education: Becoming a master teacher.* Champaign, IL: Human Kinetics.

Graham, G., Holt/Hale, S., & Parker, M. (1993). *Children moving: A reflective approach to teaching physical education* (3rd edition). Mountain View, CA: Mayfield.

Grant, J. M. (1995). *Shake, rattle, and learn: Classroom-tested ideas that use movement for active learning.* York, Maine: Stenhouse.

Halverson, L., & M. Roberton. (1984). Developing children—Their changing movement. In *Physical education for children: A focus on the teaching process,* 2d ed., ed. B.J. Logsdon. Philadelphia: Lea & Febiger.

Hammett, C. T. (1992). *Movement activities for early childhood.* Champaign, IL: Human Kinetics.

Hellison, D. (1995). *Teaching responsibility through physical education.* Champaign, IL: Human Kinetics.

Herman, J.L., P.R. Aschbacher, & L. Winters. (1991). *A practical guide to alternative assessment.* Alexandria, VA: Association for Supervision and Curriculum Development.

Hopple, C.J. (1995). *Teaching for outcomes in elementary physical education: A guide for curriculum and assessment.* Champaign, IL: Human Kinetics.

Hopper, C., Munoz, K., & Fisher, B. (1996). *Health-related fitness for grades 1 and 2.* Champaign, IL: Human Kinetics.

Logsdon, B., K. Barrett, M. Ammons, M. Broer, L. Halverson, R. McGee, & M.A. Roberton. (1984). *Physical education for children: A focus on the teaching process.* 2d ed. Philadelphia: Lea & Febiger.

Luxbacher, J.A. (1995). *Soccer: Steps to success.* (2nd edition) Champaign, IL: Human Kinetics.

Luxbacher, J.A. (1991). *Teaching soccer: Steps to success.* Champaign, IL: Leisure Press.

Lankford, Mary D. (1992). *Hopscotch around the world.* New York: Morrow Junior Books.

Mauldon, E., & Redfern, H. B. (1969). *Games teaching: A new approach for the primary school.* London: Macdonald & Evans Ltd.

McCaslin, N. (1996). Movement and rhythms. In N. McCaslin, *Creative Drama in the classroom and beyond* (2nd ed., pp. 53-71). White Plains, NY: Longman.

Morris, D., & Stiehl, J. (1989). *Changing kids' games* (2nd ed.). Champaign, IL: Human Kinetics.

National Association for Sport and Physical Education (NASPE) Motor Development Task Force. (1994). *Looking at physical education from a developmental perspective: A guide to teaching.* [Position paper]. Reston, VA: NASPE & American Alliance for Physical Education, Recreation & Dance (AAHPERD).

National Dance Association (NDA). (1994). *National standards for dance education.* Reston, VA: American Alliance for Health, Physical Education, Recreation & Dance (AAHPERD).

National Dance Association (NDA). (1996). *Dance education: What is it? Why is it important?* Reston, VA: American Alliance for Health, Physical Education, Recreation & Dance (AAHPERD).

Pate, R.R., & R.C. Hohn, eds. (1994). *Health and fitness through physical education.* Champaign, IL: Human Kinetics.

Perrone, V. (Ed.) (1991). *Expanding student assessment.* Alexandria, VA: Association for Supervision and Curriculum Development.

Preston, V. (1963). *A handbook for modern education dance.* London: Macdonald & Evans.

Preston-Dunlop, V. (1980). *A handbook for modern educational dance.* 2d ed. Boston: Plays.

Purcell, T. (1994). *Teaching children dance: Becoming a master teacher.* Champaign, IL: Human Kinetics.

Ratliffe, R., & Ratliffe, L. M. (1994). *Teaching children fitness: Becoming a master teacher.* Champaign, IL: Human Kinetics.

Rink, J.E. (1993). *Teaching physical education for learning.* 2d ed. St. Louis: Mosby.

Rowen. B. (1994). *Dance and grow: Developmental dance activities for three-through eight-year-olds.* Pennington, NJ: Princeton.

Russell, J. (1975). *Creative dance in the primary school* (2nd ed.). London: Macdonald & Evans.

Stanley, S. (1969). *Physical education—A movement approach.* 2d ed. Toronto: McGraw-Hill of Canada.

Stinson, S. (1988). *Dance for children: Finding the magic in movement.* Reston, VA: American Alliance for Health, Physical Education, Recreation & Dance (AAHPERD).

Wall, J., & Murray, N. (1994). *Children and movement: Physical education in the elementary school* (2nd edition). Madison: Brown & Benchmark.

Werner, P. H. (1994). *Teaching children gymnastics: Becoming a master teacher.* Champaign, IL: Human Kinetics.

Williams, H.G. (1984). *Perceptual and motor development.* Englewood Cliffs, NJ: Prentice-Hall.

Young, J., Klesius, S., & Hoffman, H. (1994). *Meaningful movement: A developmental theme approach to physical education for children.* Madison, WI: Brown & Benchmark.

Books for Children

Kellogg, Steven. (1995). *Pecos bill.* New York, NY: Morrow. (Also [Narrated by Robin Williams, with music by Ry Cooder]. On [CD] WD-0709, or [CS] WT-0709 (1990). New York, NY: Windham Hill/Rabbit Ears Productions, distr. by BMG)

McDermott, G. (1977). *Arrow to the sun: A Pueblo indian tale.* New York: Puffin Books. (Originally published 1974 Viking).

Sharman, L. M. (1994). *The Amazing book of shapes.* New York: Dorling Kindersley Publishing.

Piano Music

Listed by composer, musician or song/album title.

Karp, D. Spider Dance. In *The Alfred Signature Series* (piano sheet music, 1993). Van Nuys, California: Alfred Publishing Company.

Palmer, W., Manus, M., & Lethco, A. Square Dance, Red River Valley, & Oh! Susanna! In *Alfred's Basic Piano Library, Piano Lesson Book Level 2* (piano arr., 1992, pp. 31, 40-41, 45). Van Nuys, California: Alfred. (Recorded 'round and square dance' music is available from educational and physical education supply companies)

*Schumann, R. Soldier's March from *Album for the Young.* In J. Bastien, *First Piano Repertoire Album* (1981, pp. 26-27). San Diego, CA: Kjos West.

Schumann, R. The Wild Horseman. In J. Bastien, *First Piano Repertoire Album* (1981, pp. 28-29). San Diego, CA: Kjos West.

*Also available on Silver Burdett Ginn's *The Music Connection* 1995 series, Morristown, NJ, and other leading music education resources. [Ask the music teacher in your school for a piano or instrumental version of this music.]

Recorded Music

Listed by composer, musician or song/album title.

Bartok, B. Vol. I., No. 1 Allegro "Children at Play"; Vol. I, No. 4 Allegro "Pillow Dance"; and Vol I. No. 10 Allegro motto "Children's Dance" [Recorded by Zoltan Kocsis]. On *For Children* [CD] HCD 12304 (1994). Hungary: Hungaroton Classic LTD. (Recorded 1980)

Bartok, B. Volume III, Nos. 1 & 2 Allegro and Andante [Recorded by Zoltan Kocsis] On *For Children* [CD] HCD 12304 (1994). Hungary: Hungaroton Classic LTD. (Recorded 1980)

Bartok, B. Volume II, No. 29 Allegro Scherzando "Pentatonic Tune" [Recorded by Zoltan Kocsis]. On *For Children* [CD] HCD 12304(1994). Hungary: Hungaroton Classic LTD. (Recorded 1980)

Bartok, B. Volume II, No. 31 Andante Tranquillo [Recorded by Zoltan Kocsis]. On *For Children* [CD] HCD 12304 (1994). Hungary: Hungaroton Classic LTD. (Recorded 1980)

Bartok, B. Volume III, No 15 Molto Tranquillo "Bagpipe" [Recorded by Zoltan Kocsis]. On *For Children* [CD] HCD 12304(1994). Hungary: Hungaroton Classic LTD. (Recorded 1980)

Bingo [Recorded by Merit Audio Visual]. On *Folk Dances from Near and Far* [CS] Catalogue No. MAV 1043; also on [7" 45 rpm record] Catalogue No. A7S-2. Available: Wagon Wheel Records and Books, 17191 Corbina Lane #203, Huntington Beach, CA 92649 Tel 1-714-846-8169. (Also available on [7" 45 rpm record] Catalogue No. 1189; and on *Folk Dances Near and Far #3* [LP or CS] from Folkraft Records and Tapes, P.O. Box 404, Florham Park, New Jersey 07932 Tel 1-201-377-1885)

*Brahms, J. S. Hungarian Dance, No. 5, and Hungarian Dance No. 6. On *Brahm's Greatest Hits* [CD] RCA Victor 60843-2 (1991). New York, NY: RCA Victor, distr. by BMG. (Also see Hungarian Dance No. 5 on *Greatest Hits Sampler* [CD] 60896-2-RV (1991). New York, NY: RCA Victor, distr. by BMG) (Also see Hungarian Dance No. 6 on *The Music Connection**)

Danses espagnoles, and Ritual Fire Dance [Recorded by Katia and Marielle Labeque]. On *Espana!* [CD] Philips 438 938-2PH (1994). London: Philips Classics (dist. in US by Polygram Classics, New York, NY).

*Greig, E. Morning, Act 4 from *Peer Gynt Suite* [Recorded by James Galway]. On *Seasons* [CD] Catalogue No. 51828 or [CS] Catalogue No. 51829. Available: Public Radio MusicSource, *Classics*, Minnesota Communications Group, P.O. Box 64502, St. Paul, Minnesota 55164-0502 Tel 1-800-949-9999.

*Kabalevsky, D. *Comedian's* Galop [Recorded by San Diego Chamber Orch]. On *The Comedians Suite, Op 26* [CD] KIC 7042-2 or [CS] 7042-4 (1991). Port Washington, NY: Koch International Classics. (Also available on *Adventures in Music*, Grade 3, Vol 2 [LP] from Folkraft Records and Tapes, P.O. Box 404, Florham Park, New Jersey 07932 Tel 1-201-377-1885)

*Kabalevsky, D. March [Recorded by San Diego Chamber Orch]. On *The Comedians Suite, Op 26* [CD] KIC 7042-2 or [CS] 7042-4 (1991). Port Washington, NY: Koch International Classics. (Also available on *Adventures in Music*, Grade 3, Vol 2 [LP] from Folkraft Records and Tapes, P.O. Box 404, Florham Park, New Jersey 07932 Tel 1-201-377-1885)

*La Bamba [Recorded by Trini Lopez]. On *La Bamba* [CD] K-tel Latin 3514 or [CS] 3514 (1995). Plymouth, MN: K-tel International USA.

La Macarena [Recorded by Los Del Rio]. On *La Macarena Mix* [CS] Cerdisco (1995). Ariola, South America: EMSA [BMG] Argentina.

*La Raspa. On *Rhythmically Moving 3* [Produced by Phyllis Weikart] [LP, CS or CD]. Available: High/Scope Press, 600 North River Street, Yipsilanti, MI 48198 Tel 1-313-485-2000. (Also on *Folk Dances from Near and Far* [Produced by Merit Audio Visual] [CS] Catalogue No. MAV 1043C; and on *Folk Dances from 'Round the World Vol. 1* [LP] Catalogue No. RPT LP 106 available from Wagon Wheel Records and Books, 17191 Corbina Lane #203, Huntington Beach, CA 92649 Tel 1-714-846-8169) (Also available on [7" 45 rpm record] Catalogue No. 1457 and [LP or CS] Catalogue No. 3 *Folk Dances Near and Far* from Folkraft Records and Tapes, P.O. Box 404, Florham Park, New Jersey 07932 Tel 1-201 377-1885) (Also on "Recorded Dances" in *The Music Connection* 1995 [CD] series. Morristown, NJ: Silver Burdett Ginn)

Lott Ist Todt. On *Folk Dances for Everyone* [CS] Catalogue No. MAV 1044C. Available: Wagon Wheel Records and Books, 17191 Corbina Lane #203, Huntington Beach, CA 92649 Tel 1-714-846-8169. (Also available on [7" 45 rpm record] Catalogue No. 1419 from Folkraft Records and Tapes, P.O. Box 404, Florham Park, New Jersey 07932 Tel 1-201-377-1885)

Mariachi music [Popular music from Mexico]. On *Mariachis Mexicanos* [CS] EPM-99551-2 (1996). Long Island City, NY: EPM, distr. by Qualiton Imports. (Also see *Music of New Mexico: Hispanic Traditions.* On [CD] SFCD-40409 or [CS] SFC-40409 (1992) available from Smithsonian Folkways, Office of Folk Programs, 955 l'Enfant Plaza Suite 2600, Washington, DC 20560 Tel 1-202-287-3262)

Mexican Mixer [Produced by Phyllis Weikart]. On *Rhythmically Moving 3* [LP, CS, or CD]. Available: High/Scope Press, 600 North River Street, Yipsilanti, MI 48198 Tel 1-313-485-2000 (and distr. by Wagon Wheel Records and Books Tel 1-714-846-8169) (Also available on [7" 45 rpm record] Catalogue No. 1102 or [LP] Catalogue No. 1516 from Folkraft Records and Tapes, P.O. Box 404, Florham Park, New Jersey 07932 Tel 1-201-377-1885) (Also see Mariachis music above) (Also see La Bamba and La Macarena above) (Also see Danses espagnoles.)

Ravel, M. *Bolero* [Recorded by Boston Symphony Orch/Charles Munch]. On [CD] Catalogue No. 37908 or [CS] Catalogue No. 37912 (1994). Available: Public Radio MusicSource, *Classics*, Minnesota Communications Group, P.O. Box 64502, St. Paul, Minnesota 55164-0502 Tel 1-800-949-9999.) (Recorded 1951)

Rossini, G. (arr./orch. Respighi). Can-Can [Recorded by Boston Pops Orchestra/Arthur Fielder]. On *La Boutique Fantasque No. 9* [CD] RCA Victor Living Stereo 09026 61847-2 (1994). New York: BMG. (Recorded 1954-56) (Also [Recorded by [Cinncinnati Pops Orch/Erich Kunzel]. Can can, waltzes, marches, polkas. On *Gaite Parisienne* by J. Offenbach [CD] Catalog No. 28620 or [CS] Catalogue No. 29779. Available: Public Radio MusicSource, *Classics*, Minnesota Communications Group, P.O. Box 64502, St. Paul, Minnesota 55164-0502 Tel 1-800-949-9999.)

Rossini-Brittan. "March" [Recorded by Fabio Bidini]. On *Soirees Musicales, Complete No. 1-12* [CD] RCA Victor Red Seal (1995). New York, NY: RCA Victor, distr. by BGM.

Seven Jumps [Recorded by Merit Audio Visual]. On *Folk Dances Near and Far* [CS] Catalogue No. MAV 1043C; and on *International Folk Dance Mixer* [CD or CS]. Available: Wagon Wheel Records and Books, 17191 Corbina Lane #203, Huntington Beach, CA 92649 Tel 1-714-846-8169) (Also on *Rhythmically Moving 2* [Produced by Phyllis Weikert] [LP, CS, CD] available from High/Scope Press, 600 North River Street, Yipsilanti, MI 48198 Tel 1-313-485-2000) (Also available on *Folk Dances Near and Far* [LP or CS] Catalogue No. 3 from Folkraft Records and Tapes, P.O. Box 404, Florham Park, New Jersey 07932 Tel 1-201-377-1885)

Seven Steps. On [7" 45 rpm] Catalogue No. 1163. Available: Folkraft Records and Tapes, P.O. Box 404, Florham Park, New Jersey 07932 Tel-1-201-377-1885.

The Snail—A french song-play. On [7" 45 rpm record] Catalogue No. 1198. Available: Folkraft Records and Tapes, P.O. Box 404, Florham Park, New Jersey 07932 Tel 1-201-377-1885.

*Sousa, J. Semper Fidelis [Recorded by The Boston Pops]. On *This is My Country: RCA Victor 60+* [CD] 09026-61545-2 (1993). New York: BMG Classics. (Also available on *Marches* [2 LP's] Catalogue No. HYP-R11; and on *Patriotic Songs & Marches* [Recorded by D. Buck] [LP or CS] from Educational Activities, P. O. Box 87, Baldwin, NY 11510 Tel 1-800-645-3739)

*Sousa, J. The Stars and Stripes Forever [Recorded by The Boston Pops]. On *This is My Country: RCA Victor 60+* [CD] 09026-61545-2 (1993). New York: BMG Classics. (Also available on *Stars and Stripes Forever and the Greatest Marches* [CD] Catalogue No.28557 or [CS] Catalogue No. 29509 from Public Radio Music Source, *Classics*, P.O. Box 64502, St. Paul, Minnesota 55164-0502 Tel 1-800-949-9999) (Also available on *Marches* [2 LP's] Catalogue No. HYP-R11; and on *Patriotic Songs & Marches* [Recorded by D. Buck] [LP or CS] from Educational Activities, P. O Box 87, Baldwin, NY 11510 Tel 1-800-645-3739)

*Tchaikovsky, P. I. March from *The Nutcracker* [Performed by Arthur Fieldler/Boston Pops]. On *Classics for kids* [CD] 09026-61489-2 (1993). New York: BMG Classics.

*Available on Silver Burdett Ginn's *The Music Connection* 1995 series, Morristown, NJ, and other leading music education resources. [Ask the music teacher in your school for a piano or instrumental version of this music].

Note. Music recordings may be found in local record stores or via mail-order services, such as Public Radio Music Source at 1-800 75-MUSIC or Tower Records at 1-800-ASK-TOWER.

EQUIPMENT SUPPLY CATALOGUES

Listed here are a few of the many companies (local, national and international) that carry movement education and educational games, gymnastics, and dance equipment and materials for young children. We encourage you to review this list and the physical education and dance supply companies in your locality; ask your school librarian or administration for additional resource catalogues on early childhood movement education.

Chimetime—Division of Sportime
Movement Products
One Sportime Way
Atlanta, GA 30340
1-800-477-5075 *or* 1-770-449-5700
Fax 1-800-845-1535 *or* 1-700-263-0897

Flaghouse
150 North MacQuesten Pkwy.
Mount Vernon, NY 10550
1-800-793-7900; outside USA: (914) 699-1900
Fax 1-800-793-7922 *or* (914) 699-2961

Porter Athletic Equipment
9555 Irving Park Rd.
Schiller Park, IL 60176
(708) 671-0110
(gymnastics apparatus)

Toledo Physical Education Supply
Box 5618
Toledo, OH 43613
(419) 476-6730 *or* 1-800-225-7749
Fax 1-419-476-1163

UCS
One Olympic Drive
Orangeburg, N.Y. 10962
1-914-365-2333 *or* 1-800-526-4856
Fax 1-914-365-2589
(gymnastics apparatus)

U.S. Games.
P. O. Box 117028
Carrollton, TX 75011-7028
1-800-327-0484
Fax 1-800-899-0149 *or* 1-214-243-0149

Wolverine Sports
745 Circle
Box 1941
Ann Arbor, MI 48106
(313) 761-5690

About the Authors

Bette J. Logsdon, PhD, has 37 years of physical education experience—5 years in public schools and 32 years at the university level, preparing teachers with special interest in elementary school physical education. She spent the last 15 years of her career at Bowling Green State University (Ohio). During this time, she taught regularly scheduled elementary physical education classes to learn more about children, test theories, and stay abreast of the challenges facing elementary school teachers. Bette lives in Toledo, Ohio.

Luann M. Alleman, MEd, has 25 years' teaching experience in public and private schools. She has worked with children, including physically challenged students, at the elementary and high school levels, and with college students in university teacher-preparation courses. She was the first intern consultant for physical education in the Toledo School System and provided in-service training for Toledo public school elementary physical education teachers. Retired after 17 years as department chair of elementary school physical education for the Toledo School System, Luann resides in Holland, Ohio.

Sue Ann Straits, PhD, has been a lecturer in the Department of Education at The Catholic University of America (Washington, D.C.) since 1993. Since beginning her career in physical education in 1972, she has gained extensive practical experience teaching physical education and dance in early childhood and elementary education settings both overseas and in the United States. She also has conducted workshops around the world on movement education. Sue Ann makes her home in Reston, Virginia.

David E. Belka, PhD, has taught physical education classes to elementary school students and pedagogy and elementary content courses at the college level. An expert in developing and teaching games, David is the author of *Teaching Children Games*, a practical guide that explains the why and how of teaching children to become skilled games players. For more than two decades, he has analyzed, critiqued, and reviewed elementary physical education texts. David lives in Oxford, Ohio, where he is a professor at Miami University.

Dawn Clark, EdD, is an associate professor and the coordinator of dance education at East Carolina University, where she teaches dance pedagogy. She taught physical education and dance at the elementary level for five years. In 1987 Dawn earned a certificate in Laban studies; this background has been especially helpful for the *Physical Education Unit Plans* books, whose units are organized around Laban's movement themes and movement framework. Dawn is a resident of Greenville, North Carolina.

Learning Experiences in Games, Gymnastics, and Dance

Adopted by school districts across the country, these highly acclaimed unit plans are tailored to meet the needs of elementary students at every level. Increase student learning and motivation—and decrease off-task behavior—with these time-saving plans!

PHYSICAL EDUCATION UNIT PLANS FOR Preschool-Kindergarten

Learning Experiences in Games, Gymnastics, and Dance

BETTE J. LOGSDON / LUANN M. ALLEMAN
SUE ANN STRAITS / DAVID E. BELKA
DAWN CLARK

1997 • Paper
184 pp
Item BLOG0781
ISBN 0-87322-781-6
$18.00
($26.95 Canadian)

SECOND EDITION

PHYSICAL EDUCATION UNIT PLANS FOR GRADES 1-2

Learning Experiences in Games, Gymnastics, and Dance

BETTE J. LOGSDON / LUANN M. ALLEMAN
SUE ANN STRAITS / DAVID E. BELKA
DAWN CLARK

1997 • Paper
184 pp
Item BLOG0782
ISBN 0-87322-782-4
$18.00
($26.95 Canadian)

SECOND EDITION

PHYSICAL EDUCATION UNIT PLANS FOR GRADES 3-4

Learning Experiences in Games, Gymnastics, and Dance

BETTE J. LOGSDON / LUANN M. ALLEMAN
SUE ANN STRAITS / DAVID E. BELKA
DAWN CLARK

1997 • Paper
184 pp
Item BLOG0783
ISBN 0-87322-783-2
$18.00
($26.95 Canadian)

SECOND EDITION

PHYSICAL EDUCATION UNIT PLANS FOR GRADES 5-6

Learning Experiences in Games, Gymnastics, and Dance

BETTE J. LOGSDON / LUANN M. ALLEMAN
SUE ANN STRAITS / DAVID E. BELKA
DAWN CLARK

1997 • Paper
184 pp
Item BLOG0784
ISBN 0-87322-784-0
$18.00
($26.95 Canadian)

Special package price!

1997 • All 4 *Physical Education Unit Plans* books
Item BLOG0697 • ISBN 0-88011-697-8
$59.00 ($88.50 Canadian)

Prices subject to change.

DATE DUE